D0378854

MUIRHEAD LIBRARY OF PHILOSOPHY

An admirable statement of the aims of the Library of Philosophy was provided by the first editor, the late Professor J. H. Muirhead, in his description of the original programme printed in Erdmann's *History of Philosophy* under the date 1890. This was slightly modified in subsequent volumes to take the form of the following statement:

'The Muirhead Library of Philosophy was designed as a contribution to the History of Modern Philosophy under the heads: first of Different Schools of Thought—Sensationalist, Realist, Idealist, Intuitivist; secondly of different Subjects—Psychology, Ethics, Aesthetics, Political Philosophy, Theology. While much had been done in England in tracing the course of evolution in nature, history, economics, morals and religion, little had been done in tracing the development of thought on these subjects. Yet "the evolution of opinion is part of the whole evolution".

'By the co-operation of different writers in carrying out this plan it was hoped that a thoroughness and completeness of treatment, otherwise unattainable, might be secured. It was believed also that from writers mainly British and American fuller consideration of English Philosophy than it had hitherto received might be looked for. In the earlier series of books containing, among others, Bosanquet's *History of Aesthetic*, Pfleiderer's *Rational Theology since Kant*, Albee's *History of English Utilitarianism*, Bonar's *Philosophy and Political Economy*, Brett's *History of Psychology*, Ritchie's *Natural Rights*, these objects were to a large extent effected.

'In the meantime original work of a high order was being produced both in England and America by such writers as Bradley, Stout, Bertrand Russell, Baldwin, Urban, Montague, and others, and a new interest in foreign works, German, French and Italian, which had either become classical or were attracting public attention, had developed. The scope of the Library thus became extended into something more international, and it is entering on the fifth decade of its existence in the hope that it may contribute to that mutual understanding between countries which is so pressing a need of the present time.'

The need which Professor Muirhead stressed is no less pressing today, and few will deny that philosophy has much to do with enabling us to meet it, although no one, least of all Muirhead himself, would regard that as the sole, or even the main, object of philosophy. As Professor Muirhead continues to lend the distinction of his name to the Library of Philosophy it seemed not inappropriate to allow him to recall us to these aims in his own words. The emphasis on the history of thought also seemed to me very timely: and the number of important works promised for the Library in the very near future augur well for the continued fulfilment, in this and other ways, of the expectations of the original editor.

H. D. LEWIS

MUIRHEAD LIBRARY OF PHILOSOPHY

General Editor: H. D. Lewis

Professor of History and Philosophy of Religion at the University of London

MUIRHEAD LIBRARY OF PHILOSOPHY

EDITED BY H. D. LEWIS

CONTEMPORARY
INDIAN PHILOSOPHY

SERIES II

CONTEMPORARY INDIAN PHILOSOPHY

SERIES II

EDITED BY

MARGARET CHATTERJEE

Ph.D. (Delhi)

Reader in Philosophy in the University of Delhi

LONDON. GEORGE ALLEN & UNWIN LTD
NEW YORK. HUMANITIES PRESS INC.

First published in 1974

ISBN 0 04 199005 6
U.S.A. ISBN 391–00347–X

Printed in Great Britain
in 12 point Fournier type
by Unwin Brothers Limited
The Gresham Press
Old Woking, Surrey

PREFACE

This volume has been designed to present a selection of discussions by contemporary Indian philosophers on problems of current philosophical concern. It has not aimed at providing accounts of any of the traditional systems of Indian thought. At the same time, unlike in the case of compiling volumes on contemporary philosophical thinking in other countries, an editor concerned with Indian philosophy is confronted by the fact that there is a tremendous corpus of classical writing that constitutes India's philosophical heritage and that many Indian philosophers today are occupied with its exegesis. The relation of the contemporary Indian philosopher to this heritage is something to which, say, the relation of an American thinker to the pragmatist movement, or of a British thinker to the empiricist tradition, or of a German thinker to Kant and Hegel, scarcely offers a parallel. The traditional way, in philosophy as in society itself, is still very much alive in India. For this reason some contributions have been included which reflect this tradition, a tradition which is eager to vindicate its relevance, indeed its modernity.

Within the short compass of fourteen chapters it was not possible to include many other distinguished names, some senior and some in the younger age group which, had space permitted, one would have liked to include. Regret must also be expressed that no topic falling within philosophy of science or political philosophy could be included. The range of interests shown is, even so, wide. In this our contemporary thinkers follow 'the tradition', which was, without a doubt, one of great diversity.

I am very grateful to Dr J. J. Lipner for making an index of subjects for this book and noting some mistakes in the proofs.

April 1973   MARGARET CHATTERJEE

CONTENTS

THE CONTRIBUTORS

DAYA KRISHNA, M.A., Ph.D.(Delhi), is Professor of Philosophy in the University of Rajasthan, Jaipur. He is the author of *The Nature of Philosophy*, *Considerations towards a Theory of Social Change*, and *Planning, Power and Welfare*.

D. Y. DESHPANDE has been Professor of Philosophy at Vidarbha Mahavidyalaya, Amravati (Nagpur University), since 1965. He is Founder-member and Secretary of the Indian Philosophical Association since 1949 and editor of the *Journal of the Philosophical Association* since its inception in 1953.

RICHARD DE SMET, Ph.D. (Gregorian University), Member of the Order of the Jesuits, is Professor of Philosophy, De Nobili College, Poona, since 1968. Though a Belgian by birth he has lived twenty-seven years in India in such close connection and collaboration with Indian scholars that many of them claim him as one of themselves. He has been intimately associated with the preparation of the Marathi *Encyclopedia of Philosophy* to which he is the most prolific contributor. Apart from over 200 published articles he is well known for such books as *The Theological Method of Śaṅkara*, Louvain, 1954, *Philosophical Activity in Pakistan*, Lahore, 1960, and *Religious Hinduism*, Allahabad (3rd ed.), 1969.

N. K. DEVARAJA, M.A., D.Phil. (Allahabad), D.Litt. (Lucknow), was Sayaji Rao Gaekwad Professor of Indian Civilization and Culture at Banaras from 1960–7 and has been Director of the Centre of Advanced Study in Philosophy, Banaras Hindu University, since November 1967. He is the author of *An Introduction to Śaṅkara's Theory of Knowledge* (1962), *The Philosophy of Culture* (1963), *The Mind and Spirit of India*, and *Hinduism and Christianity* (1969). He is also well known as a poet, novelist and literary critic in the Hindi language.

V. A. DEVASENAPATHI, M.A., Ph.D. (Madras), is Professor of Philosophy at the Centre of Advanced Study in Philosophy, University of Madras, since 1964. He is the author of *Śaiva Siddhanta, Towards Conquest of Time* (Principal Miller Lectures) and *The Ethics of the Tirukkural* (Sornammal Endowment Lectures)—all published by the University of Madras—and of *Human Bondage and Divine Grace* (Tiruppanandal Endowment Lectures) published by Annamalai University.

T. M. P. MAHADEVAN, M.A., Ph.D. (Madras), is Director, Centre of Advanced Study in Philosophy, University of Madras, since 1964. He is the author of *The Philosophy of Advaita*, *Gauḍapāda—A Study in Early Advaita*, *Outlines of Hinduism*, etc.

J. N. MOHANTY, M.A.(Cal.), Ph.D. (Göttingen), is currently visiting Professor, Graduate Faculty, New School for Social Research, New York. He was Vivekananda Professor of Philosophy in Burdwan University from 1962–8, Acharya B.N. Seal Professor of Mental and Moral Science, University of Calcutta, from 1968–70, and has been George Lynn Cross Research Professor of Philosophy, University of Oklahoma, since 1970. He is the author of *Nicolai Hartmann and A. N. Whitehead: A Study in recent Platonism*, Calcutta, 1957, *Edmund Husserl's Theory of Meaning*, The Hague, 1964, 1969 (2nd ed.), *Gaṅgeśa's Theory of Truth*, Santiniketan, 1966, *Phenomenology and Ontology*, The Hague, 1971, *The Concept of Intentionality*, St Louis, 1972.

RAJENDRA PRASAD, M.A. (Patna), A.M., and Ph.D. (Michigan), is Senior Professor of Philosophy, Indian Institute of Technology, Kanpur. He was Sectional President of the Indian Akhila Bharatiya Darshan Parisad in 1963 and of the Indian Philosophical Congress in 1967, General President of the Indian Philosophical Association in 1969, and of the Akhila Bharatiya Darshan Parisad in 1970. He edits the *Indian Review of Philosophy*, the quarterly journal of the *Indian Philosophical Congress*, and edited for some time *Darshanik Triamasika*, the quarterly journal of Akhila Bharatiya Darshan Parisad. He has contributed numerous papers in *The Philosophical Quarterly*, *Philosophy: East and West*, *Philosophy and Phenomenological Research*, etc.

BINAYENDRATH RAY taught philosophy in Dacca and Delhi and retired from Delhi University a few years ago as Reader in Philosophy. He is author of *Consciousness in Neo-Realism* (Oxford Univ. Press), and contributed to *History of Philosophy*,

Eastern and Western, edited by S. Radhakrishnan and published by Allen & Unwin, 1952 (1st ed.).

SUSHIL KUMAR SAXENA, M.A., Ph.D. (Delhi), is Reader in Philosophy, Delhi University. He is the author of *Studies in the Metaphysics of Bradley*, 1967, published by Allen & Unwin in their Muirhead Library series. He is a leading interpreter of Hindustani (that is, North Indian) music and Kathak dance and is a music and dance critic and composer. He has written several articles on aesthetical subjects in *Diogenes, Marg,* etc.

PRANAB KUMAR SEN, M.A., D.Phil. (Cal.), is Reader in Philosophy, Jadavpur University, Calcutta. He is at present researching in Oxford University on a Commonwealth Academic Staff Fellowship. He has written widely on logical problems in *The Visva-Bharati Journal of Philosophy, The Journal of the Indian Academy of Philosophy, The Journal of the Philosophical Association,* etc.

SIBAJIBAN (Bhattacharyya), M.A. (Cal.), is Professor of Philosophy in the University of Burdwan. He has contributed articles and reviews to *Mind, Analysis, Journal of Symbolic Logic, Notre Dame Journal of Formal Logic, Philosophy and Phenomenological Research, Philosophy: East and West,* etc.

RAMAKANT SINARI, M.A., Ph.D. (Bombay), is Professor of Philosophy at SIES College, Bombay. He researched in the University of Pennsylvania and the State University of New York at Buffalo from 1964–5. In 1969–70 he was an invitee to the Fifth East–West Philosophers' Conference at the University of Hawaii and a Visiting Professor of Philosophy at Elmira College, New York. He is the author of *Reason in Existentialism*, Popular Prakashan, 1966, and the *Structure of Indian Thought*, Charles C. Thomson, 1970, and has published papers in *Philosophy and Phenomenological Research, Philosophy: East and West, The Philosophical Quarterly, Anviksiki,* etc.

S. VAHIDUDDIN, who did his graduate studies in Osmania University, Hyderabad, and has a Ph.D. from Marburg, was Professor of Philosophy in Delhi University from 1967 to 1973. He studied in the Universities of Berlin, Marburg, Heidelberg and Paris, and while doing his doctoral work at Marburg was closely associated with Rudolf Otto. During 1959–60 he lectured in many Universities and other educational institutions in U.S.A. He has contributed many papers on philosophy of religion, aesthetics, and Islamic thought, in Indian and overseas journals.

ABOUT THE EDITOR

MARGARET CHATTERJEE, who is Reader in Philosophy in Delhi University, was an Exhibitioner at Somerville College, Oxford from 1943–6. She took her Ph.D. from Delhi University in 1961. She was President of the History of Philosophy Section of the All India Philosophical Congress in 1969. She is the author of *Our Knowledge of Other Selves* (1963), *Philosophical Enquiries* (1968) and *The Existentialist Outlook* (1973), and has contributed papers in *Kant-Studien, Religious Studies, Philosophy and Phenomenological Research, The Journal of Aesthetics and Art Criticism, Anvikshiki, The Visva-Bharati Journal of Philosophy, Diogenes, Man in India,* etc.

Chapter 1

LOGIC AND ONTOLOGY

by

DAYA KRISHNA
University of Rajasthan

Logic is supposed to be neutral to ontology. The search for something which will hold true in all possible worlds, or even if there were to be no world at all, has had a perennial fascination for the philosophical mind. The criteria of universality and necessity which seemed to belong to mathematics made it the ideal paradigm for knowledge, at least in the Western tradition of thought deriving from the Greeks, particularly Pythagoras and Plato. But however universal and necessary mathematical knowledge may seem, it certainly cannot lay claim to the exhaustiveness of such knowledge. Not only does mathematical knowledge continue to grow, but no one seems to think that it can ever stop growing. Though it may grow as a matter of fact, there seems nothing in principle which will ensure that it must be so, specially with the view most philosophers of mathematics entertain about mathematical knowledge.

The claim of mathematics to be considered as knowledge has always posed problems for so-called tough-minded philosophers with the empiricist conviction that ontological status be granted only to that which is encountered in sense experience. They find it difficult to deny it the status of knowledge and even more difficult to accept that it is such. To accept it as knowledge is inevitably to raise the question, 'knowledge of what?'. It is difficult to accept that it is knowledge of that which is encountered in sense experience, as this would not only rob it of that element of universality and necessity which has been the reason for its perennial fascination for the rationalist philosophers in the West, but also make the whole field of transfinite mathematics impossible in principle, unless, of course, it were to be accepted that infinity can be directly encountered in sense experience. If we add the perspective of growth to our reflection on the kind of knowledge that mathematics happens to be, then it would be even more difficult to accept that it is not knowledge of anything whatsoever.

The possibility of growth in principle with respect to the sort of knowledge that mathematics happens to be, appears *prima facie* to be in conflict with the purely logical and deductive nature which is usually ascribed to it. In fact, a certain sort of finality seemed to characterise Euclidean geometry and Aristotelian logic from the earliest point of their inception until almost the middle of the nineteenth century when the elaboration of non-Euclidean geometries revealed the purely postulational character of the Euclidean axioms which were supposed to have been self-evidently true. The assimilation of geometry to algebra earlier in Descartes and the subsequent attempts to translate each branch of mathematics in terms of the others revealed the basic unity of all mathematics and the articulation of this unity in terms of the notion of sets and the possible operations that could be performed on them. The deductive character of various geometries revealed the foundational nature of the process of deduction and thus made many people seek in logic the foundations of mathematics. The same thing was achieved by the formal properties of the operations on sets which were shared by certain other operations which happened to be more obviously logical in character.

Logic has generally been regarded as being concerned with relations between sentences or propositions. Mathematics, on the other hand, may be said to be concerned with relations between numbers. The ontological question, then, in the case of the two may be said to relate to the status we wish to accord to sentences or propositions on the one hand and numbers on the other. To the extent that propositions are regarded as pseudo-substitutes for sentences, the same may be said with respect to numbers as the referents of marks which are supposed to stand for them. The problem, then, shifts to the so-called semantic function and the issue relates to the question of whether all referents have to be of the same ontological type. The fact that the sign or symbol which performs the referential function happens to be sensory in character is irrelevant to the issue. It has perhaps necessarily to be such for the purposes of communication, unless one is prepared to accept the possibility of direct telepathic communication amongst human beings. What matters, however, is that which is referred to and whether it is only of the type that is apprehensible by the senses.

The whole thrust of recent philosophical thought in Anglo-American countries seems to be towards the devising of ways and means to escape the cognitive necessity of postulating the reality of entities other than those which are, or could be, directly apprehended in or though sense experience. Quine and Goodman's almost half-conscious confession epitomises this.[1] Yet the naive equation of all that is apprehended through the senses with reality flies in face of the fact that the illusory *appears* as real. As Shalya has forcefully argued recently, the concept of reality itself is a theoretical concept and is correlative to a systematic context.[2] Otherwise, the distinction between the real and the unreal will collapse, and there would be no such thing as unreality at all. Yet, if what is to be considered as 'real' were to be the result of the acceptance of a criterion, then we would have the problem of the justification of the criterion on our hands unless we are prepared to grant the possibility of multiplicity of criteria with no rational grounds for choosing between them.[3]

The fear of granting ontological reality to abstractions that

[1] 'Any system that countenances abstract entities we deem unsatisfactory as a final philosophy.' (*Journal of Symbolic Logic*, December 1947.)

[2] Yashdev Shalya, *Jñāna Aur Sat*, Rajkamal Prakashan, Delhi, 1967.

[3] See the discussion in my book *The Nature of Philosophy* (Progressive Publ., Calcutta, 1955, Chapter III).

seems to haunt so many Anglo-American philosophers in this ultra-abstract age may find some explanation in the acute observation of K. C. Bhattacharyya that because of the extent to which we identify ourselves with the body, we cannot but help regarding the sensory world alone as pre-eminently real and all the rest as its shadow. On the other hand, the very moment we begin to identify ourselves with mind or intellect or reason, the perceptual world begins to appear as a shadow of the world grasped by faculties other than sense experience.[1] As in the normal human knowing process, senses and intellect both play an inalienable role, and as man is simultaneously both body and mind, what is regarded as real and what as the shadow depends on the valuational primacy one accords to the one or the other. The ontological denigration of abstraction, then, may be seen as a correlate of the sensate value system of modern man which regards body as the primary reality of man. However, just as for the rationalist–idealist philosophers, body with its correlate the sensory world is the focal point of ontological attack, so is the empiricist philosophers' battle against abstractions, which, like some of the ancient demons of Hindu mythology, rise and multiply faster than they are killed.

The attempted reduction of mathematics to logic reduces the ontological issue to the referent of logic alone, and as logic does not ostensibly seem to be *about* any specific entities, the necessity of granting ontological status to anything other than those encountered in sense experience evaporates also. Logic seems to be concerned with the elaboration of rules which, if followed, would always ensure the deduction of true consequences from true premises. The rules are, to use the usual terminology, 'truth preserving'. How do we know whether the rules are such as to necessarily ensure truth preservation? The only answer that could possibly be given might relate to the fact that no one has yet been able to derive a false conclusion from true premises by following the rules, or that the

[1] K. C. Bhattacharyya, *Studies in Philosophy,* Vol. II, Calcutta, Progressive Publ., 1958.

term 'true' means derivability according to the rules, thus
making it impossible in principle to call any conclusion
'false', if it were derived according to the rules. In the first
case, the argument would be essentially inductive in nature
and would suffer all the problems and the limitations which
inductive reasoning usually does. It could not preclude the
possibility that someone could show such a derivation in the
future and thus show the rules to be incapable of achieving
what they were supposed to achieve. If, on the other hand, we
adopt the second alternative to obviate this contingency, the
notion of truth becomes purely syntactical and the characterisation of logic as truth preserving loses all sense. For, if truth
means derivability according to rules, then neither premises
nor conclusions could be regarded as true or false on their
own.

The desire to provide a semantic underpinning to logic
derives perhaps from the desire to make logic *applicable* and
thus *useful*. The parallel analogue with mathematics would,
however, also raise the same questions with reference to logic.
There would have to be a distinction between pure and applied
logic and Einstein's famous remark about the relationship
between pure and applied mathematics would also apply to
their relationship.[1] On the other hand, the practically oriented
may take comfort from the fact that whatever the theoretical
difficulties, the relationship between pure and applied logic
will continue to be established and may be as fruitful as in the
case of mathematics. However, such a consideration, if taken
seriously, might strike at the root of most philosophical
perplexities which, in any case, happen to be purely theoretical
in nature. The application question, on the other hand, if
closely analysed, may reveal some special problems in the case
of logic which do not arise in the case of mathematics. The
usual field of the application of logic is in the realm of the
arguments which people give. If we admit that the substitution
of concrete premises in place of the usual sentential variables

---

[1] To the extent it can be applied, it is not exact and to the extent it is exact, it
cannot be applied.

makes the *slightest* difference to the correctness of the formal-ised argument, then the so-called application will become *completely* nugatory in practice. To put it another way, there can be no such thing as the 'approximation' of a concrete argument to a purely formalised one, as is usually the situation in the case of the application of mathematics. Concrete points and lines can be said to approximate the idealised points and lines of geometry and it is this feature that leads to 'degrees of precision' in scientific measurement which can be carried to any length depending upon our needs.[1] Concrete arguments are either correct or incorrect; there is no middle ground for them, no more or less, no indefinite approximation to an ideal which is never reached.[2]

The same appears to be the case with respect to what may be called the new field of 'applied logic' as contrasted with what may be considered as the traditional one. Hardly anyone would think these days of applied logic as consisting of arguments where concrete premises are substituted for sentential variables. Rather, it is in computer programming where it is the logical connectives that are given a mechanical or electrical analogue, that we find the field of applied logic *par excellence*. However, the computer, by being built around the function of the logical connectives, only simulates the formal-ised argument schema and behaves fundamentally like the human manipulator in a formalised derivation according to the transformation rules of a deductive system. It, thus, is more akin to the usual mathematical calculator and should, in the strict sense, not be considered as belonging to the field of applied logic at all.

The dependence of the notion of truth preservation on the

[1] There are supposed to be some intrinsic limits to measurement deriving from Heisenberg's principle of uncertainty and perhaps the absoluteness of the velocity of light as postulated in Einstein's theory of relativity, but that does not basically affect our contention.

[2] The problems arising from the substitution of concrete sentences for the senten-tial variables has been discussed in the author's article 'Law of Contradiction and Empirical Reality', in *Mind*, April, 1957 and 'Types of Coherence' (*The Philosophical Quarterly*, July, 1960). For an extensive critique of the later article, see Dharmendra Kumar, 'Types of Coherence—a Refutation' (*The Visva-Bharati Journal of Philosophy*, Vol. IV, 1965).

prior notion of truth, and that too in its semantic aspect, raises not only a host of issues which have not been attended to in the literature on the subject, but also makes logic depend upon ontology in a sense which most pure logicians may not consider very welcome. Traditionally, one could not think of a valid argument, unless it conformed to the syllogistic rules, which required, amongst other conditions, the presence of at least one universal premise for its validity. As is well known, however, it is impossible *in principle* to establish the truth of a universal proposition unless it is just a summation of a finite set of instances, however large they may be. If it is impossible to establish the truth of a universal proposition and it is also essential that it function as one of the premises in a valid argument-form, then it is obvious that it could never be known whether the rules had ensured truth preservation or not. The usual way out is to *assume* the truth of the premises, *ignore* the fact that the truth of at least one of them cannot be established in principle, assert an 'if–then' relationship between the premises and the conclusion, and establish its validity on the basis of its being in accordance with the rules of derivation. Yet, however convenient this solution may appear in practice, it is obvious that it cannot justify the validity of the rules themselves on the ground that, if followed, they will always ensure the impossibility of deriving a false conclusion from true premises. Thus, in a fundamental sense, logic in its traditional presentation could not ensure the fulfilment of its central task which was supposed to be that of truth preservation.

Does modern logic fare any better in the performance of that very function which it agrees is the central task of all logic, whether traditional or modern? In a sense, the concept of 'truth functionality' may be regarded as the central point of modern logic, and the explication of the concept of derivation or proof its central concern. Truth functionality is itself a function of the notion of 'truth values' on the one hand and that of 'truth operator' or 'logical operator' on the other. Truth values, as everyone knows, may be as many as one wants as long as their number is more than one—logic would perhaps have no function if sentences could not have any other truth value except one.[1] As for logical operators, the one logically significant thing about them is the number of minimum sentences they require to form a new sentence. As this can vary from the minimum of one sentence to as many as one chooses to imagine, we have the whole range from monadic to *n*-adic logical operators. The actual number of logical operators, then, is a function of the *decision* with respect to the number of truth values we accept for our logical system and the minimum number of sentences which we want our operators to operate upon. However, as any *choice* is bound to be *arbitrary* in the matter, and as it is basically a *selection* out of the infinite possibilities between which there can be no *logical* grounds of choice, any particular choice is bound to be a special case of generalised logic.

The situation arising from this indefinite infinity of logical operators is usually met in the literature by showing the definability of *all* such operators in terms of a few fundamental ones, such as conjunction and negation or disjunction and negation. This definability or rather describability in terms of a few operators does not *annul* the distinction between different operators and thus the proposed solution can only be regarded as spurious in character. The operators continue to be different, whether they are described in one way or another.

The indefinite multiplicity of logical operators, each distinctive from all the others and irreducible to any one of them in any significant sense of the term, arises due to different factors. One relates to the minimum number of sentences which a particular operator requires to form a new sentence, while the other relates to the possible truth values that a sentence may have. As there is no intrinsic limit to either of these, the indefinite multiplicity of logical operators would follow from either of them, taken either singly or jointly. The question regarding the meaningfulness of such an indefinite extension on either count should strictly be treated as an

---

[1] This is not entirely correct as logic without the operator of negation has been tried. The attempt, however, only shows that very little can be done with it.

extra-logical question on the truth-functional view of logic. Yet, such is the hangover of these extra-logical interests even for the so-called truth functionalists that they continue to ask questions such as what is the meaning of *n* truth values which a sentence is supposed to have in many-valued logics. The usual reassurance given is in terms of finding the *interpretation* in terms of probability values which may range anywhere between 0 and 1. The limits are supposed to provide the usual truth values of falsity and truth in a two-valued logic, but it is obvious that there is no necessity in such an interpretation. The indefinite multiplicity of possible truth values could as well be correlated with natural numbers ranging from one onwards, without making the situation any different except that there will be no upper limit to the series and if the notion of truth were to be identified with such a limit, there would be no such thing as truth.

The objection that the number of numbers in the two series is the same, as they can be put in a one–one correlation, is besides the point. In fact, it is wrong to think that because the two series are the same in respect to the number of their numbers, they are the same in other respects also. The point made above that while the one series may be said to have an upper limit, the other cannot, suggests a basic difference in at least this aspect of the matter. But this is not the only difference. We may, for example, significantly ask what is the next number in the series of natural numbers, although it would be meaningless to ask the same question regarding the series of rational numbers. Now, if we accept Ryle's criterion that if the same question cannot be meaningfully asked of two sets of entities, then they should be held to be basically different, we would have to accept that the series of natural numbers and the series of rational numbers are fundamentally different in spite of the fact that they have the same number of numbers. The situation on Ryle's criterion is, in fact, even more desperate. The criterion demarcates types or categories of objects. If so, the two series would have to be assigned to different categories on Ryle's criterion. The philosophers of mathematics may take their choice and reject Ryle's criterion or accept the discomforting conclusion that the two series are categorically different.

The redundancy of the probability interpretation of *n*-valued logic is, however, only one aspect of the matter. The deeper problems lie in respect to the notion of truth functionality itself when considered in relation to *n*-valued logic. In two-valued logic, whether the logical operator happens to be monadic, dyadic or *n*-adic, there is *always* an operator which in all conditions gives T and another which in all conditions gives F. These are known as tautology and contradiction, respectively. On the same analogy, in an *n*-valued logic we would have *n*-types of operators which in all cases would give the same value because of the nature of the operators themselves. Yet, what exactly would it mean for operators other than those that are tautological or contradictory to have the same value in every case? To ask this question is to realise that either the notion of truth functionality has little sense as far as logic is concerned or that the concepts of truth and falsity are irrelevant for the type of study that modern logic aspires to be. The usual two-valued truth-functional logic with its values of truth and falsity symbolised as T and F masks this dilemma which comes into the open the moment logic is generalised as a truth function of *n*-values. It is then that the arbitrariness of the names designating the so-called truth values is revealed, for the moment we have more than two of such values, we realise that as far as truth-functional logic is concerned, what is important is their number, that is, whether they are one or two or three or four, or any other number. Any further characterisation is basically irrelevant.

If the notions of truth and falsity are irrelevant to truth-functional logic, then what could possibly be meant by truth preservation being the central task which the rules of logic are supposed to ensure? There *is* no truth to preserve as the so-called truth values are essentially a misnomer. It is, if we may be allowed to use a slightly modified form of Ryle's well known phrase, a systematically misleading name, but once

this is realised, some of the restrictions imposed on the sentential variables on which the truth-functional operators are
supposed to operate, would also seem otiose. For example,
there would seem no reason for saying that the sentential
variables should range only over declarative sentences, as they
alone can be true or false. In a certain sense, the extension of
logic to such fields as the logic of imperatives suggests that the
restriction is basically unjustified. The reason why it has
usually been regarded as a necessary restriction may then be
seen to follow from the mistaken understanding about the
nature of two-valued logic. If there can be such a thing as a
logic of imperatives and if imperative sentences are not
supposed to be either true or false, then the whole idea of
logic as the elaboration of rules which are truth preserving
falls to the ground. There is, in such a case, not even the
pseudo-reference to truth which at least seemed a character of
the sentence-types with which two-valued truth-functional
logic was supposed to deal. An imperative sentence is not true
or false, and hence the question of whether what *follows* from
it is true or false is besides the point.

The extension of logic into other fields does not merely
bring into question the notion of truth preservation as the
central task of logic in the manner it has been traditionally
conceived. In some of the developments, it may be said to
question the very centrality of the notion of truth functionality for logic, which was supposed to have been given to it
by modern developments in logic. If, for example, there is
such a thing as a logic of belief statements such as Hintikka
and others have tried to develop, and if 'I believe that' is not a
truth-functional operator as has been usually contended, then
it is obvious that logic need not concern itself with truth-
functional relations at all.

The meeting point of what may be called the ontological
and epistemological issues with respect to logic may perhaps
be found still better in the case of what is called 'quantificational logic'. This logic relates to those types of argument
forms where the derivation of the conclusion depends upon the

quantificational character of the premises concerned. Here all the restrictions on the dropping and adding of quantifiers are meant to *ensure* that no false conclusion be derivable from premises that happen to be true. How could it ever be *proved* that the rules *do* ensure this? As already pointed out in the case of the supposedly necessary universal premise in the traditional syllogistic argument, what is required necessarily happens also to be in principle impossible of being ever established as true. The difficulties arising from this situation are not confined to traditional logic alone. Rather, the troubles besetting modern logic seem to be compounded still more.

First, except for a few eccentrics like Fisk, almost all the modern logicians seem to argue for a fundamental ontological difference between the two quantifiers. The universal quantifier, according to the new orthodoxy, should be interpreted as ontologically neutral. In other words, its truth should not be taken to entail the existence of any entities whatsoever. The converse is supposed to be the case with the so-called existential quantifier. Yet the two are supposed to be interchangeable. In fact, the rules for the translation of the one into the other are usually given along with the contention that the two are also radically different in their ontological commitments. Perhaps it is felt that there are no difficulties because the translation is done in terms of a negation of the other quantifier along with a negation of the property or properties which were supposed to be possessed or not possessed, as the case happened to be. Also, when translated into the usual language of meaning, the two appear to be equivalent, even though according to many of these logicians themselves it is difficult to have any satisfactory criteria of synonymy. But no such considerations or appeal to meaning seem relevant to the issue concerned. The ontological difference was intended to relate to the *form* alone, but if the forms themselves are considered to be interchangeable, then there seems no ground for contending that there is an essential ontological difference between the two.[1]

---

[1] An analogous problem, though without ontological overtones, arises in relation to traditional logic when it formulates a rule that from two negative premises no

The problems arising with respect to the use of the quantifier 'all' are, however, not confined to those mentioned in the last paragraph alone. They arise even more insistently and openly in what is known as the logic of classes or the set theory. In quantificational logic they are usually masked by the notion of a 'universe of discourse', which is just a euphemism for saying that we are not talking about 'all', but only about 'all of a certain type'. However indefinite may be the extension generated in this way, it is defined by the possession of a property or properties, as the case may be. But the notion of an unrestricted 'all', not confined to the possession of this or that property, comes into the open only when we begin to talk of classes and discover the universal class.

What exactly is this universal class? It is usually considered to be a result of the operation of union on a class and its complementary class. As the complementary class is formed of all those members which do *not* possess the said property, the class formed of all those who either possess or do not possess a property is supposed to be the universal class of which everybody has to be a member since either one possesses the property or one does not possess it. As the non-possession of the property is defined by exclusion in the manner of the Buddhist doctrine of *Apoha* it may be taken as exhausting the universe in the manner of the traditional formulation of the Law of Excluded Middle as '*A* must either be *B* or not-*B*'. But it is well known that the Law is not accepted by everybody and to the extent it is rejected, it would affect the notion of a universal class which, at least in its usual formation, seems built upon it.

The 'universality' of the universal class, however, does not depend only on the acceptance or rejection of the Law of Excluded Middle. It may be affected significantly by other considerations also. For example, is the notion of 'exclusion'

conclusion can be drawn, forgetting that by its own rules of obversion, any proposition could be changed into another equivalent proposition whose quality is opposed to that of the former. Thus every negative proposition can be transformed by obversion into an affirmative proposition and *vice versa*. Thus either no conclusion could ever be derived from any premise *or* it could always be so derived, for all affirmative propositions could be turned into their equivalent negative forms and all negative propositions into the equivalent affirmative ones.

B

to be applied only to those types of objects to which the property may significantly be said to apply? In other words, is it to be confined only to what is called the 'universe of discourse', in the literature on the subject? For example, does the complementary class of all things which are unified by the non-possession of the property 'blue' include such things as music or $\sqrt{2}$? In case it does not, the universal class is universal only in name, as everything is not its member. On the other hand, if it is allowed to have them as its members, not only does the whole notion of 'pseudo-question' along with that of meaninglessness on which so much of modern philosophising rests, fall to the ground; but some serious difficulties are created for the traditional formulation of the Law of Contradiction also. Usually, it is formulated as 'A cannot be both B and not-B', but if not-B is interpreted without the restriction imposed by the universe of discourse, it would lead to the absurd situation that something cannot be, say, both blue and square as 'square' would have to be included under the domain of 'not-blue'.[1] If, on the other hand, it is formulated in its modern form as 'A sentence cannot be both true and false' or rather 'A declarative sentence cannot be both true and false', then its formal truth would be only a consequence of the prior assumption that truth and falsity are the sort of properties that belong to sentences and that they are *exclusive* of each other. Yet, whether any properties are *exclusive* of each other is a factual question, and no *a priori* decision can be reached in the matter. On the other hand, if it is treated as a purely definitional matter, it would certainly make it necessarily true but only at the cost of rendering it completely insignificant. In a certain sense, the word 'declarative' in the modern formulation does just this, for it is defined in terms of the properties of truth and falsity, though it does not explicitly specify that they are absolutely exclusive of each other.

The trouble with exclusion of properties is that, at least in respect to those which concern the empirical domain, it is not

---

[1] On this and other related problems see the author's article 'Law of Contradiction and Empirical Reality' (*Mind*, April, 1957).

clear whether they really exclude each other or not. As Körner has argued, there can always be the possibility of a situation arising in the case of predicates applicable to the empirical realm where it is not clear as to which of the predicates applies. As both of the supposedly exclusive predicates seem to apply legitimately to the situation, one can only conclude that either both are applicable, or neither is. This has given rise to what has been called the logic of inexact predicates. However, if the inexactness is intrinsic to the predicates or to their applicability, one wonders how any logic could remove it.

The ontological problem raised by intrinsically inexact predicates has seldom been considered in detail by those who have tried to build a logic of inexact predicates. The problem relates to the question of whether such a situation is to be interpreted as indicating an intrinsic ambiguity or indeterminateness in reality itself or as an inalienable limitation or defect in the condition or constitution of human knowledge. Usually, such a dilemma has been felt in relation to the problems raised by certain facts in physics, both at the microscopic and cosmic levels. But the issue is of wider import. Yet, except for Kalidas Bhattacharyya,[1] whose work is little known outside India, few have attempted to deal with it in a focal manner.

However, the ontological implications of the logic of classes centre even more around the notion of a class of *all* classes. The issues arising in this connection are well known and relate to what in the literature on the subject has come to be called *Russell's Paradox*. The paradox is basically a paradox of self-reference, and the issue relates to the question of whether the notion of a genuine totality is capable of being intelligibly conceived without giving rise to self-contradiction. The consensus is that it cannot be so conceived, and the usual way out is to adopt some version or other of the *Theory of Types*. But as the theory prohibits in an *ad hoc* manner that any

[1] Kalidas Bhattacharyya, *Alternative Standpoints in Philosophy*, Calcutta, Dasgupta, 1953.

class may be a member of itself, it generates an unending series of classes of classes, each of an order higher than the other. In other words, it makes the notion of an achieved totality impossible in principle.

It may be contended that the ontological thrust of logic lies elsewhere. After all, the central crux of logic lies in the if–then relationship, for it only says that *if* one accepts something, *then* one has also to accept something else. Even with respect to truth functionality we can only say that *if* one accepts a certain number of truth values which a sentence may have, and *if* one also accepts that certain connectives require a certain minimum number of sentences to form a new sentence, *then* it follows that there will be so many distinct truth-functional operators in the system. Logic, in this perspective, makes no assertions. Or rather, it only asserts hypothetical relationships. As the central logical contention is that one cannot simultaneously accept something and reject that which necessarily follows from it, the relation of implication becomes really basic to it. Thus, even though it is only one of the dyadic operators in a two-valued truth-functional logic, yet, in a sense, it is more fundamental than others.[1] Whether this fundamental character can be accepted and articulated while remaining within the boundaries of truth-functional logic, is difficult to say. Still, whether fundamental or not, the ontological commitment of logic may be thought of as lying in the assertion of the realities of relations, rather than of anything else.

If logic cannot be possible without assuming the reality of relations, then they would have to be provided with a reality, for logic would not like to commit suicide and argue for its own impossibility. As Russell argued long ago, the reality of relations, particularly those of the asymmetrical kind, implies a pluralistic world. *Ergo*, if logic implies the reality of relations and the reality of relations implies a pluralistic world, we might conclude that the reality of logic implies a pluralistic

[1] This point arose in a discussion with Dr R. S. Bhatnagar of the Philosophy Department of the University of Rajasthan, Jaipur, and I am thankful to him for it.

ontology. But is logic real? Bradley had argued, before Russell, for the unreality of relations, and long before him, the Buddhist philosopher Nāgārjuna had argued for the unreality of anything which anybody held to be real. But, does everything include everything? Does it include itself, for example? If it does not, how can it talk of everything? If it does, surely we have, besides the usual paradoxes of self-reference, the peculiar problem of the unreality of that which proves the unreality of everything else? If it does not, we have the problem of the ontological reality of that process or argument which declares everything besides itself to be unreal.

The problem of the ontological presuppositions, implications and status of logic is important as there has occurred in recent times a concerted and persistent attempt to develop a logic with no ontological commitments whatsoever. In a certain sense, the claim of logic to be true in all possible worlds had already implied it. Nagel had explicitly argued for the ontological neutrality of logic in his well known article entitled *Logic without Ontology*.[1] This could perhaps be understood as the implication of the essentially analytical view of logic which has been entertained by most logicians and philosophers. It would be interesting in this connection to ask about the position of those who do not subscribe to the analytic-synthetic dichotomy and, in fact, have attacked its very foundations. The position of Quine is well known in this respect, but it does not seem to have been noticed that once the distinction is given up, it would be impossible for logic not to have ontological implications. Also, the so-called contingent character of any ontology will infect logic also, unless the converse infection is allowed to make ontology necessary.[2]

Now, logic does not seem to be about any entities whatsoever. Not even in the *prima facie* sense in which mathematics seems to be about numbers. If it is *about* anything, it is perhaps

---

[1] E. Nagel, *Logic without Metaphysics*, Glencoe, Illinois, 1957.
[2] For some aspects of this problem see the author's article 'The Synthetic *a priori*—some considerations' (*Philosophy*, April, 1961).

about sentences and the relationships between them; not about any *specific* sentences, but rather sentence forms of which particular sentences may be regarded as exemplifications. As for relationships, it is perhaps the one designated by the phrase 'following from' that may be said to be its specific concern. The ontological question with respect to logic would thus centre around the ontological status of sentences and those of sentence forms, and the relation of 'following from' which is supposed to hold between them.

What sort of entity is a sentence and what sort is the sentence form with which logic is supposed to be concerned with? However one may conceive of sentences, it would be difficult to think of them as natural entities, and if they are not natural entities, sentence forms could hardly be considered as such. If anything, they would have to be regarded as abstractions from a type of entity which itself could not be considered as 'natural' in any relevant sense of the term. Yet, sentences are the sort of things that are seen and heard, or even felt and touched as in the case of persons who are blind and use braille—but to the extent that they are *only* such, they cease to be sentences. To use an older terminology now out of fashion, visibility or audibility or even tactuality is not their essence, even though without them they could perhaps never be known.[1] The being of a sentence, so to say, lies completely outside itself—something which is hard to accept. Yet if there are no such things as sentences, there would perhaps be no such things as sentence forms either, and it is difficult to see how there would be any logic if this were so.

The desire to free logic of any ontological implications has resulted in the elaboration of logics which will be 'true' in all possible worlds, or perhaps even if there were to be no world. But it is difficult to understand what is exactly meant in this context. First, to the extent that logic is supposed to be analytically true, it is difficult to make sense of the idea that it has to

---

[1] We say 'perhaps', for if telepathy were to be a fact, it would have to be admitted that one could 'know' what is conveyed without its being embodied in something which is apprehensible by the senses.

be true of *any* world. Perhaps the analogy is with the notion of *application* in mathematics. If that is the analogy, then it also follows from the analogy that the application is something extra-logical which does not affect the logical validity of what is sought to be applied. Perhaps this is what is meant by the picturesque phrase 'true in all possible worlds'. But if this were so, then it would be necessarily so by definition, and the question of finding if it were actually true or not of all possible worlds would not arise.

On the other hand, what exactly is meant by a 'world' is not made clear. Does an object of sense experience count as a 'world'? What about the senses themselves? Are they to be considered as their own objects, or are they to be regarded as outside the 'world'? Whose sense experience is to constitute the world? Also, are all sense experiences to be given an equal status, or is a distinction to be made between them? If so, on what grounds? Do these grounds lie within the world or outside the world? Similarly, what is meant by the adjective 'possible' in this context? What would it mean for a world to be impossible? Since the distinction itself is usually drawn on grounds of logic, the notion of a 'possible world' comes to mean that which is not self-contradictory or in other words permitted by logic.

The so-called ontological problem is usually supposed to arise with respect to individual constants and how they are to be interpreted in case they are admitted in logic.[1] The problem becomes complicated by the issue of whether the inference rules concerning Universal Instantiation and Existential Generalisation are to be allowed such constants. The first thing to note in this connection is that the problem arises only in relation to quantificational logic. It has no place in the sentential or the propositional calculus. The reason for this lies in the fact that the argument forms of quantificational logic depend on 'all' and 'some' which themselves are onto-logical in character. *Some* is interpreted in a sense which commits oneself to an empirical ontology, whether one wants

[1] The case arising in respect of classes has already been discussed earlier.

it or not. As most of the logicians happen to be empirically inclined in present times, they are happy with the interpretation and feel that it logically underwrites their empiricism. The *all*, on the other hand, is not only treated in such a way as to raise the problem of the ontological status of hypothetical entities and relationships, but also to give rise to the problem of counterfactual conditionals. Further, as we pointed out earlier, the *all*, in any empirical sense, is intrinsically incapable of being comprehended because of the simple fact that in any empirical perspective time has inevitably to be taken as real. If, therefore, logic is not to have any ontological implications, quantificational logic will have to be banished from the realm of logic.

This is generally masked by the fact that the usual interpretation of *all* and *some* is found in the realm of mathematics which does not seem infected by temporality. But the moment we leave that realm, ontological issues begin to crowd on every side. Mathematics, of course, raises its own ontological problems, especially those that concern the assumption of 'actual infinities'. But, however great the problems arising from this field, they do not arise from the nature of the quantifiers, especially when they refer to the empirical domain.

Further, the attempt to free logic of ontology thrives on a distinction between what logic is *about* and logic itself. However valid this distinction may be in limited contexts, it fails to make sense when the basic ontological issue is in question. If, for example, logic requires an indefinite supply of symbols, each distinguishable from the other, then an ontological pluralism has to be accepted if logic itself has to *be*. Similarly, as the symbols have to be apprehensible by the senses, not only has the reality of the senses to be admitted but also the reality of space in which the *different* instances of the same symbol may occur. This, of course, ignores the distinction between logic and meta-logic, but in any discussion of ontology it is bound to be so. Those who will like to stick to the distinction will have to accept an ontology of infinite hierarchies of 'meta-metas', with some of the same consequences we have earlier discussed in relation to the theory of types. The choice between the paradoxes of self-inclusion and the difficulties of infinite regress may be left to the taste of individual philosophers. But the sleight of hand and the self-deception which lie behind the talk of an ontology-free logic need to be exposed so that the philosophically unwary are not taken in.

Chapter 2

ARE THERE SENSATIONS?

by

D. Y. DESHPANDE
Vidarbha Mahavidyalaya, Amravati, Nagpur University

The word 'sensation' has for long been part of the common currency of psychology and philosophy, both of which inform us that our knowledge of the external world is derived ultimately from our sensations. Yet it is to be feared that neither psychologists nor philosophers are entirely clear about the meaning of the word. When one considers the accounts given of the nature of sensations, and in particular the conclusions which philosophers draw from them, one cannot help feeling that there is something basically wrong about the whole thing. I propose in this short paper to examine this concept as it is used by philosophers, and to try to remove some at least of the confusion and ambiguity which are associated with the notion in philosophical literature.

I

Professor Ryle has shown clearly[1] that the psychologist's and the philosopher's use of this word 'sensation' is a technical one, quite different from any ordinary use of the word. The ordinary non-technical use of the word is that in which we speak of the sensations of toothache, of giddiness, of nausea, and the like. Another ordinary word for sensation in this sense is feeling. However, in addition to these sensations the

[1] See his paper 'Sensation', in H. D. Lewis (Ed.), *Contemporary British Philosophy*, 3rd series.

psychologist and the philosopher also speak of an entirely different kind of sensations, viz. those which they call 'the sensations of the special senses', i.e. the sensations of sight, hearing, touch, taste and smell, and they imply, even expressly state, that these two kinds of sensations are two species of the same genus. That this claim of the psychologist and the philosopher is false, and that it is even doubtful if there are sensations in this technical sense, is what I intend to show in the following pages.

As a representative statement of what psychologists mean by sensation I quote a few lines from Stout.

'Sensations consist in the immediate experiences which arise in connection with brain changes excited by processes in the sense-organs, primarily initiated by stimuli outside the body, and also by processes within the body taking place independently of external stimulation. If the eye is stimulated, we immediately experience colour sensations; when the ear is stimulated we experience sensations of sound. Similarly sensations of taste, smell, warmth or cold arise in connection with other stimuli acting at or near the surface of the body, while sensations such as nausea, cramp, fatigue, and hunger arise in connection with stimuli acting upon the internal organs.'[1]

Here is a clear statement of the way the word sensation is used by the psychologist. It will be obvious from it that to him sensations are 'immediate experiences', that we experience sensations, and finally that sensations of the special senses are a species of the same genus of which the sensations of nausea, cramp, etc., are another species. Stout goes so far as to say that *primarily* sensations are immediate experiences induced by stimulations of sense-organs, and only secondarily those which are induced by 'the stimulation of internal organs'.

I wish to argue that this account is fundamentally mistaken. For the sake of terminological convenience I shall call sensations like fatigue, cramp, nausea, etc., 'Sensations-1' and those of the special senses 'Sensations-2', and I shall first try to show

[1] *A Manual of Psychology* (4th ed.), p. 7.

that there is a fundamental difference between the two kinds of sensations, a difference which forbids us to subsume them both under the same genus.

The difference between the two kinds of sensations at once becomes apparent if we consider how they are described. When we see a blue object, the psychologist tells us that we experience a sensation of blue or of blueness, and this expression 'sensation of blue' seems at first to be exactly parallel to the expression 'sensation of fatigue'. But apart from the odd fact that *of* in the expression 'sensation *of* blue' is followed by an adjective, which it perhaps never is outside of psychology books, the meaning of *of* in the two expressions is quite different. When we speak of the sensation of fatigue we imply that fatigue itself is a sensation. 'The sensation of fatigue' means the same as 'the sensation fatigue', just as 'the feeling of fatigue' means the same as 'the feeling fatigue' and implies that fatigue itself is a feeling. When we say that a person answers to the name of Brown, I think we have an expression in which *of* functions in precisely the same way grammatically. 'A person of the name of Brown' simply means 'a person of the name Brown', and the preposition *of* is simply the sign of apposition. Now it is obvious that in the expression 'sensation of blue', *of* has an altogether different meaning. Blue or blueness is not itself a sensation, and the expression 'sensation of blue' is not of the same kind as the expression 'sensation of fatigue'. It is of the form 'awareness of blue' or 'knowledge of blue', where *of* signifies the relation of knowledge and its object. The point might be summarised by saying that when we have a sensation of fatigue, we have fatigue (which is a sensation), whereas when we experience (as the psychologist says) a sensation of blue, we experience blue which is not a sensation at all. In the first case there is an awareness, viz. a sensation; in the second there is an awareness *of* something which is not itself a sensation.

This argument based on the analysis of linguistic usage can be further reinforced by introspective examination. When we see or hear anything, do we experience any sensations or feelings? I think it is obvious that when I see anything I do not feel any sensation either in the eye or anywhere else in the body.[1] To be sure, when looking at a very bright light, I do experience pain in the eye; but normally seeing does not involve any sensations in the eye, and even in this exceptional case pain is no part of seeing. Similarly with regard to hearing. A very loud noise, such as the report of a gun, might cause a painful sensation in the ear; but this painful sensation is no part of hearing, and in normal hearing such sensations are absent, and so on with the rest of the senses. It therefore seems as if, contrary to the accepted view, there are no sensations of seeing, hearing, etc.

II

It might be objected on behalf of the psychologist that the sensations of the special senses are not of course bodily feelings like fatigue, cramp, nausea, etc., and the fact that such sensations are not present in seeing, hearing, etc., does not prove that there may not be sensations of another kind present in those modes of perception. Let us therefore enquire whether there are sensations of this second kind, and if there are, what their nature is.

The psychologist tells us that sensations are immediate experiences, and also that they are immediately experienced; he uses these two expressions with such complete indifference that it is obvious that he regards them as synonymous. However, it must be admitted that they are very far from being synonymous. The first description informs us that sensations are experiences; the second that they are experienced, that is, they are objects of experience—a vastly different affair. Put together the two descriptions seem to suggest that our experience of sensations is an experience of the second order. For if sensations are immediate experiences, and they are also immediately experienced, then our experience of sensations (referred to in such expressions as 'we immediately experience sensations of sight') will be an experience of an experience. It

[1] See Ryle, *op. cit.*, p. 432.

seems unlikely that this implication was part of the intention of the psychologist.

Perhaps it is possible to defend the indifferent use of these two expressions; it might be maintained that they *are* synonymous. For in a sense to be an experience is to be experienced: for how could anything be an experience unless it was experienced? Would not 'unexperienced experience' be a contradiction in terms? By this it is not meant that every experience is experienced in (or made the object of) a second experience, but simply that it is experienced in the self-same experience. To say that pain is an experience and that it is experienced, surely means one and the same thing. They certainly do not imply that when I experience pain I have some second-order experience. I think that this argument is plausible and is probably sound. If so, nothing more is involved in saying that we immediately experience sensations than in saying that our sensations are immediately experienced, and the two expressions may be treated as synonymous.

Having cleared up this apparent complication, let us now turn once again to the psychologist's account of Sensations-2. We at once notice that whereas his statements that sensations are immediate experiences and that they are immediately experienced are true of Sensations-1, they are not of Sensations-2. My experience of a Sensation-1, say nausea, is nothing more than my nausea. But can we say the same thing about my experience of an S2 (Sensation-2), say a sensation of colour? Is my sensation of a colour an experience? If it is, I should be able to describe it. For example, I can describe an S1 as fatigue, or cramp, or nausea; and these I can further characterise qualitatively and quantitatively. Fatigue may be mild or intense; a pain may be shooting, throbbing or splitting, but when we turn to an S2, say a sensation of colour, we find that we are unable to describe it by its intrinsic properties. Whatever description we give of it turns out to be a description not of the sensation but of its object. How does a sensation of colour differ from that of sound? Or a sensation of blue from that of red? The differences pointed out are found to be differences in the objects, i.e. of colours from sounds, or of blue from red. Whether the sensations themselves differ from one another is very difficult, if not impossible, to say for the simple reason that they do not lend themselves to inspection. In fact all that one finds when one looks for *sensations* of colours and of sounds, is colours and sounds; of the sensations themselves there is never a hint. If anyone should doubt this, let him try to differentiate between the sensation of colour and that of sound without mentioning colours and sounds.

But surely psychologists speak of the attributes of sensations? And by these attributes, they surely mean attributes of the sensations themselves? Well, as a matter of fact they do; but it is sad to see how completely they fail to accomplish what they profess to be doing. Stout, for example, enumerates five attributes of sensation, viz. quality, intensity, protensity, extensity, and local signs; and he tells us that sensations differ from one another in one or more of these respects. Let us consider some of these attributes. We are told as regards the first attribute, viz. quality, that every sensation has its characteristic quality. A sensation of colour, for example, differs from a sensation of sound in quality; so does a sensation of blue differ from that of red. No doubt a colour is qualitatively different from a sound, and so is blue qualitatively different from red, but how are we to find out whether the *sensations* of colours and sounds or of blue and red do so differ? For the sensations themselves (as distinct from the objects of those sensations) are nowhere open to view. Or consider the case of extensity, another attribute of sensation. Sensations are said to have an attribute called 'extensity' which is different from the extension of things, e.g. 'when a thing is first seen as a speck in the distance and then its appearance gradually grows bigger as it is approached, the change is a change in the extensity of the visual sensation'.[1] Here is an extraordinary statement by a famous psychologist that the apparent size of a thing is the quality of the visual sensation! If sensations are what they are reported to be, viz. experiences, it is not easy to see how they

[1] Stout, *op. cit.*, p. 127.

can have a size, either apparent or real. This clearly shows that the alleged attributes of sensation are in reality qualities of the objects of those sensations, and the complete failure of the psychologist's attempt to describe sensations by reference to their intrinsic properties supports the suspicion expressed above that perhaps there are no such things as what psychologists call 'sensations of the special senses'. For if there are immediate experiences answering to the descriptions of S2, there is no reason why they should forever baffle us in our attempts to track them down. Sensations-2, if there are such entities, must be transparent; and their existence must be inferred or postulated. However, inferred or postulated entities can hardly be described as immediate experiences, nor can they be held to be the starting point of all our knowledge of the external world.

III

I think it will be instructive to enquire here into the causes which may have led philosophers and psychologists to postulate sensations of the second kind and to extend the application of the ordinary word 'sensation' to these postulated entities. I think that the following considerations most probably led them to do this.

It must have been obvious to psychologists and philosophers alike quite early in their career that the ordinary verbs of perception, viz. see, hear, feel (touch), taste and smell, take as their grammatical objects names of physical objects and processes. Thus we say, 'I saw an orange', 'I heard a train', 'I felt his hand on my shoulder', and so on. It must have been equally obvious to them that a physical object, say an orange, cannot be perceived in its entirety by any one sense. An orange is not something only visible; it is also something which can be touched, tasted and smelt. So if by 'seeing' one meant (as was not unnatural) a purely visual mode of knowledge, what one sees would not be an orange, but only its visible aspect or look. Similar difficulties would arise with regard to the other senses also. There was therefore a need for a word to denote the awareness peculiar to each sense, and the word which naturally suggested itself was sensation, owing partly to its kinship with the word sense in such phrases as 'the sense of sight', 'the five senses', etc., and partly to the fact that the word sensation was already in use, though in a totally different sense, viz. as meaning feeling. For similar reasons the use of the word sense as a verb (to sense), meaning to become aware by any one of the five senses, was introduced. It came to be believed then that sensing was the activity proper to each sense, and sensation was the peculiar kind of knowledge which each sense gave.

IV

A question which will raise its head at this point is the following: If there are no sensations (of the special senses), then how does perception take place? What part do the senses play in perception? Surely the senses have something to do with perception! The usual view about perception and about the role of the senses in it is that in every perception there is sensation, and that perception consists in amplifying the sensation or in construing or interpreting it in the light of past experience. Perception consists of transforming a sensation into a knowledge of a physical object. But if we say that there is no such thing as the sensations of the special senses, then what are we to say of the part the senses play in perception?

I think that our denial of Sensations-2 need cause us no insuperable difficulties. We can say that perception does not involve Sensations-2, but it does involve sensible awareness of sense-objects. I think that what philosophers have called sense-data are such objects.

Now I wish to make one thing absolutely clear—I do not wish to advocate or defend the sense-datum theory. In its full-fledged form, it is not merely a theory of perception, but also a theory of metaphysics. I am aware that the theory gets into serious trouble regarded either as a theory of perception or of the constitution of the physical objects. Nor do I wish to suggest that the theory could be so presented as to obviate all criticism. All I wish to say is that the sense-datum is the kind of thing which one becomes aware of by one's senses, and that while perception cannot involve sensations (S2) for the simple reason that there are no such things, it does involve some activity of the senses. The senses present to us their immediate objects, out of which then the mind construes a perception of a physical object. Between Sensations-2 and sense-data I favour the sense-data because we are certainly aware of them, whereas we are certainly never aware of Sensations-2. The larger questions of epistemology and metaphysics I leave to those who are qualified to tackle them.

Chapter 3

TOWARDS AN INDIAN VIEW OF
THE PERSON

by

RICHARD DE SMET, S.J.
De Nobili College, Poona

It was rather unexpected to hear Dr T. M. P. Mahadevan
declare on the 5 March 1973, while inaugurating the seminar
he had convened at the University of Madras on the concept of
the 'person', that 'if the *Brahman* of Śaṅkara is anything it is
surely not impersonal'. Dr Mahadevan is a strict adherent of
Śaṅkara's non-dualism (*Advaita-vāda*) and it had become
usual since the Max Müller era to hear such non-dualists assert
contrarily that the *Brahman* of Advaita is impersonal. We were
then witnessing an important linguistic change. The reason
for it seems to be a better understanding in the Indian philosophical circles of the idea of 'person' as originally developed
by Christianity for its own philosophico-religious uses and
further elaborated along the centuries by Western thinkers.
This better understanding may owe something to the increased
participation by Catholic scholars in the many seminars,
conferences and congresses of the diverse philosophical
associations of India, especially during the last twenty years.
More recently, interest in the person has been enhanced by the
writings of Strawson whose M and P predicates are now
haunting the minds of a large number of Indian philosophers.

The uncertain status of the notion of 'person' in India is
conditioned by the fact that it is foreign to the Sanskrit tradition and has no adequate rendering in any of the Sanskritic

languages. When dealing with man or the Deity Indian philosophy always worked with other concepts which rarely
imported the holistic signification of 'person'. It will be useful
to attend to the chief ones among them.

The term *ātman* whose original meaning is that of the
reflective pronoun is used philosophically to designate the
various results of the analysis of a being: the gross body, the
vital energies called *prāṇas*, the outer senses, the inner sense
which is threefold, viz. *manas* (mind), *ahaṃkāra* (ego-sense)
and *buddhi* (intellect-will), the unmanifested matter (*avyakta*)
which emanates all these, the individual monad (*jīva* or
jīvātman) embodied (*dehin*) in them, and the divine Absolute
which is the ultimate basis and sustainer of their whole
hierarchy and, hence, is called supreme *Ātman* (*paramātman*).
Each inner *ātman* acts as an internal cause (*upādāna*) giving
reality to the element which precedes it in our enumeration but
it does this without synthesising with it, i.e. only as a support.
Hence, it is never equal to the whole being and misses the
integrality of 'person'. Even to call it a self and to speak of a
hierarchy of lower and higher selves is open to much ambiguity.
This Upanishadic analysis remains an elementary praesupposi-
tum of Indian thought and had to be recalled.

A closer equivalent of 'person' is *puruṣa* which means male,
man. Philosophically, it was assumed to designate a sentient
and usually an intellectual monad such as man's 'soul' (*jīvātman*), a god or a godly power, or 'the God within', but also, as
in some verses of the Gītā, to designate a cosmic entity, such
as primordial matter. Monadic also is *jīva*, the living one,
which denotes the sentient principle within living beings.

As to *vyakti* which is in current use today in the sense of
'individual', it denotes strictly the individual within a genus so
that when said of God, for instance of the three Persons of the
Christian Trinity, it is a source of ambiguity and of difficulties
in comparative religion.

When the term 'person' came to the notice of Indian
intellectuals, it had already a long history of its own. Originally
a designation of the stage-mask of Greek and Roman actors, it

had quickly taken the meaning of stage-part or dramatic hero. Hence, the Stoics found it convenient to refer to man as endowed by God with a part to play on the world stage. This interpretation allowed the Roman law courts to call person a subject of legal rights and duties, i.e. a citizen as opposed to a slave. The dignity thus conferred upon the term 'person' induced the Christians to adopt it (not without some ambiguity at first) to designate the Three (Father, Son or Word, Spirit) in the one divine Essence and the One in two distinct natures (divine and human) otherwise known as Jesus Christ, the Word made flesh. Since Christians believed in the brotherhood of all men, they also began to consider them all as persons, whether free or slaves, citizens or foreigners. This development was summed up in the basic, though imperfect, definition coined by Boethius: a person is an individual subject whose nature is rational.

The medieval Schoolmen realised that 'person' belonged to the realm of responsible action, intellectual and morally free, as the ultimate subject of single attribution of all predicates implying intellectual agency. Consequently, Aquinas refined Boethius's definition finally to declare that 'person' means an integral and unitary self-subsistent subject characterised by intellectual consciousness, moral freedom and all properties ensuing from these defining notes. Prominent among these properties were privacy, inalienability of end-in-itself, ownership of natural rights, moral responsibility, being a source of values in its own right, and capacity of initiating interpersonal relationships. It is to be noted with a regard to the Indian valuation of self-denial that such relationships demand a fair degree of selflessness and that this elaborate definition did not favour ethical individualism. It was also such that it could with due precision apply analogically to the divine as well as to human persons.

Such is the concept of the person which remained dominant up to Kant himself, but it is during the latter's time that Jacobi chose to restrict the extension of the term 'person' to the category of human individuals so that its application to the

Godhead would be merely anthropomorphic. The trend he thus inaugurated was followed by a number of thinkers of the nineteenth century and influenced the translators of Sanskrit works towards the turn of the twentieth century. In their hands Śaṅkara's distinction between the qualityless Absolute (*nirguṇa Brahman*)—equivalent to the *Deus simplex* of Christian theology—and the anthropomorphic qualified Godhead (*saguṇa Brahman*) became the distinction between the impersonal and the personal *Brahman* or between the Absolute (*Brahman*) and God (*Īśvara*). Today it is practically impossible to convince the Hindus that the personal God of Christianity is really the Absolute and as a rule the non-dualists among them consider that the Christians have inherited only an anthropomorphic conception of the Deity.

Against this background it becomes understandable that modern Indian thinkers have hardly been attracted by the person as a topic for reflection or have perceived its interest only on the level of the human individual as treated in the various brands of modern humanism. Yet the materials for an Indian recognition of the person are present both in the theologies and in the various anthropologies of the Indian tradition and it will now be our task to explore them and to discern their value.

The Integrated Individual of Vedic Times

In Vedic society an individual enjoys the full dignity of man only in so far as he is a *yajamāna* (sacrificer), i.e. is entitled by his *varṇa* (caste-rank) to employ priests to perform sacrifices (*yajña*). The prototype of *yajña* is the primordial sacrifice of the Great Male or Man (*Mahā-puruṣa*) through whose ritual dismemberment the universe in all its parts and categories of beings has come to be, as recalled in *Ṛgveda*, x, 90, and to be established spatially and temporally in its perfect order called *Ṛta*, the Truth. What man experiences as untruth (*an-Ṛta*) is the deterioration of this order manifested in droughts, diseases and other derangements of nature. Sacrifice is the special technique by which he is able to overcome this deterioration and restore the whole (*sarvam*), including himself, in its orderly integrity. By correctly performing the daily and other sacrifices, he feeds and duly praises the 'gods' (*deva*) who are, as it were, the cosmic engineers who keep the universe in perfect running order, and thus he secures anew the original wholeness and wholesomeness (*sarvam bhavati*) for himself, his family, his society and his world. He is never a mere individual, insulated by his empirical limits or by any hankering after self-sufficiency, but the centre of a network of links with the beings of the three worlds. Prolonged by his wife, children, cattle and pasture lands, hierarchically complemented by the members of the other *varṇas*, he is the ally of the gods and the friend of a world the secret of whose regulation he possesses in the knowledge which he calls *Veda*.

The Vedic seers incline increasingly to derive the universe not from blind Necessity but from a personal Originator and Ruler whose mysterious nature and agency they grope towards imagining. In these gropings lies the dawn of metaphysics. Unfathomable, abiding before and beyond the being of his creatures and the non-being of their temporal causes, alive (breathing yet windless) by his own energy, he is the unnamed 'that One' (*tad-ekam*) though given many a title. In the search for an expression of his creatorship, all the modes of production known to the Vedic man are tried and found wanting: the weaver's yarn-stretching (*tan-*), the builder's foundation-laying (*dhā-*), the blacksmith's forging (*takṣ-*), the architect's measuring (*mā-*), the bird's brooding (*tap-*), the mammal's semen-emitting (*sṛj-*), the lord's commanding (*vāk-*) and the priest's sacrificing (*yaj-*). The very plurality of these approaches which cancel one another secures the transcendence of that Father and Lord of the creatures (*Prajā-pati*) who encompasses them all. In his mysterious Personality man finds the source of his dependent being, the support of his life and the security of his well-ordered world. A centre through this Centre, a subsistent through this Subsistent, he also finds in him the dealer of his *varṇa*-status and the weaver of his complementarities.

Never will the conception of man in this subcontinent again be so holistic and attentive to his many-relatedness. Analysis with its sharp tooth will tear it to pieces and an astonishing variety of anthropologies will vie to displace it. Yet even today it appears to survive below the level of sophistication especially in so far as the caste-system continues to regulate the relations and interactions of Indian people and their religiosity remains focused on both the *devas* and the transcendent One. Indeed, the enduring presence of this conception is the basic datum discerned and analysed by the modern anthropological study of man and society in India.[1]

Man, the Meeting-place of the Cosmic Powers in the Brāhmaṇas and Upanishads

The interrelated but opaque man of the Vedas was destined to be analysed and almost split up during the next centuries, a fate not unlike that of the atom of modern physics. This process started with the equivalence discovered in the *Brāhmaṇas* and *Āraṇyakas* between the sacrifice, the cosmos and man the microcosm in the light of the myth of the self-sacrificing universal *Puruṣa*. The selfsame *devas* fed through the sacrifice had to be not only the great functionaries of the macrocosm but also the internal powers at work in man. His vital energies (*prāṇas*) and his psychological functions (*indriyas*) had to be deities (*devatā*) competing within him for their hierarchical ranking but not different from the power-wielders of the macrocosm. Like the ritual sacrifice, he himself was their meeting-place and he could through introspection develop a new Vedic knowledge of the henceforth internalised sacrifice by which he would discover in himself the very Power that gave efficacy to the sacrifices, the mysterious *Brahman*.

In the Upanishads, the search is on for this *Brahman* as the innermost *Ātman* of man and of every contingent being. Every layer of man, the material, the biological, the psycho-

---

[1] Cf. for instance, D. G. Mandelbaum, *Society in India*, 2 vols, Univ. California Press, 1970.

logical, the intellectual, in turn yields some great entity (a *puruṣa* or an *ātman*) which is measured up to the ideal of greatness, supremacy of power and absoluteness conveyed by the *brahman*-idea. Even beyond pure Consciousness reflection attains remarkably the ultimate transcendence of Bliss (*Ānanda*). These two together constitute the earliest adequate definition of *Brahman*: *Vijñānam ānandam brahma, Brahman* is Consciousness, Bliss (*Bṛhad-āraṇyaka* Up., iii, 9). Uppermost as well as innermost it stands at the apex of everything in the transcendent simplicity of its fullness. Of man and the universe it is the Essence (*svarūpa*), not in the sense of what they are but of that from which they are: 'That from which these beings are born, by which once born they live, into which they enter when they die, that is what you must try to understand, that is *Brahman*' (*Taittirīya Up.*, iii, 1). Ground, support, inner witness and ruler, goal of all contingent beings, it is most immediate to them, their highest *Ātman* indeed, yet it surpasses them all. If we try to name it by any one of their names, it shakes it off and we must say, '*neti neti*, it is not thus, not thus' (*Bṛh. Ār. Up.*, iv). For it is non-dual (*advaita*) and in it 'there is no disjunction between seer and sight' (*ibid.*).

It is therefore understandable that if one wishes to coincide by a direct awareness with this inmost Absolute, one should begin with mortification (*tapas*) and train oneself to apophatic self-denial. This is the doctrine of Bhrigu who mortified himself and attained to the successively better realisations that the *Brahman* is the matter from which all food derives, or better the breath of all life-breath, or better still the mind of all minds, or higher than that the Consciousness of every discerning consciousness, and finally the Bliss shadowed in every bliss (cf. *Taitt. Up.*, iii, 2–6). There is a direct connection between this doctrine and the desire for renunciation which becomes frequent in the Upanishads:

'Once Brahmins have come to know this *Ātman* who transcends hunger and thirst, sorrow, confusion, old age and death, they rise above their desire for sons, riches, etc., and wander forth to lead a beggar's life. They, first, lead a child-like life (*bālya*) in learning (*pāṇḍitya*); then, they reject these two and become silent sages (*muni*); lastly, they put away both silence and its opposite with disgust, and become *Brāhmaṇas* (knowers of *Brahman*).' (*Bṛh. Ār. Up.*, iii, 5).

According to all this, the Upanishadic man is no longer a solid organism externally related to the beings of the three worlds but a complex assembly of a whole scale of cosmic powers apart from which he seems to be nothing. He is not exactly their host or even their meeting-place but rather the very form of their active encounter, not their containing shell but a particular shape of their manifestation. On a higher level of introspective analysis even those powers are swallowed up by the mighty *Brahman* and in their humiliation man finds both his most complete self-denial and his highest exaltation for he is driven to say, I am not this body, nor these senses, nor these higher powers, I am not even this individual ego, but I am *Brahman* (*ahaṁ brahmāsmi*).

This is not a proclamation of pantheism for *Brahman* is not identified with anything finite, and not even of acosmism for the finite as such is not denied altogether, but it is the entrancing discovery that the Absolute stands transcendingly in the heart of man and of every contingent being. Man is not absolute but the Absolute is within him. Man is no longer the solid centre of many outgoing relationships but he has found the inner relationship of total dependence on the firmest and most solid Existent (*Sat*) from which he receives his whole existence and of which he is but a contingent manifestation. He is no longer a focus but an irradiation. The whole universe is the great wheel of *Brahman* (*brahmacakra*) in which all things get life and subsistence; in this wheel man is like a wild gander fluttering about till he recognises the Impeller of the wheel; then, blessed by him, he goes to immortality (cf. *Śvetāśvatara Up.*, i, 6).

The permanent value of this Upanishadic anthropology lies in this, that it roots man most ontologically in the divine

Absolute and establishes for the centuries to come the crea-
turely dimension of his personality. It was, however, pregnant
with an ambiguity of wide consequence. Indeed, it could be
developed in two opposite directions: either as a valuation of
man as a wonderful creature of the perfect Absolute and a
manifestation of its splendour, or as a devaluation of man who
is like nothing compared to the fullness of being of the
Brahman-Ātman. But already the Upanishads inclined to the
latter. Helped by the growing popularity of the discipline of
renunciation (*sannyāsa*) this became the chief trend of Upanishadic interpretation, not, however, without some sporadic
manifestations of the other alternative especially in the
Vaishṇava or the Shaiva theologies.

Man as the Renouncer
The *sannyāsin* undertakes deliberately to be the opposite of the
Vedic householder. He withdraws through a radical decision
from the ties of family and the bonds of society, frees himself
from the duties and rights of his *varṇa*-status and sets himself
in the margin of society and its hierarchical framework. Turning
away with a shrug of contempt from the honoured triad of
human goals, wealth (*artha*), love (*kāma*) and duty (*dharma*),
he devotes himself exclusively to the pursuit of a new and
supreme goal, *mokṣa*, the complete liberation from the round
of rebirths (*saṃsāra*) and its cause, action of all kinds, good as
well as evil. His ideal is *nivritti*, studied passivity, as opposed to
pravritti, the goal-seeking activity of the caste-man. He is
dead to the world, desireless, indifferent, beyond good and
evil.

What he represents is not exactly spirituality but transcendence of which he is the living symbol. It is not the spiritual character of intellectual knowledge which judges of all
things but its power of abstraction which can ultimately
dissolve all concreteness and take its stand in pure consciousness. It is not man's sovereign will to act as he decides but his
more radical freedom to break asunder all his ties and even the
meshwork of his ensnaring ego. *The sannyāsin is the hero of*

pure transcendence. He witnesses to this dimension of intel-
lectuality of our 'freedom from' which is usually hidden by the
commitments of our 'freedom to'. He has isolated it like a live
wire, dangerous but fascinating. However, by isolating it he
has also deprived it of its essential accompaniments within the
riches of human personality. Fortunately, *sannyāsa* will be
confronted by other trends and from their interaction new
insights will be born which will compensate its austere narrow-
ness.

The Man of the Caste-system

During the same period when renunciation became the chosen
mode of life of many, Indian society reinforced its *varṇa*-
organisation into a caste-system. To the *dharma-sūtras* (law-
guides) which belonged to the Vedic *śruti* (revelation) there
were now added *dharma-śāstras* (treatises of law) exemplified
by the famous Laws of Manu. These belong to *smṛti* (tradition) and were elaborated, essentially from the standpoint of
the Brahmins, in order to codify in exact detail the hierarchical
framework of the castes, the rights and obligations of each
caste and, within the caste, of individuals as members of joint
families (joint in the community of habitation, commensality,
cult and ownership) and exogamic *gotras* (clans), the multi-
tude of prohibitions arising from the polarity between ritual
purity and impurity, and the categories of delicts and punish-
ments.

In the exacting bonds of this caste-system, man finds the
security of stability, but his freedom is severely curbed from
birth to death. Social mobility almost disappears and social
conformism determines even his most private acts. The
system, while satisfying to the extreme the social requirements
of the human person, leaves no scope to his individualistic
tendencies or only an exceptional one. This unavoidable exception concerns *sannyāsa*. Renunciation, indeed, though it
contradicts the whole system as an escape from it, is reluc-
tantly permitted and the countersocial goal it pursues, *mokṣa*,
is allowed as an addition to the three traditional 'ends of man'

(*puruṣārtha*). Although permitted, renunciation is carefully regulated. It is only at the end of his useful social life, after he has begotten children, given them in marriage and settled everything for their welfare that a man is allowed to leave his sacrificial fire and, with or without his wife, retire to the seclusion of the forest and eventually wander forth, homeless, tieless and utterly free.

This is a compromise devised to contain the dangerous spreading of the way of renunciation by confining it to that part of man's life when he becomes a burden on society. The fact that it remained largely theoretical because it was over-ruled by the absolute claim of the great representatives of *sannyāsa* does not withdraw its signification. It proved that the human person cannot be reduced to its social dimension and that no amount of regulation can smother its deep-seated desire for emancipation.

The Monadic Man of Jainism and Sāṅkhya

In this world of caste-men and renouncers, Mahāvīra Jina gave a new life to a probably older form of renounced life. With him, man as a monadic individual is exalted in the transcendency of his spirit. Ignoring (and probably ignorant of) the Upanishadic *Brahman*, ground of the world and inner ruler of man, and, as a characteristic renouncer, the claims of the caste-society, he proclaims the eternity, inherent consciousness and potential omniscience of the *jīva* (living one), the monadic soul-substance which he affirms to exist not only in man but in every possible aggregate of matter (*pudgala*). We may note the egalitarian aspect of this affirmation. Inequality, however, though unnatural, is very much a fact of the mundane existence of the *jīvas* through the round of their rebirths (*saṃsāra*). Encapsulated in a diversity of envelopes made of gross matter (called *ajīva*, non-living, non-soul), the *jīvas* share their variety in shape, weight, size and organic modifications; they are subjected to their temporality and all their limitations; and the opacity of matter obscures their natively perfect sight and maintains them in parviscience. Graver still, their embodiment exposes them to the evil effect of activity whether of body, mind or speech. Actions, indeed, affect the soul through a more penetrating kind of materialisation. Like dyes permeating a cloth they colour it, each one in its own shade, and this tainting obfuscates their knowledge most internally. This conception of action, *karman*, as a dye-stuff (made of eight kinds of atoms of subtle matter) has puzzled many, yet it is logical enough once the distinction of the spirit from all non-spirit (including action) is admitted as an ontological difference between heterogeneous substances. What is less logical is the admission of a contamination of the one by the others.

This view of man commands a discipline of dematerialisation and, to coin a word, of 'dekarmanisation' accessible to all regardless of their caste and culminating in monastic renunciation. The laity must begin with the five vows (*vrata*) of non-killing, truthfulness, non-stealing, chastity and non-coveting. These are practised with the help of three restraints (*gupti*) and ten pious duties (*dharma*) including fasts and other mortifications. Those who feel fit for perfect renunciation then enter the monastic life which frees them from all duties to society except preaching the 'way of the Jinas'. They live a life of extreme asceticism, minutely regulated, and aim after the highest purification which some of them anticipate symbolically by a state of permanent nakedness. If their death, which may follow upon a complete fast undertaken voluntarily, coincides with utter freedom from karmanic matter, they attain the release of *nirvāṇa* (going off, like a flame that ceases to burn). Their *jīva* no longer weighted by any atom of *ajīva* and cleansed of any taint of *karman* ascends to the summit of space and recovers the blissful omniscience and freedom of the pure spirit. Godlike (in a universe void of God) but individual, it stands forever in the self-sufficiency of its all-knowingness.

Non-theistic Sāṅkhya resembles Jainism but is more radical in its conception of the individual spirit. The latter, called *puruṣa* (man) or *jña* (knower), is never really but only apparently embodied. Hence, it is never really affected by

matter nor tainted in any way by activity which is the exclusive province of unconscious matter (*pradhāna* or *prakriti*). Its
illusory feeling of repeated embodiments in the sorrowful
round of births is due to its own reflection in the mirrorlike
density of matter. It is a mere fallacy which the Sāṅkhya
teaching suffices to dispel, apart from any asceticism, by the
finality of its demonstration of the inamissible purity of every
puruṣa. Whenever this truth is grasped by a *puruṣa*, he at once
recovers the untroubled awareness of his isolation (*kaivalya*).
Pure, unrelated, he is then neither omniscient nor parviscient
but a solitary light shining upon nothing, indifferent and
serene.

The relevance of these twin conceptions to an integrated
Indian view of personality lies perhaps in this that they have
obeyed man's urge to reach his spiritual core with the dangerous fearlessness of any intellect fascinated with the purity of
abstraction. Analysis here is completely cut off from synthesis.
The fullness of its starting-point, which is necessarily the
whole 'phenomenon of man' taken in the concreteness of his
very much 'incarnated' activities and experiences, is so
impoverished by the analysing process that there is no real
accounting for it at the end. This, indeed, is not simply a
process of sifting by which the more precious element is
distinguished from the others but a process of utter rejection
of the non-spiritual. Further, the spiritual itself is hypostatised
into a pure ego and thus is a solidified abstraction unlike the
transcendent and universal *Ātman* of the Upanishads.

The Evanescent Man of Early Buddhism

Analysis again is very much at work in the teaching of Buddha,
but he shuns entirely the tendency to turn abstractions into
substances. What captivates his attention is the mobility and
constant changingness of the human phenomenon. The
paradigm of reality is not substance but action which is
instantaneous and followed immediately by its consequence.
Man is like a stream of five conjoined currents (called the five
skandhas or aggregates) corresponding to what we normally

conceive as matter, sensations, perceptions, mental constructs and consciousness. No abiding support underlies this stream to give it ontic continuity, neither *jīva* nor *puruṣa*, nor *ātman* of any kind. 'Physical forms are like foam; sensations like bubbles; perceptions like mirage; mental constructs like the flimsy trunk of a banana tree; and consciousness like phantoms' (*Saṃyutta Nikāya*, III). 'What is called mind, or thought, or consciousness, is produced and disappears in a perpetual revolving of day and night. Just as, O monks, a monkey sporting in a wood seizes now a branch and then another, so also what is called mind is produced and vanishes in a perpetual passing from day to night' (*ibid.*, II).

When we perceive ourselves as a permanent ego, we are as deluded as the child who takes a spreading flame for a swift-running animal. The end of this illusion is *nirvāṇa*, the blowing out of the imagined ego.

'As a flame blown out by the wind disappears and cannot be named, even so the monk when released from name and body disappears and cannot be named—He who has disappeared, is he non-existent?—No measuring is there of him that has disappeared whereby one might know of him that he is not; when all qualities are removed, all modes of speech are removed also' (*Sutta-nipāta*, 1075–6).

Buddha's teaching is curiously reminiscent of modern physics, his flame-man of its bodies, dances of electrons, but physics does not pretend to be an ontology. As Śaṅkara will show, he leaves out of account the resisting fact of the *cogito* which is the door for the reintroduction of spiritual subsistence. But he stands forever as a warning against any facile solidification of man according to the constructs of his desires and instinctual drives. Only the ego belongs to the realm of naming, the true person cannot be reached by the modes of speech. Whether this apophatism did imply in Buddha's mind beyond a rejection of predicamental personality even a denial of any post-predicamental person remains a matter of dispute, but as apophatism it is salutary.

What also deserves to be emphasised is Buddha's contribution to the humanisation of man. While he rejected any Jaina-like extreme asceticism he preached a way of non-violent morality (*śīla*), meditational concentration on selflessness (*samādhi*) and devotion to wisdom (*prajñā*) which transformed the ways of the people of India and of the successive waves of their invaders. In his own life he exemplified a pattern of most attractive virtues (mildness, kindness, compassion, moderation, wisdom) which later legend expanded and hieratised so that he became more and more an ideal Personality (called significantly *mahā-puruṣa* and *bhagavān*), emulated by his monks and venerated with loving devotion (*bhakti*) by the masses of the laity. Thus on the level of transcendence a new ideal of personality was slowly taking shape on the very ruins of the ego-tainted conceptions he had so successfully contradicted.

The Open Person of the Bhagavad-Gītā

In order to understand the genius of the author of the Gītā as manifested peculiarly in his renovated conception of personality, it is essential to realise that all the above anthropologies were alive and in conflict when he undertook his creation. Their conflict was felt most keenly in the opposition between the fast gaining conceptions of the Buddhist and other Renouncers and the resisting Brahmanic views of a society which defended its caste organisation and its sacrificial tradition. If their tension was to be overcome otherwise than through their sterile effort of mutual destruction, a bridge had to be built, a synthesis formulated which would reconcile their respective values. This is why the Gītā was composed.

The first element of this synthesis is the unpromising dualism of Sāṅkhya: man is an embodied spirit (*dehin*) in a body (*deha*) pertaining to material nature (*prakriti*). Whatever changes happen to him, whether birth, death, activity or suffering, happen to this body only whereas the *dehin* is an impassible knower. 'Never is it born nor dies: unborn, eternal, everlasting, primeval; it does not slay nor is it slain: weapons

C

do not cut it nor does fire burn it, the waters do not wet it nor does the wind dry it' (cf. ii, 16–25). Yet lodged in *prakriti* it experiences the changes that take place in it as if they were its own and thus has the feeling of revolving through the round of births and deaths, but the knowledge of not being at all an agent suffices to deliver it from sorrow.

This dualism provides as it were two separated spans which must be linked if the bridge is to be constructed. Not unlike Descartes who secures the unity of man's thinking self with his body through an indirect recourse to the truthful God, the author of the Gītā overcomes his *dehin-deha* dualism through his well-articulated monotheism. Krishna, the divine *Puruṣottama* (supreme Person), is the universal *Paramātman* and, as such, the absolute basis (*pratiṣṭhā*) of the *Brahman* (14, 27). This *Brahman* is threefold: it is the *Brahman* of the sacrifices, it is the perfect stillness which the renouncers emulate, and it is the 'great *brahman*' (*mahad-brahman*) of the universe. The latter stands for the totality of *prakriti* which comprises both material nature (i.e. the *prakriti* of Sāṅkhya) and all the *ātmans* or *dehins* or *jīvas*, i.e. all the conscious entities. These, indeed, constitute the higher (*parā*) as opposed to the lower (*aparā*) *prakriti*. This complete *prakriti* 'is mine', says Krishna. It is the same as *mahad-brahman*. Now, 'great *Brahman* is to me a womb, in it I plant the seed: from this derives the origin of all beings. In whatever womb whatever form develops, of those great *Brahman* is the Womb, I the Father, giver of the seed' (14, 3–4).

An often misunderstood simile extends this teaching from the origin to the whole activity of beings: 'in the religion of the heart of all beings dwells the Lord, twirling them hither and thither by his uncanny power [like puppets] mounted on a machine' (18, 61). The machine, indeed, is the lower *prakriti* in which the *dehins* are inserted by their bodies. Thus they share in activities which appear to be their own but which are really the Lord's. Now the Lord's activity is always disinterested (*niṣkāma*) since its fruit can be no gain for him and is produced only for the benefit of beings. Once man understands this, he can easily be converted to *niṣkāma karma*, i.e. cease to desire the fruits of actions and yet accept his role as the instrument or occasion (*nimitta*) of those actions willed by the Lord and produced through the Lord's *prakriti*.

The traditional Vedic view that man is a sacrificer by divine ordination finds here its point of reinsertion. All obligatory duties can now be considered as sacrifices and ought to be performed as such; and the Lord Krishna is not only the ordainer but the recipient and proper object of all sacrifices (5,29; 9,24; etc.). Once action is thus reinterpreted as sacrifice, it becomes immune from any charge of binding man through fetters of selfishness or self-centredness. Man restored as sacrificer, loses all ego-rooted desire and lives beyond fear in serene freedom.

The superiority of the Gītākāra's conception may be expressed comparatively by a short apologue. It has been said that Jina, like a dog, attacked the arrow (*karma*) that tortured him thus increasing his pain (through austerities) whereas Buddha, like a lion, attacked Desire, the shooter of the arrow. Buddha, however, saw no final liberation except through monastic renunciation and contemplative inactivity. Krishna while disarming the hunter Desire did not confine the lion to a cave but gave him the freedom of the forest to pursue all his natural and traditional activities.

For him, indeed, man though essentially a passive knower and experiencer is related to action in a very special way. Unable to escape it owing to his link with *prakriti*, he is faced with two possibilities, either to pass into its bondage by greedily desiring its fruits or to find his very freedom by assuming it disinterestedly. The latter demands that he recognise all activity as but the actuation of divine will and accept sharing in it as in a pure sacrifice, thus imitating the transcendent disinterestedness of the Lord. If he does this, he finds the authenticity of his engagement in history. History, indeed, far from being a senseless succession of changes, has an immanent purposiveness since through it God works unceasingly to procure the welfare of his creatures. Man by identifying himself with this work becomes himself an agent of this purpose.

The very fact that there are two possibilities implies man's freedom of will. After instructing Arjuna in all this, Krishna exhorts him to do as he chooses. Arjuna is called, not obliged, to take his refuge in Krishna. If he takes this first step through a deliberate surrender in faith, he begins to tread the path of loving devotion (*bhakti*) which will transform his historical existence into a dedication to God through serving his creatures. Beyond this *bhakti* of selfless service which Krishna deems inferior still (*aparā*) he will reach the highest (*parā*) *bhakti* which is unitive love in eternity.

Thus the Gītā conception of man is highly personalistic notwithstanding its unpromising *sāṅkhya* basis. Man in dependence upon his Lord is an agent, a sacrificer, a being capable of free choice, of selfless commitment to meaningful history, of religious faith and love, of acceptance of divine grace, of personal surrender to the supreme Person. This exalting personalism marks even the Gītā conception of the Deity. None of the great teachings of the Upanishads concerning the absolute *Brahman* is neglected but the notion of *Brahman* or even Paramātman is itself transcended insofar as it is said to have a basis. This basis is Krishna as the supreme Puruṣa (*Puruṣottama*), the Absolute as Person, Bhagavān, Dispenser of grace, not only loved but Lover in the eternal union of perfect mutual *bhakti*. This view inaugurates the personalistic monotheism which will characterise the religions of *bhakti* of the succeeding ages.

The Bodhisattva as the Ideal Man in Mahāyāna Buddhism

After the innovations of the Gītā concerning both God and man, Buddhism itself could not remain the same. The masses were now presented with a better Bhagavān than Buddha for Krishna was not only a rival human teacher of liberation but God himself manifested as a man without any loss of his infinite power and wisdom. The way he taught was not an

unnatural path of withdrawal from secular duties in order to
secure complete renunciation but a way combining active
commitment with indifference to its fruits in a sacrificial
spirit of single-minded devotion to God and his work.
Further, instead of a denial of any *ātman*, the embodied spirit
of man was assured of eternity and called to a bliss of mutual
parābhakti.

Without betraying the essentials of their doctrine, the
Buddhists succeeded in opening up a 'great career' (*mahāyāna*) which would in some fashion emulate these attractive
developments.

In Mahāyāna, we observe a fast mutation of buddhology
towards apophatic monism. A sort of gnosticism exalts the
supramundane (*lokottara*) nature of the Buddha at the expense
of his historical birth. In the *Lalitavistara* he is made to
declare: 'I am the God who transcends gods (*devātideva*) . . .
but I shall conform myself to the world . . . Gods and men in
unison will proclaim, 'He is God by Himself only' (*svayaṃ
eva devaḥ*)'. Increasingly, his historical existence is conceived
as purely apparitional (*upapāduka*) and his human body as a
mere accommodation to the world (*lokānuvartana*). What
matters henceforth is his *dharma-kāya* (law-body) which is
made of the five features of his teaching: morality, concentration, wisdom, liberation and his awareness of this liberation;
it is in this *dharma-kāya* that men are invited to take their
refuge. By the year AD 400 this conception has reached its full
expression in the works of Asaṅga. The *dharma-kāya* is
simultaneously the true doctrine of the Buddhas, their spiritual
body, their proper nature, and the absolute of reality. Hence, it
is the transcendent, absolute, eternal and infinite essence of all
things. However, the very purity of this essence is expressed in
terms of void (*śūnya*) through a persistent denial of all sub-
stantiality. Though it has become a homologue of the
Upanishadic *Brahman*, it is never conceived as fullness
(*pūrṇa*) but only as the apophatic opposite of all our positive
conceptions.

Nevertheless, if it is the deepest essence of beings, then

everyone has in himself the 'germ of Buddhahood' (*tathāgata-garbha*); which means that the 'great career' (*mahā-yāna*) of a Buddha is open to all. Whoever enters it is a *bodhisattva*, one who has his being in enlightenment, and stands as the concrete ideal to be imitated by all men, for he conquers successively the ten perfections. His career is described minutely. He is born with an inclination to accept the true doctrine and easily becomes a beginner. Thence arises in him the thought of enlightenment in the form of two wishes, namely, to obtain enlightenment and to lead all beings to it. He then commits himself by a vow before an elder *bodhisattva* to fulfil these wishes which he does through preaching, meditating, honouring the Buddhas with a ritual cult, cultivating the ten perfections and even transferring upon others his acquired merits. Thus he becomes not only a hero of charity, morality and wisdom but a merciful saviour. Yet, he is not simply to be revered, trusted and invoked, but actually to be emulated. Indeed, he is not a Platonic ideal or an inaccessibly divine goal but he is in his own way what each one is really able to become. How to characterise his humanity? Not only by utter selflessness which is the renouncer's ideal but by the most universal and unrestricted service of others. Personality here breaks forth beyond the 'ego-barrier' not, however, to become lost beyond any reach but rather to become open to all and to encompass them with boundless wisdom and compassion.

Man as the Reflection of the Absolute according to Śaṅkara
It is common knowledge that Śaṅkara teaches that *Brahman*, the Absolute, is the supreme *Ātman* of the individual or, as he says, of the knower-agent-and-enjoyer. The latter alone is the ego that says 'I' and 'mine'. But is this ego some kind of entity and which one? In *Upadeshasahasri* 18, Śaṅkara provides the following answer:

'The appropriator is the ego-sense which always stands in proximity to this [absolute Consciousness] and acquires a reflection of it. . . . Only when there is a reflection (*ābhāsa*) of

the inner Witness can words like "I", "thou", etc., by referring
to the reflection, indirectly indicate the Witness. They cannot
designate the latter directly in any way. . . . Because the ego-
sense bears a reflection of the *Ātman*, it is designated by words
pertaining to the *Ātman*; just as words pertaining to fire are
applied to torches and the like though only indirectly. . . .

'The reflection of a face is different from the face since it
conforms to the mirror; and in turn the face is different from
its reflection since it does not conform to the mirror. The
reflection of the *Ātman* in the ego-sense is comparable to the
reflection of the face while the *Ātman* is comparable to the
face and therefore different from its reflection. And yet ordinary knowledge fails to discriminate them.'

What is the ontological status of this ego-like reflection? The
reflection of a face in a mirror is not a property either of the
face or of the mirror or even of both together since it depends
only on a certain relation between them. Further, due to this
very dependence, it is not a reality in its own right (*vastu*);
rather its 'true reality' is the face compared to which it is
'unreal' (*asat*). All this applies to the human ego which exhibits
the marks of the *per se* Consciousness it reflects but is in
itself dependent, contingent, and as unable to support itself as
any reflection apart from its prototype.

Yet, the awareness that the ego is merely a reflection of the
Ātman is not only 'the only door or bridge (*dvāra*) by which
we can pass from the ordinary meaning of "I" or "thou" to
what they mean indirectly, namely, the *Ātman*', but is also the
key of any correct anthropology. Śaṅkara's comment on
Brihad-āraṇyaka Up., 4, 3, 7, shows clearly the instrumental
role of the ego-reflection in the integration of the human
person:

'As an emerald dropped for testing into milk imparts its
lustre to it, so this Light of the *Ātman*, through being within
the heart, i.e. the *buddhi* (intellect), because it is more subtle
than it, unifies (*ekīkṛ—*) and imparts its lustre to the body and
the organs including the heart. . . . The *buddhi*, being diaphan-

ous and next to the *Ātman*, puts on a reflection (*ābhāsa*) of the Consciousness-Light of the *Ātman*; this is why even discriminating men happen to identify themselves with the *buddhi*, first. Then the reflecting Light of Consciousness falls upon the *manas* (mind) . . . then on the sense-organs . . . and lastly on the body.'

Or as he says when explaining *Gītā* 18, 50: 'The *Ātman* is extremely pure. And the *buddhi*, being almost as pure, can put on a reflection of that aspect of the *Ātman* which is Consciousness. And the *manas* can put on a reflection of the *buddhi*, etc. Hence, worldly men see the *Ātman* in their body only.'

Thus in conceiving the human person as an aggregate but internally unified by the absolute *Ātman via* the reflection-like ego, Śaṅkara integrates the great utterances of the Upanishads without consenting to either pantheism or acosmism. Unfortunately, his anthropology did not gain the attention it deserved and many among the later Vedāntins, even of his own school, veered towards either of these very directions which he had so carefully avoided.

Conclusion

It is not possible within the compass of these pages to sketch out any more of the other views of man or God elaborated in India. Those outlined here are sufficiently typical to provide features which seem characteristic of the approach to the mystery of the person in this ancient but ever alive culture.

There is obviously a tension at work between the two aspects of active transcendence and cosmic-social relatedness. Secular thought, whether Vedic or Dharmashastric, attempts to resolve it into an equilibrium but this remains unstable because of the radical demands of the renouncers in favour of complete transcendence. To many of them this means the transcendence of the pure spirit in man, illusorily enmeshed in nature but able to recover its purity through the escape of a total isolation (*kaivalya*) from nature. To others the transcending element is not even a spirit but a mere spiritual dynamism beyond any substance-like ego and in regard to which the whole world is like a mirage while from the standpoint of the world it itself appears utterly evanescent. To others still, the transcendence which affirms itself within man is to be viewed as itself transcended by a spiritual Absolute which escapes any classification. Whether *Brahman* or Dharmakāya, this Absolute is ultimate and commands a reordering of all other conceptions.

Paradoxically, while the discovery of such an Absolute relativises all the transcenders it transcends, it has also given rise to a new kind of anthropologies less cut off from the world and, we may even say, open to it though fully imbued with the sense of spiritual evaluation inculcated by the renouncers. There is indeed a remarkable affinity between the conceptions of the *Gītā*, of Mahāyāna and of Śaṅkara insofar as their very focusing on an ultimate Absolute (though the latter be differently conceived) allows them as it were to turn compassionate eyes to the world and to adopt a humanistic stance within their religious perspective. This is obvious in the case of Arjuna or of the *bodhisattvas*, less so in the case of Śaṅkara. Even apart from his exhibiting the humanity and virtues of the merciful teacher and from his upholding the relative validity of the empirical world and its *pramāṇas*, we find in his theory of the ego as arisen in the image and semblance of the *Brahman-Ātman* and of the integration of the whole human aggregate around this reflection-ego a more holistic conception of the human person than in the Absolute-less doctrines.

It seems then that in India human personalism is bound to be very meagre unless it is lit up and supported by a religion of the Absolute which itself tends to be a personalism of the Divine beyond all anthropomorphisms.

Bibliography

The following list is a fair representation of recent writings by Indian authors concerning the Person. It comprises those available at the Centre of Advanced Study in Philosophy of the University of Madras (with acknowledgement to the Library Assistant, Mr Abdul Rawoof). Simply reading their titles will reveal much of the background allegiance and standpoint of their writers.

BOOKS

Concept of Man, A. Radhakrishnan and P. T. Raju, London, Allen & Unwin, 1960.
Concept of Self, Kamala Roy, Calcutta, Firma K. L. Mukhopadhyay, 1966.
East–West Studies of the Problem of the Self, P. T. Raju and Albuney Castell (Eds), The Hague, Nijhoff, 1968.
Idea of Personality, P. N. Srinivasachari, Madras, Adyar Library, 1951.
Individuals and Societies, D. Chattopadhyaya, Bombay, Allied Publ., 1967.
Ramakrishna-Vivekananda Vedanta and Human Personality, Coimbatore, Ramakrishna Mission, 1966.
Nature of Self, A. C. Mukerji, Allahabad, Indian Press, 1938.
Personality, Rabindranath Tagore, London, Macmillan, 1961.
Philosophy, Logic and Language, Kalidas Bhattacharyya, Bombay, Allied Publ., 1965, pp. 116–54.
Sankhya Conception of Personality or a New Interpretation of the Sankhya Philosophy, Abhay Kumar Majumdar, Calcutta Univ., 1930.
The Subject as Freedom, K. C. Bhattacharyya, Amalner, Malkani, 1930.
Towards the Universal Man, Rabindranath Tagore, London, Asia Publ., 1962.
Vedanta: Its Doctrine of Divine Personality, K. Sundarama Iyer, Srirangam, Vani Vilas Press, 1926.
Way of Humanism, East and West, Radhakamal Mukerjee, Bombay, Academic, 1968.
Concept of Mind in Indian Philosophy, Sarasvati Chennakesavan, Bombay, Asia Publ., 1960.
Our Knowledge of Other Selves, Margaret Chatterjee, Bombay, Asia Publ., 1963.

ARTICLES

'The Concept of Person in Strawson and Vedanta', in C. Sampurna, *Indian Philosophical Annual,* 6, 181–8, 1970.
'The Concept of Self in Buddhism', in Kalidas Bhattacharyya, *Philosophical Quarterly* (India), 34, 77–87, 1961.
'The Dynamism of Personality', in S. N. Roy, *ibid.,* 24, 35–40, 1951.
'Early Trends in the Indian Understanding of Man', in R. V. De Smet, *Philosophy East and West,* 22, 259–68, 1972.
'God as Personal and Impersonal', in H. M. Joshi, *Pathway to God,* 7, 60–8, 1972.

'Humanism and Indian Thought', in A. Chakravarti, *Journal of the Madras University*, 9 (1), 1937.

'The Role of Man in Hinduism', by R. N. Dandekar, in K. W. Morgan, *The Religion of the Hindus*, New York, 1958.

'Man in Hindu Thought', in R. N. Dandekar, *Annals of the Bhandarkar Oriental Research Institute*, 43/1–4, 1–57, 1963.

'Humanistic Transformation', in P. T. Raju, *Aryan Path*, June 1951.

'Identity of the Self', S. C. Chatterjee, *Philosophical Quarterly* (India), 24, 217–24, 1952.

'Individual and Society in Indian Social Thought', in N. A. Nikam, *Indian Philosophical Annual*, 6, 41–3 ,1970.

'Individualistic Trends in Gandhian Thought', in Kanak Khanna, *ibid.*, 5, 160–5, 1969.

'Karma and Avatara, a New Direction to the Doctrine of Incarnation in Hinduism', in K. R. Sundara Rajan, *Saiva Siddhanta*, 3, 146–8, 1968.

'Karma and Grace', in C. Ramalinga, *ibid.*, 3, 5–8, 1968.

'Mind and Consciousness, a Comparison of Indian and Western Views', in Sarasvati Chennakesavan, *Philosophical Quarterly* (India), 26, 247–52, 1954.

'Phenomenological Approach to a Metaphysics of Personality in the Light of Advaita', in Debabrata Sinha, *ibid.*, 29, 83–6, 1956.

'Self and Others', in Kalidas Bhattacharyya, *ibid.*, 31, 145–56, 1958.

'Self and the Body', in K. C. Gupta, *ibid.*, 32, 43–8, 1959.

'Self and the Ego', in Bhasker S. Naik, *ibid.*, 7, 171–6, 1931.

'Self, Reality and Salvation in Christianity and Buddhism', in Mervyn Fernando, *International Philosophical Quarterly*, 12, 415–25, 1972.

'Some Implications of the Concept of Personality in Social Philosophy', in S. H. Kelshikar, *Philosophical Quarterly* (India), 31, 11–18, 1958.

'The Theistic Concept of Progress', in V. A. Devasenapathi, *Saiva Siddhanta*, 2, 36–8, 1967.

'Towards a Philosophy of Transcendental Personalism', in S. Vahiduddin, *Philosophical Quarterly* (India), 23, 17–22, 1950.

Chapter 4

THE ONTOLOGY OF VALUES

by

N. K. DEVARAJA

Centre of Advanced Study in Philosophy, Banaras Hindu University

Traditionally, philosophy has been very much concerned with the investigation of the nature of reality. This concern has generally based itself on the supposed antithesis between appearance and reality. While the antithesis is conspicuously present in the thought systems of idealistic philosophers from Aruni and Plato, Nāgārjuna and Śaṅkara, down to Kant and Bradley, it is not unknown to philosophers of other persuasions. Thus the materialistically inclined thinkers, drawing inspiration from the physical sciences headed by physics, make a distinction between primary qualities on the one hand and secondary and tertiary qualities on the other, and declare the latter to be in some sense less real than, and so mere reflections of, the former. In his well known work *The Nature of the Physical World* Sir Arthur Eddington draws a distinction between the *apparent* table visible to our eye and the *real* table located in what he calls 'the shadow world of physics'. However, the idealists and the materialists including the scientists differ on one crucial point. The idealists believe reality to be in some sense spiritual or at any rate non-physical; this reality according to them can be investigated and known only by the metaphysical intellect. Materialists as well as the scientists, on the contrary, consider reality to be physical in the final analysis; they further believe that this reality can be investigated by the methods of science. Another important difference that divides the philosophers of the two camps concerns the location and the status of values. Idealistic thinkers are inclined either to identify the highest value with the ultimate, spiritual reality or to derive the former from the latter. Materialistic thinkers, on the other hand, are generally inclined to equate values with either feelings of pleasure and pain or things leading to the feelings of satisfaction and dissatisfaction in conscious beings.

If reality be constituted by the phenomena of nature, or by spatio-temporal facts, it cannot possibly form the subject matter of philosophy. Nevertheless philosophy can and may reflect on the categories used by the several sciences to describe and explain their respective domains. Philosophy may also reflect on the mutual bearings of different sets of descriptive and explanatory concepts. In other words philosophy, being a second-order activity, may legitimately scrutinise the conceptual tools used by the different scientific investigators, with a view to assessing the efficacy of those tools in terms of the avowed purposes of those investigators. However, the philosopher's interest in the conceptual systems fashioned and used by the several sciences is logico-epistemological rather than ontological. The philosopher *qua* philosopher, for instance, is hardly interested in the nature of, say, electricity or heat; what interests him is the movement of, or the method of approach adopted by the human (scientific) mind that enables man to achieve the understanding of a particular form of energy which is practically useful and which is consistent with the rest of his knowledge. The philosopher may also wonder at the varieties of the modes of explanation adopted by different scientific workers and the types of understanding achieved by them.

Why, it may be asked, is the philosopher not interested in the knowledge of the nature of electricity and is interested in the activity of the scientist seeking to understand and explain the phenomenon called electricity? A plausible answer to this question is: because the philosopher is interested in understanding the nature or workings of the human mind including the mind of the scientist. This is a thoroughly traditional answer, for do not the Upanishads and Socrates exhort us to know ourselves? However, while accepting the traditional view of philosophy, I would like to make the following amendment to it: Man desires to understand himself or his mind or self, because he is interested in improving the quality of his being or mind. Thus it appears that there is qualitative distinction between the curiosity of the scientist and that of the philosopher. Scientific curiosity is primarily directed on the objective world that the scientist seeks to understand and explain in a disinterested spirit; the practical or utilitarian applications of scientific knowledge are consequent products of scientific curiosity and knowledge. The only natural or intrinsic aim and reward of scientific activity is aesthetic delight following upon the satisfaction of the aforesaid curiosity. The philosopher's reflective activity differs from that of the scientist in two important respects. First, in reflecting over a form of the mind's life or activity the philosopher, so to say, vicariously enjoys the life in question. So to say, the philosopher appropriates to his own reflective consciousness those aspects of the scientist's (or, for that matter, the artist's) activity that make it interesting—without having to bother at all about the tiresome labour that the scientist (or the artist) had to undergo in collecting and organising his conceptual (or intuitional) materials. Second, the philosopher cannot contemplate the data relating to the mind's activities in a neutral spirit. While enjoying the contemplation of those activities the philosophic mind gets necessarily involved in the evaluative assessment of them. The philosopher reflects over science (or the activity of the scientist) and art (or the symbolised activity or experience of the artist) because he finds them intrinsically interesting or valuable. Speaking generally, philosophy may be defined as the study of the value bearing forms of human life or activity incarnated in public symbols. The philosopher's interest in any other matter or matters is ancillary to his study of the forms of life or consciousness that are bearers of values (or disvalues) of diverse kinds.

A number of opinions have been advanced with regard to

the nature of philosophical problems and the proper method of attacking or dealing with those problems. For one thing, most of the modern philosophers find it difficult to adopt the speculative methods of traditional metaphysics, whether idealist or materialist. While the followers of the later Wittgenstein like to analyse the meanings of familiar words and explore the implications of ordinary language, the phenomenologists engage themselves in the analysis of 'one's own consciousness of the world' with a view to defining the structures that are essential to experience or knowledge. As against the phenomenologists the existential philosophers seek to understand not so much the foundations of knowledge as the foundations of human action. All these philosophers, however, seem to be agreed that philosophical thought should have relevance in terms of or with reference to our day-to-day life and experience, and should eschew speculation that resists checking against experience accessible to normal men and women.

There can be no doubt that the physical world revealed to us in sense experience holds the first place in our knowledge. Even the idealists who deny reality to this world are generally not inclined to deny the fact of its existence or appearance. Thus, while the spatio-temporal world is unreal according to the Advaita Vedānta it is not non-existent. The physical world of course includes other living beings with bodies. I am also conscious, as was Descartes, of my own existence as a knowing (and also as a desiring, feeling and willing) subject, but this consciousness or knowledge does not reveal much as to my actual essence. In any case there has been a lot of speculation in regard to the true essence of the knowing subject. In contradistinction to the speculations about the self, there has been a good deal of agreement concerning the nature of the objects encountered in sense experience. What I am trying to suggest is this, that we should start our thinking about values either with the physical world as it figures in our experience, or in our active encounter with that world and our fellow humans. Inasmuch as the human beings whose relationships with me figure prominently in my life and experience, form part of the visible world, that world must occupy an important place even in my reflections about man and his values.

The first thing encountered by me in experience is the world of physical objects having diversity of colours, shapes or forms, weights and volumes, and other characteristics and functions ascertainable through their visible effects. This world may be called the empirical realm, and the characteristics and functions exhibited by it may be termed empirical qualities or empirical meanings. The term 'meaning' here, it may be noted, has no semantic significance. A meaning, as used here, signifies any aspect of an entity that is attended to and observed. The term 'meaning', as applied to an object or an aspect of an object or entity attended to, is intended to underscore the fact that our activities of attending and knowing are in general interested or interest-bound. An object interests me either because it serves some purpose or because it appears to be worth noticing in its own right. This situation may be expressed by saying that an object, in order to catch my attention, must bear one or other meaning for me. Man certainly lives in the environment of physical nature comprising living and non-living entities; however, in a more important sense, he lives in different realms of meanings. Roughly speaking there are three kinds of meanings that interest man and attract his attention. These are empirical meanings, pragmatic meanings and aesthetic or spiritual meanings. It may be noted here that all the three kinds of meanings may inhere in the same object or entity. (The term entity here signifies any object or configuration of objects, any chain of events, processes or activities, or any complex of concepts or ideas that may possibly be made the object of attention.) The different kinds of meanings call for different types of reactions. In principle, empirical meanings in their purity are matters only for observation, or detached contemplation; they need not involve either affective or volitional responses. Thus I may learn in a purely detached spirit about the temperature at the North Pole, the depth of the

Pacific Ocean, the distance of Venus from the earth, or the date of a certain battle fought by Caesar. However, it is seldom that I read about history, or even about the north pole, completely without some sort of feeling or emotion. Accompanied by feeling or emotion the purely empirical cognition assumes for me aesthetic or pragmatic overtones, and begins to have a bearing on my affective or volitional life. That life inevitably involves interference with my career as a creator and enjoyer of values.

The pure observer may be a *sthitaprajñā* (well-poised). In case a person attains that state through knowledge and self-discipline, the state may be regarded as a value produced or attained by the person concerned. If, however, a person is apathetic towards his surroundings through lack of vitality or chronic depression, he will be a mere observer in the sense that he would not seek to produce or enjoy any values in relationship with the environmental objects.

However, most of us are seeking to fulfil our diverse needs with the help of the objects present in the environment. In other words the objects making up our environment bear pragmatic (or, occasionally, aesthetic) meanings for us. The pure scientist investigates empirical meanings in a spirit of intellectual adventure accompanied by aesthetic delight, but the moment he seeks to harness nature to his use he enters the realm of pragmatic meanings. His manipulation of empirical phenomena or meanings is successful to the extent to which his knowledge of those phenomena is dependable and his manipulative activity conforms to that knowledge. Man cannot take liberties with the physical objects characterised by fixed dispositions, but he can use them to gain his practical ends. These ends belong to the order of pragmatic meanings; they consist of the satisfactions indicative of man's effective, healthful existence and survival. The ends include comforts of various kinds as well as power over or possession of means that contribute to satisfaction of diverse kinds.

The most important locus of the pragmatic meanings are the physical objects which are in relation to the conscious human beings. It is true, in a general way, that the physical objects and forces have pragmatic significance for man in virtue of their fixed dispositions. Thus, copper wires can be used as carriers of electric current because they are good conductors. Similarly, milk and eggs are used as foods because they supply protein, minerals, etc., to the body. Obviously, the utility of an object for man depends on the one hand on its characteristic nature or disposition, and, on the other, on the needs of the person making use of it. Further, it may be noted that every object known to us has a number of properties and attributes, and every living being has a number of needs, and different needs on different occasions. A chair is generally used by me for sitting, but it may be used as a shield against a person attacking me with a club or knife; it may also be used to hit and drive out a hostile person or animal. The scientists, working over centuries, have accumulated important information about the characteristic nature and behaviour of a large number of elements and their compounds, and of several forms of energy, thus investing innumerable objects and phenomena with unsuspected pragmatic significance. Thanks to the labours of countless scientists man today enjoys far greater control over natural forces, over health and disease, etc., than his predecessors living in the pre-scientific ages.

As stated earlier, pragmatic meanings or values of things can be said to be existent only in relation to living beings. Here a distinction may be drawn between the values or meanings that are relational, and those that are relative. Edible objects such as milk and eggs have pragmatic or utility value in virtue of their own composition as well as the constitution of the living beings whom the former tend to nourish. There exists, so to say, a natural *rapport* between the edible objects of various descriptions and the diverse kinds of living organisms. To the extent to which the organisms need food materials of different kinds, even as they need air and water, the former cannot subsist and live without the latter. On the other hand, men in the past have lived without many an object that we use and seem to be in need of today, e.g. chairs and tables, electric fans and bulbs, automobiles and aeroplanes, guns and atom bombs. The utility or value of these latter kinds of objects is relative to the needs developed by the modern civilised human beings. Some of these needs are understandable in terms of man's desire for comforts, while others are related to his desire for power, or amusement, or knowledge, etc. Thus the printing press, books and newspapers cater to man's need for knowledge and information, the cinema and the theatre to his recreation and aesthetic enjoyment, and so on. However, in practice it is difficult to separate natural utilities from the non-natural ones, even as it is difficult to distinguish between the natural and the artificial needs of mankind. While man also makes use of objects present in the natural environment, he has also learnt to use his knowledge and ingenuity in controlling and augmenting the production of those objects, e.g. cereals, milk and eggs. He has also learnt to manufacture and produce artificial foods, medicines and the like. Apart from the objects contributing purely to man's pomp and luxury most of the objects invented and manufactured by man are intended to fulfil or serve his natural needs of nourishment, movement and transport, fighting for protection against and overcoming enemies, and the like, in more efficient ways. Viewed in this light the elaborate paraphernalia of our civilisation may be regarded more or less as an extension of the natural powers of man in directions of more efficient and organised fulfilment of his manifold needs, physical and mental.

Man differs from animals in three important respects. First, in virtue of his more complex nature he has a larger number of needs including psychological, moral and spiritual needs. Second, man commands a far greater variety of means for fulfilling his various needs than the animals. Third, in virtue of his intelligence and imagination man attacks his manifold needs, both at individual and at collective levels, in a complex organised manner involving consideration of the future and the relative importance of diverse needs and the modes of their satisfaction.

It happens that a man, wielding influence and power can use

other human beings as instruments for attaining his own pragmatic ends. In fact, the conduct of a modern man living in a modern town or city consists as much of transactions with men and women as with physical objects present in an industrial environment. Qualitatively speaking our relations with our fellow humans are much more significant than those with physical objects. We can look upon other human beings either as persons mainly that are ends in themselves, or as conscious entities merely that can be used as means for the furtherance of our own ends. It is obvious that our relations with other human beings involve, and should involve, moral values or considerations that are more or less absent in our dealings with physical objects and even the animal world.

What, then, is the ontological status of the pragmatic or utilitarian values? Are they objective in any sense, or should they be looked upon as purely subjective? It is difficult to give a simple reply to these queries. While a distinction may be drawn between qualities that are relational, and those that are relative, it is not always possible neatly to divide the two types of qualities. However, in so far as the existence and survival of the animals including man depends on certain properties of the objects needed for nourishment and continued existence of the former, those properties may be considered objective from the viewpoint of those beings. Objects, those found in nature as well as those manufactured by man, acquire one or other pragmatic meaning or value under the gaze of the conscious human beings engaged in pursuing their diverse ends. There is a sense in which objects of various kinds are but means to the several kinds of satisfactions sought by man. Since it is not possible for man to catch hold of and hoard satisfactions directly, he seeks to possess objects that are instrumental in the attainment of the desired satisfactions. Thus it is that man learns to covet objects of various kinds, and wealth and power and influence, that enable him to obtain the desired objects with ease. It is in this sense that wealth and power may be said to belong to the order of pragmatic or utilitarian values. However, man also learns, through an intricate network of associations, to seek wealth and power as ends in themselves.

To the extent to which human agents invest physical objects with pragmatic meanings or values in their conscious pursuit of diverse ends, those meanings or values may be regarded as being supervenient on empirical meanings or qualities. For instance, I invest the chair before me with a new meaning or value the moment I intend to use it as a shield or as an object with which to hit an adversary. Not that the new meaning or value is wholly unrelated to the characteristic nature of the chair, but the relation or connection is a function on the one hand of my need and purpose at a particular moment and, on the other, of the creative ingenuity that makes me see or find a particular meaning or utility in the object before me. The use of the chair as a shield or as an object to hit with marks a departure from its traditional use, and so is a function of my operative intelligence or ingenuity. In a broader context man's use of wood to make a chair with is itself an instance of his creative interference with the course of nature, i.e. with the growth and continuance of trees as trees. In this sense the production of pragmatic or utilitarian values by man may be taken to be an index of his freedom.

We shall now pass on to the consideration of the spiritual values consisting roughly of moral, aesthetic and religious values. It may be suggested that cognitive or intellectual values should also be included among spiritual values, for is not Truth a spiritual value? We have already conceded that the philosopher may reflect on the activity of the scientist seeking truth about nature. However, scientific truth itself, except in so far as it has a bearing on moral and religious truth, may not interest the philosopher. In any case we shall not, in this paper, occupy ourselves with problems relating to the pursuit of scientific truth. We shall confine our attention only to the aforesaid forms of the spiritual values. Our special concern is to investigate their relationship to the empirical world.

It was stated above that the so-called pragmatic meanings or values supervene on the empirically given qualities; it is our contention that moral meanings or values supervene on the pragmatic meanings or values contemplated and created by conscious human agents. Second, a situation or action can have moral meaning only if it involves a relation between two or more persons. There may be actions and situations having pragmatic meaning or significance that involve relationships between one or more persons on the one hand, and the environment of physical objects on the other, but no important relationship between the persons themselves. Such actions and situations will be devoid of moral significance. It follows from this that the area of pragmatic meanings or values is wider than that of the moral values, even as the sphere of empirical meanings is larger than that of the pragmatic meanings. Thus my knowledge of the possible number of stars in a particular galaxy has no pragmatic significance in the present state of man's knowledge, though it may have aesthetic meaning of a sort. Likewise, if a hundred workers are engaged in transporting, say, bricks from one place to another, and if their movements and wages do not promote conflict, then their activities, while having pragmatic meaning, have no moral import.

Moral considerations (i.e. moral meanings and values) make their appearance or come into play when questions relating to the distribution of the pragmatic goods in accordance with the deserts of different persons are raised. Such questions may arise between any two parties that are in a position to exchange goods and services of diverse types. In virtue of the services, goods or considerations extended by X to Y, X seems to himself and others to acquire some rights in his relationship with or over Y. In a modern society ruled by a money economy a person may also acquire rights by giving or spending money to or for another person. The fundamental concept in morality seems to be that of desert; the principle of justice is a derivative of that concept. Another important notion affecting our moral judgements is that of 'fittingness or requiredness' which seems to be an extension of the notion of desert in its application to the total complex comprising persons and the environment or the complex of circumstances wherein their actions take place. A person deserves to be paid in terms of money, or honour, or recognition and reputation in virtue of what he has done or accomplished, but he deserves to be helped by his fellow-being in virtue of the unforeseen difficulty or difficult circumstances in which he happens to find himself involved. Those who are in a position to help a person caught in a difficult situation or adverse circumstances with either no inconvenience or little inconvenience to themselves, are obliged to give their help.

Neither the attributes of 'fittingness' and 'desert' or 'deserving' nor those of 'justness' or 'rightness' inhere in collocations of circumstances or in actions as redness inheres in roses or greenness in leaves. The attributes or qualities in question exist or have being only for human observers endowed with some intelligence and a peculiar kind of awareness called moral sensitiveness. It may be noted here that the pragmatic qualities or meanings of objects, and situations too, are often relative to the purposive consciousness of the human percipients. However, there remains a difference between man's perception of pragmatic meanings on the one hand and his awareness of moral meanings on the other. The pragmatic meanings of objects, collocations of objects and actions are ultimately related, however indirectly, to the inherent needs of man implanted in him by nature. Quite a few of these needs are common to both man and other animals. On the other hand man's perception of moral qualities seems to be connected with the feeling of sanctity that he entertains with respect to the abstract concepts called 'desert' and 'fittingness'.

We may now briefly consider the aesthetic qualities and values perceived and cherished by man. The aesthetic qualities seem to belong in the first place to perceptual phenomena, e.g. objects in nature and the bodies of living beings. However, their incidence often depends on the age, health and mood of the observer. In this respect the aesthetic qualities are relational, like the pragmatic qualities or values apprehended by the living beings in their instinctive perception and living. Just as man has learnt to produce artificial objects bearing prag-matic meaning, and also to attach, through causal association pragmatic importance to such human virtues as efficiency, power of decision and the like, similarly he has learnt, through various types of association, to see beauty in various forms of human conduct, human character and action, and in works of art. The essence of aesthetic qualities seems to consist in the suggestion of impulses and activities associated with life; perceptual phenomena, including collocations of symbols, appear to act as mere symbols of such impulses and activities. It is noteworthy that we see moral and aesthetic attributes or qualities not only in tangible forms of actions and movements, but also in such symbolic activities and gestures as kind and courteous speech. Croce was wrong in thinking that a work of art appeals to us only in virtue of the intuitional or sensory elements incorporated in it; such a work, e.g. a play or novel, may evoke strong reactions in us in virtue of an intense moral conflict depicted in it.

The subject of religious values is more controversial than that of any other types of values. It is generally supposed that religious life and value have reference to supernatural beings or Being, or a supernatural order of existence. Whether the existence of such supernatural, and not merely supersensible, entities as God or gods can be established through reason is a moot question. It may be pointed out that such important thinkers as Śaṅkara, Ramanuja and Kant have affirmed the impossibility of proving the existence of God by inference or logical arguments. While the mystics belonging to different theistic religions are found who claim to have had a direct vision of God, there are religio-philosophical systems that find it unnecessary to posit the existence of a God distinct from the individual soul. This is true not only of Buddhism and Jainism but also of the Sāṅkhya-Yoga and the Advaita Vedānta. For the Advaitin the highest religious experience can consist only in self-vision or self-realisation. There is no logical provision for encounter with an 'Other' in the aforesaid systems.

We have no intention here to enter into the interminable

controversy about the reality of God and a supernatural order of existence. Instead, we shall confine our attention to the behavioural expressions of the religious values. Here again we shall assume that a sort of consensus as to the essential traits of a religious person and religious conduct exists among the leaders of thought belonging at any rate to the major religions. The consensus finds expression in the respect and reverence shown to the so-called saints, or persons with a saintly disposition. What are the essential marks of a saint or a saintly person? The saintliness of a person or character, it may be submitted, cannot be characterised in terms of one or other set of beliefs, metaphysical or religious. For all we know, the saintly disposition may co-exist with different sets of such beliefs. A saintly person may be a Buddhist or a Christian, a Jaina or a Hindu. Further, a Hindu saint may be a devotee of a personal God, or an Advaitin following the path of knowledge.

One essential mark of a saint seems to be indifference to the goods that produce conflict and divide men, both individuals and groups, from one another. In other words, the saint is indifferent towards competitive goods comprising wealth, power, fame and the like that kindle the flames of desire, envy, anger and hatred. Having freed himself from these negative sentiments, the saint is able to develop the attitude of disinterested friendliness and compassion towards all living beings.

Religious charm and attraction seem to supervene on a life that has risen almost wholly above the pragmatic order of values. A measure of detachment towards these values is needed even for the man who proposes to be just in his dealings with his fellow beings. In the last analysis man's predilection for justice should be taken to constitute an innate disposition in him; it cannot be a derivative of his concern for the pragmatic or utilitarian values connected with the needs of his existence and survival. There can be no naturalistic explanation of man's basic moral sentiments. Probably man's sense of justice is ultimately rooted in his power of imagination coupled with the capacity for empathetic identification with the life situations of others. Likewise the possibility of man's being able to rise above the pragmatic concerns of life seems to depend on his ability to evoke in himself a vivid sense of death or the perishable character of life with its struggles and achievements.

The above account of the values steers clear of assumptions of such substantive entities as the soul and God or Godhead. The conception of the soul as a simple or non-composite entity, which is to be met with both in Indian and in Western thought, is scarcely able to do justice to the moral and emotional complexities of man's life as known to us. This consideration is particularly relevant in the context of Indian conceptions of the *Ātman*. The Cartesian mind is supposed to be a thinking substance; one wonders how such a substance can account for the moral, affective and volitional dimensions of human life. The same criticism would apply to the different conceptions of the *Ātman* to be met with in Indian systems of thought.

However, it seems necessary to suppose that as animal life evolves to higher stages of existence, it grows in complexity through the emergence of the powers of imagination and thought on the one hand and the moral, aesthetic and religious sensibilities on the other.

Values or value-aspects of things certainly enter into our experience for otherwise there could be no intelligible talk about them. On the other hand it will be seen that values are not cognisable through sense experience. My thesis is that the values can only be suggested by sense experience as also by linguistic and other symbols. We shall illustrate this point with a reference to the types of values discussed above.

First take the case of pragmatic or utilitarian values. These were divided by us into two classes or types, relational and relative. The colour and the smell of an edible object may appeal to the instincts of an insect, bird or animal, but these apparently attractive and alluring features may turn out to be deceptive. The capacity for instinctive perception is much too limited in man to be reliable, and civilised human beings generally depend on other sources of knowledge of the food values of objects than instinctive like or dislike. Such features of objects such as colours and smells, I suggest, are merely the signs of the nourishing properties of the edible objects for different organisms. We talk about such properties in terms of calories, vitamins, salts, etc., that have little to do with the visible features of objects. In other words we cannot refer to even the relational pragmatic or utilitarian qualities of objects as we do to the sensory qualities of things. This is still more true of the pragmatic qualities that are relative to our conscious purposes. For this reason a layman can hardly make any sense of the movements of a compounder preparing a mixture, or an engineer giving orders for moving certain materials, unless the relevant purpose or objective is explained to him by a competent authority. Pragmatic meanings or values being thus invisible, the moral meanings or values that are dependent on those meanings in the sense of being supervenient on them are *a fortiori* invisible. The pragmatic meanings are, so to say, suggested or symbolised by the order or manner in which visible objects and movements or activities are disposed; likewise, the moral meanings are suggested or symbolised by the order or arrangement of pragmatically meaningful actions and relations. While the pragmatic meanings are directly suggested by the visible movements of objects and persons, the moral meanings are but indirectly related to these movements. A parent scolding a child and a police officer maltreating a pickpocket are apparently engaged in actions aimed at producing pragmatically negative or harmful results, but they may be morally justified. This example also clearly brings out the distinction between pragmatic and moral meanings or values.

As observed earlier, the visible features of objects are merely the *signs* of the qualities that appeal, positively or negatively, to our aesthetic sensibility. These latter qualities cannot be directly expressed in language. This means that the aesthetic qualities of objects including actions or deeds and characters, can only be *suggested* by arrangements of references to either sensory or pragmatic qualities or meanings. The validity of this thesis is recognised by the influential school of *Dhvani* in Indian poetics. It also finds support in T. S. Eliot's notion of the 'objective correlative'.

The mechanisms of our knowledge and expression of the religious values resemble those involved in the apprehension and expression of moral and aesthetic values. The angelic sweetness and charming friendliness and repose characteristic of the saint resemble aesthetic qualities in that they are suggested by the state of complete adjustment and equilibrium achieved by him. His overflowing kindness expresses itself in acts and expressions of compassion. The bearing and conduct or activities of the saint act as *signs* to make us see his spiritual qualities. Thus the personality of the saint seems to mark the meeting point of the good and the beautiful, or the point where goodness, in its overflowing sweetness, transforms itself into graceful harmony in relation to the world of nature and man.

Chapter 5

GOD, MAN AND BONDAGE

by

V. A. DEVASENAPATHI

Centre of Advanced Study in Philosophy
University of Madras

I

'Man is born free but is everywhere in chains', said Rousseau. Since his day, men have achieved freedom in several ways. Political freedom has been restored in many areas of the world which were formerly under foreign domination. Likewise freedom has been won in the economic, social and intellectual spheres. All these may be valuable in their own way, but do they constitute fundamental freedom? We may recall the following words of Alban Widgery:

'As I reflect on my own past life, I am conscious of the great extent of human bondage. Men are chained by the constitution of Nature with its laws; they are bound by social conventions. I have found more irksome the slavery of work through the years of my professional career. I had to do particular things at specific times and places, whatever my inclinations were. The compulsion on me was no less than that of the whip on the back of a slave. Most men I have known have suffered similarly. I am appalled when I think how many persons spend the greater part of their waking hours like cogs in a machine, more rigidly bound than the serfs of earlier ages. We can never escape from all forms of bondage, but at least, with retirement from my profession, I have gained freedom from its enforced routines' (*A Philosopher's Pilgrimage*, Allen & Unwin, 1961).

There is recognition in the foregoing quotation that life is associated with bondage. This is interesting in the context of Indian philosophy which has concerned itself from very early times with reflection on human nature and on the problems of existence in general and of human existence in particular. In spite of the surface or initial pessimism in Indian philosophy, we find that the various systems get over this pessimism in their own way. *Life or existence in itself is not bondage or evil but the way we live it makes it so.* This may sound strange in view of the general impression that Indian philosophy considers *saṁsāra* (transmigratory existence through several births) to be bondage (*saṁsāra bandha*) and that *mokṣa* is release from such bondage. On closer scrutiny we find that the several systems, with the exception of Cārvāka (Indian materialism), link it up with *Karma* which in one phase is the product of thought, word and deed. *Karma* in its other phase implies moral freedom for, though our past determines our present, if we are wise, we shall learn from our past and make our future, a fulfilment of our life, not an additional burden to carry. Thus, if life is a bondage it is largely of our own making.

To go back to the problem of bondage, we find different answers to this in Indian philosophy. The *Cārvāka* who accepts only sense perception as a valid means of knowledge finds this problem an irrelevant and unanswerable one. His concern is with the living present and with how best to enjoy it. He does not bother to ask himself whether the present could have been different and, if so, whether we can do anything about the future. Metaphysical problems are ruled out.

The Buddhist recognises bondage. In so far as the 'no-soul' (*nairātmiyavāda*) could be taken to be his view, there is no permanent entity which is in bondage. Enlightenment consists in recognising the enslaving effects of 'deeds', not in admitting the existence of a 'doer' in addition.

The Advaitin accepts *saṁsāra* as an empirical fact, but release consists in the *awareness* that Brahman alone is real, that the world is *mithyā* (non-real) and that the finite soul (*jīva*) is non-different from Brahman. All our woes arise from failure to realise that the soul in its essence and real existence is Brahman. If *mokṣa* is something to be attained by the soul, something which is not there all along, there is the liability of what is thus acquired being lost. The supreme truth is that there is no *attainment* of freedom. There is only the awareness that in his essence, man, being non-different from Brahman, is ever free. If we may so put it, bondage is the illusion that he is not free. Since ontologically the One (if the category of number is permissible) alone is, in the ultimate analysis there is no bondage, no release.

The Hindu theist (Vaiṣṇavaite and Śaivite) gives a third answer. He recognises bondage as something real which can be overcome only by the grace of God. How did it start? He does not answer this question directly or explicitly. He says it is beginningless (*anādi*). He does not attribute it to an original fall. In other words, he considers it a mystery, but he is certain that though bondage is beginningless, it is not, thanks to the grace of God, endless. In emphasising Divine grace, his answer differs from the answer of the Buddhist. *Karma* is not the only or the paramount factor. Divine Grace supersedes *Karma*.

We may look at the problem from another perspective, the perspective of health. According to the Advaitin, disease is a present fact but not the whole truth of the situation. Health is the natural state, disease is a passing aberration. A human being is not a permanent patient. He is a healthy person. Likewise freedom is the natural state and bondage is a phase that ultimately has no significance. The Buddhist answer is concerned, not so much with an analysis of the real nature of the patient as with his present state of sickness. The emphasis here is on the sickness with a view to its removal. The theist's answer combines the insights of the other two. No doubt its ontology is different, pluralistic, unlike the Advaitin's and, unlike the Buddhist's, definitely committed to the acceptance of permanent entities, not moral processes. Health is the goal and the natural state; but disease which racks the patient is too much of a painful reality to be written off as ultimately not real.

The most important feature in the third answer is the recognition of a Being, who unlike the human doctors liable to fall ill themselves, is ever the ideal and actuality of health. He is the Doctor who cures souls of the illness of transmigratory existence (*Bhavarogavaidyanātha*). That birth is not an evil or disease *in itself* could be gathered from descriptions of the lives of some of the saints sent by God to fulfil certain missions for the spiritual uplift of humanity. From the utterances of the saints themselves we find that they welcome birth if it could be used in worship of God and in service to His creatures. 'I am prepared to take countless births if I could engage in golden service to His devotees.' Even spiritual uplift is not the primary consideration. 'Even if I am to be born as a worm grant me the boon not to forget your feet', sings Tirunavuk-karasar (seventh century AD), who, finding his sustenance in the Lord, dedicated his life to service. All the denunciation we come across of life as bondage or evil is to be understood as directed against the misuse of life, resulting in repeated trans-migratory existence. In fact the privilege of being born as a human being, sound in body and mind was emphasised for the opportunities for dedicated worship and service it brings as against birth in sub-human (even superhuman) forms or defective human forms. In such a life there is true or funda-mental freedom, true spiritual health, if we may say so.

To the question why we should accept bondage, the theist's answer is as follows: If there is nothing like a primal bondage obstructing the soul's intelligence, the soul will be like the Lord Himself, since its essential nature is intelligence. It will not be limited in intelligence. It will be omniscient, omni-potent, and autonomous. Besides, what does *mukti* (or *mokṣa*) mean? It means freedom. To the question, 'Freedom from what?' the answer is that it is freedom from the primal bondage (*āṇava*). A detailed discussion of this follows in the next section.

If the Hindu theist speaks of God, souls and bonds, how does he interpret the Vedic declaration that Reality is one? Here is his answer: 'When the Veda says, "One", it means

that the Lord is One. Thou who sayest "one"; understand
that thou art soul bound by the fetter. The Veda means that
as there can be no letters, if the primal vowel *a* is not, so there
can be nothing if the Lord is not'.

The theist considers Divine Grace as the solution to the
problem of human bondage. Hindu theism has had a place in
Hindu philosophy for more than two millennia. Currently
also it influences the thought and life of a considerable section
of the Hindu community. Can it have any appeal to the
philosophers of the West? Many changes have taken place in
the philosophical climate of the West. Is theism philosophically
'demonetised' and has it ceased to be 'legal tender' in the West?
Presumably not, though there might be some depreciation of
this currency. There is enough interest in Western academic
circles, judging from even a few titles like the following books,
to enable us to consider theism as a live force: *God Talk* and
Twentieth Century Religious Thought, both by John Macquarrie:
The *Ontological Argument* by Jonathan Barnes: *The Argument
from Design* by Thomas Macpherson: *Religious Experience* by
T. R. Miles. Let me then turn to Hindu theism, and more
specifically to Śaivite theism which has contemporary relevance, to consider in some detail the answer to the problem of
human bondage.

II

Among the systems of Indian philosophy, it is in the *Nyāya*
that we come across arguments for the existence of God.
Udayana, a Nyāya writer has formulated the arguments which
may be summarised thus:[1]

1. The world is an effect. Like other effects, the world also
   points to an efficient cause or agent. Such an agent has
   the knowledge and power to create the world.
2. We notice a physical order in the world. This indicates a
   Controller or Law-giver.

[1] M. Hiriyanna, *Outlines of Indian Philosophy*, London, Allen & Unwin, 1951,
p. 243.

D

3. The moral government of the world suggests a Moral Governor who dispenses justice according to *Karma*.

4. Udayana argues that there is no proof to the contrary and that none of the means of valid knowledge can be used to prove the non-existence of God.

S. Radhakrishnan says that there is an argument in the Yoga system which reminds us of the classical ontological argument. He has rendered as follows the argument formulated by Vyāsa:

'His pre-eminence is altogether without anything equal to it or excelling it. For, to begin with, it cannot be excelled by any other pre-eminence since whatever might seem to excel it would itself prove to be that very pre-eminence. Therefore, that is the Iśvara wherein we reach this uttermost limit of pre-eminence.'[1]

Though the place of God in the *Yoga* system is not an important one, it is interesting to see in the foregoing what indeed bears resemblance to the ontological argument. The theistic Vedāntins do not give arguments for the existence of God, because according to them, inference can give, at best, only a First Cause. It can never give us the God of Religion, the Being who possesses infinite auspicious qualities. Hence they accept the existence of God on the authority of the Scriptures. All the same the first line of a Tamil Vaiṣṇava mystical classic, the *Tiruvāimolli* which is a scripture for the Tamil Vaiṣṇavites describes God as, 'He who possesses an excellence such that there can be nothing higher', with a nuance in the Tamil word *uyar* that suggests the possibility of an increase in the excellence should anything draw near it. This is reminiscent of the lines, 'As a mother bird each fond endearment tries, To tempt its new-fledged offspring to the skies.'[2] Thus there is an ontological note with an undertone

---

[1] S. Radhakrishnan, *Indian Philosophy*, London, Allen & Unwin, 1940, Vol. II, p. 369.

[2] Oliver Goldsmith, *The Deserted Village*.

that the Supreme Excellence allures the souls to brighter worlds of excellence by leading the way.

The Śaiva Siddhāntin, like the Naiyāyika, gives arguments for the existence of God, but he makes it very clear that these arguments will not be of avail any more than the Scriptures themselves, unless Divine Grace illumines the understanding. His arguments are similar to the Naiyāyika's:

(*A*) Arguing from the world as an effect to God as its efficient cause: The argument is set forth as a five-membered syllogism by a commentator who shows that it has all the merits of a valid syllogism and none of the defects of an invalid one.

We may dwell at some length on this point. In the Indian syllogism, example is an important step. The example given for establishing the Creatorship of God is the potter. The critic argues that the example is defective on the ground that as a potter is subject to ignorance and *Karma*, these will come to apply to God also. The Siddhāntin replies that the potter may be ignorant of many things but not of pot making. Likewise the Universal Creator cannot be ignorant of the universe or the mode of its creation. The Universe is the total effect we are trying to account for. Hence God, its Creator cannot be ignorant of anything.[1]

Incidentally, the Siddhāntin's position with regard to the question of whether God is only the efficient cause or also the material cause is interesting. Those who say, like the Śivādvaitin for example, that He is both, argue that unless He is both, the promissory statement of the Scripture, 'By knowledge of the one, knowledge of all is brought about' (*ekavijñāna sarvavijñana pratijña*) would be falsified. By knowledge of clay, the material cause, knowledge of all things made of clay is brought about. Even so by knowledge of God, the material cause, knowledge of all things would result. The Siddhāntin accepts scripture as a valid means of knowledge, but he interprets this statement in a different way. Śiva is the Lord of the universe: (1) knowledge of the owner implies

---

[1] S. S. Suryanarayana Sastri, *The Śivādvaita of Śrīkaṇṭha*, Univ. Madras, 1972, Note E, p. 101.

knowledge of his possessions; and (2) he who understands the king may be said to understand his ministers as well.[1]

Let us consider these two points in some detail. The purpose of creation may be understood better by knowledge of the Creator rather than by knowledge of the objects of creation. The Siddhāntin draws not merely on the resources of reason and inference but also on those of the Scriptures and of personal religious experience. The religious experience that shines through the songs of the Śaivite saints bears testimony to their awareness of a Being who performs the functions of creation, etc., for the purification and perfection of souls. In spite of trials and tribulations their faith remains unshaken. This may be an obsession but it seems to be a magnificent obsession! What is more, down the centuries, there has been an unbroken continuity of such faith and of exemplars of such faith. In the light of their experience, statements (1) and (2) made above gain in significance which, as bald arguments they may not have. Taken as mere arguments, they may appear to be circular reasoning, but they are grounded in religious experience. He who knows God as Paśupati (the Lord of the flock) knows that all the possessions are for the rearing of the flock. The material universe is not a vain display of the Lord's creative power. It is referred to as the sport of the Lord, no doubt, but sport is to be understood not as an idle pastime in which what is play to the Sportsman is pain and death to His creatures, but as something creative done with effortless ease. The material universe is meant by the Lord to be 'a vale of soul making', a means for the growth and development of souls. Hence, not only the world but also all occurrences therein have their accessory value. (2) He who knows the king, knows his ministers. Political realism or cynicism says, 'Every people gets the government it deserves', but it is religious faith that assures every soul that it is under the Spiritual Government of a King of kings, which it does not, and cannot ever, deserve. Membership of the Kingdom of God is a free gift that has no relation to one's desert.

---

[1] *The Śivādvaita of Śrīkaṇṭha*, p. 158.

If God is only the efficient cause, what is the status of the material cause? Broadly speaking three answers may be referred to here. The first treats God as both the material and the efficient cause. To the question whether in creation, etc., God will not be subject to the changes that the universe is subject to, the answer given is that the changes are *in* God, not *of* God. Those who consider this answer unsatisfactory argue that the changes in God, if real, will affect Him also. Hence the changes cannot be real, but only appear to be so. Their answer is that the One (God) alone *is*, the many *appear* to change and pass. The third answer is that the stuff out of which the Universe is made exists beginninglessly (*anādi*) with God. To this, the objection is (*a*) that to accept anything as existing co-eternally with God is to limit His infinitude and (*b*) that God, on this assumption, becomes not a Creator in the full sense of the term but only a worker who works with material that is given to Him, not made by Him and hence limited by such material.

The Siddhāntin, who holds the stuff out of which the Universe is made to exist beginninglessly with God, says that all accounts of Creation are with reference to the second and subsequent creation (Creation is not a unique event for Hinduism in the sense that it occurs just *once*. Creation is periodic). As for what happened in the first creation, it is a matter beyond our understanding; it is a mystery. Thus the first creation is left an open question. The word 'beginningless' means 'we do not know what happened long, long ago'. As for God's infinitude being limited by the co-existence of anything, animate or inanimate, it all depends on our conception of the infinite. If we think of it on material lines, one object by its very existence, limiting the existence of another, God cannot be infinite, but if God is Spirit, there is no question of another spirit or matter limiting Him. Besides, the real Infinite allows and actively encourages the finites to grow like unto Itself; it is the pseudo-infinite that would grudge or deny the finites possibilities of such growth.

(*B*) We may now proceed to state briefly the second argument. It is that *Karma* is not a self-administering principle. Souls cannot justly allocate the fruits of their deeds to themselves. Hence there must be God who tempers justice with mercy and governs the moral world (*Karmādhyakṣa*). *Karma* is powerful so long as our moral education is not complete. Once we have learnt the lessons of morality, Divine Love takes over from Moral Law (or *Karma*).

(*C*) Going through two excerpts in John Hick's *The Existence of God* (Macmillan, New York) it occurred to me that some oft quoted lines of Tirumūlar's *Tirumandiram*, a Śaivite canonical work, hint at or are suggestive of teleology or design. Kierkegaard is against the use of arguments. He says that Socrates presupposes God's existence and seeks to interpenetrate nature with the idea of purpose. A study of nature *without faith* in God would only confuse us by instances of dysteleology, lack of design, etc. Elsewhere in Hick's book, I came across the statement that when the Psalmist or Prophet calls Israel to behold the glory of God in nature, it is not proof to doubting minds they offer but spiritual nourishment to hungry souls, 'not arguments but sacraments'. In the light of these ideas the following lines in the *Tirumandiram* acquired a fresh significance for me:

'Do not deny the existence of the Almighty Who in His Justice commanded fire to abide in the middle of the sea (to prevent its overflow on the land). He is the Lord of the gods. He showers His grace day and night.' Maybe we have here the echoes of an argument from design *and* the traces of a sacrament! When Tirumūlar says, 'Even if we deny His existence, the Lord mightily exists', in the wake of the lines which say, 'Direct your thoughts as far as they can go. Speak the truth to the extent possible', there is the suggestion that, perplexities not withstanding, the spirit of Truth will lead us to God. One who goes through the Siddhānta works is left in no doubt, despite all the discussions and argumentation, that God's grace is the paramount factor in our spiritual enlightenment. Arguments at best can clear the way for, or confirm faith, they cannot create it.

The Siddhāntin uses three categories *Pati* (Paśupati, the Lord of the flock), *paśu* (souls) and *pāśa* (bonds). These may be also rendered as the Unbounded, the bound, and the bonds. Addressing ourselves to the human predicament (the *paśu* or the bound) for the time being, are we aware of any bondage, any curb to our freedom? The obvious bonds are political, economic and social, but at the back of these, the trouble seems to be something intimately connected with ourselves, something which neither modern medicine nor psychotherapy is able to diagnose or deal with. Hence freedom is, and has to be, at some deeper level if it is to be meaningful at all. In the absence of true freedom, freedom in the political, economic and social areas turns out to be insecure and uncertain. Freedom has a negative and a positive aspect, freedom *from* and freedom *for*. The Siddhāntin's conception is that it is freedom from the triple bonds (*āṇava*, *māyā* and *karma*) and freedom for worship of God and service to His creatures.

Āṇava is egoism, the deep-rooted sense of 'I' and 'mine'. This is said to be natural to the soul because it is a beginningless characteristic of the soul. It is the inevitable tendency of the soul—till the attainment of grace—to see and relate everything to 'I' and 'mine' and to be self-centred. Appar, a Śaivite saint of the seventh century AD has compared this tendency to the number nine which reduces all its products to itself (e.g. $9 \times 47 = 423 = 4 + 2 + 3 = 9$) finally. Someone has described this tendency caustically, if quaintly, thus: the tendency which makes one say, 'If it is a wedding, I must be the bridegroom, and if it is a funeral, I must be the corpse'. It is tragi-comical that all our efforts to boost ourselves result only in our humiliation. Paradoxically what saves us from humiliation is humility, we 'stoop to conquer'. All our life (according to the Hindus, all our lives, since we have many), we learn this one lesson, that we must cease to be self-centred and become God-centred. An unintended side-effect of this process is that we achieve greatness through humility. The *Tirukkural*, a Tamil classic, says 'Greatness ever stoops low. Pettiness preens itself in self-praise'. Thus egoism is closely linked up with ourselves or personality as the husk in a grain. In a way, while it is the grain that grows, it cannot grow without the husk, but at some stage dehusking is necessary for the grain to be itself and to be useful. At the growth stage the husk is necessary; at the use stage, it has to go. It is this *āṇava* which is responsible for all our woes, which gives a wrong orientation to our thoughts, words, physical deeds and to our feelings. Giving us a false sense of self-importance it is *āṇava* that causes our knowledge be rooted in falsehood. The falsehood is not that the self does not exist but that it arrogates to itself supreme value. So, it is not a counterfeit coin in the sense that it is totally unrelated to a given currency and so has to be treated as non-existent, but it is counterfeit in claiming a value that does not belong to it. This *āṇava* is our primal bondage. Substituting for pride the word *āṇava* we can recall the words of G. K. Chesterton: 'Pride is a poison so very poisonous that it not only poisons the virtues; it even poisons the other vices.'[1] When he says that of all spiritual diseases, egoism is the most intolerable, we are reminded of Appar's words that it is also incurable except by Divine Grace. Egotism ('all "sweet" talk ending up with oneself') or vanity is only a shade less reprehensible than egoism. For, while the egotist would like others to exist if only to constitute an audience for his talk, the egoist is so self-centred that he does not even bother whether others exist or not.

So long as man is in the grip of such egoism and it seems to be the common human lot, what schemes for political, economic or social advancement can be of avail? From this primal bondage follow other complications, viz. those resulting from *māyā* and *karma*. *Māyā* is the stuff from which the world we live in, the bodies we tenant and the objects of our experience are made. God has meant these to be the means of our spiritual growth. We are to use our body and the objects we possess in worshipping God and serving His creatures, but, thanks to *āṇava* we identify ourselves with our body and

---

[1] G. K. Chesterton, *The Common Man*, London, New York, Sheed & Ward, p. 249.

develop a possessive attitude to all things (and, indeed, to persons too). This misuse reprimanded by all theists is aptly described by a Christian thinker thus: We use God to enjoy the world, whereas we ought to use the world to enjoy God. The world is not an end in itself, it is a means to an end or *the* end, namely God.

To resume the Siddhāntin's account, our body and the world we live in are defiled (hence treated as a *mala* or impurity) by selfish use and thus become a bond. Trying to possess the world, we come to be possessed by it. *Māyā* wrongly used under the influence of *āṇava* is responsible for *mamākāra*, the possessive spirit. Instead of being enslaved unwittingly by this possessive spirit, to allow ourselves to be possessed by God is our true freedom.

The third bond is *karma*. *Karma* literally means action, but action that includes our thoughts and words. Thoughts, words and physical deeds which are good constitute spiritual merit (*puṇya*), those which are bad constitute spiritual demerit (*pāpa*). Here again, *āṇava* comes into the picture. To develop a sense of moral responsibility and assume agency for action is a step in moral growth. But corrupted by egoism, the tendency is to claim credit for good action without doing it and to try to escape blame for wrong action after having actually done it. Even more insidious is the work of egoism when it makes us claim credit for good action when we have actually done it with a feeling ' "*I*" have done this' (*ahaṅkāra*). For growth in morality consists in doing good action in a spirit of self-forgetfulness. God wants us to grow *from* a state of normative morality where we endeavour to do good, overcoming our inclinations to the contrary, where there is tension, *to* a state of natural morality, where selfless goodness has become the very breath of our being.

To learn to use our body and our so-called possessions in worshipping God and serving His Creatures, to do good with no thought of reward or self-advancement—this is the way to overcome our bondage. Where the self has got rid of its egoism, there is true freedom. Removal of egoism is possible only by the grace of God. In fact, the end and aim of spiritual evolution, as willed by God, appears to be the emergence of souls from a state of egocentrism to a state of theocentrism, through use of their freedom. As this evolution takes a long time, many births are said to be necessary. The souls that have won through to freedom in God do not cease to have their ontological entitativeness. They have a richer life as a consequence of having overcome all sense of 'I' and 'mine'.

III

Have the above ideas any contemporary relevance? As one who has had at least a 'nodding acquaintance' with other systems of philosophy, Indian and Western, and other religions, besides Śaiva Siddhānta and Śaivism, do I find these ideas intelligible, coherent and helpful as a guide to life? I believe I can honestly say I do. I have always felt that traffic is not one way, East to West alone, but also West to East. Western absolutism and theism have helped me in my understanding of their Indian counterparts, for, I believe that the major trends of thought in each tradition, absolutist, theist and humanist are basically similar. Likewise in regard to religion, I owe a deep debt of gratitude to other religions, chiefly to Christianity. I may be a Hindu (or Śaivite) of sorts, but definitely a better sort than if I had not learnt anything of other religions. The faiths of other men have been a challenge and inspiration to me.

I have never been able to understand philosophy merely as a view of life, and not also as a way of life. (Is it a mere view in the West? If so, how are we to understand the expressions, 'stoic' or 'platonic' ways of life?) While grateful for such clarification in thought as analysis of language has brought us, and for such insights as existentialism and phenomenology have given us, I believe that philosophy and religion in their traditional forms are still significant for us and might continue to be so. They may differ in emphasis, the former stressing theory and the latter practice, but none the less closely related for all the difference in emphasis.

To grow from a state of savagery into sainthood (as Arnold Toynbee holds) appears to me to be the meaning of history. All history is spiritual history. A saint is a person completely redeemed from self-centredness, who by his thoughts, words, and deeds, indeed by his mere presence, helps people to overcome their egoism. Thus if he is a lover of God, by the same token he is a lover of all living things. Śaivism says, 'Realising that Śiva (God) lives in every form of life, be kind to them'. Again we have the saying, 'Those who do not love God do not love His devotees. Those who do not love every living thing do not have love for themselves either.' This is significant for self-love, which is the obvious level at which unredeemed persons function, is seen to be pointless if it has not blossomed into love of others. 'Others' according to Śaivism (and Hinduism in general) would include souls at the sub-human levels also. Thus the society which calls forth our efforts on its behalf is the grand community of every living thing. Social service is not confined to humans alone. Everything alive is on probation for promotion to a higher level of life. Hence we owe a duty to help each one in its spiritual evolution.

The practical aspect of this philosophy of religion is to strive by our efforts to help others but to maintain ourselves without seeking the help of others: to borrow the words of Thomas Carlyle, 'not to increase the numerator, but to decrease the denominator', so that without multiplying our wants, we reduce them to a necessary minimum so that we can serve others. Is this austerity? May be it is, but it ushers in spiritual prosperity for all. I find the following ancient Tamil verses helpful in understanding this type of social philosophy:

It is demeaning to beg saying, 'Give'.
It is more demeaning to say, 'I won't give'.
It is ennobling to say, 'Take'.
It is more ennobling to say, 'I won't take'.

Another verse says 'Not to beg of others—but not to refuse to give when others beg'. This is a state of self-sufficiency, in which the sufficiency of the self is not of itself but because the self lives, moves and has its being in the Supreme, self-radiating Its Love for all.

Chapter 6

CONTEMPORARY RELEVANCE
OF THE INSIGHTS OF ADVAITA

by

T. M. P. MAHADEVAN

Director, Centre of Advanced Study in Philosophy, University of Madras

I

Advaita is non-dualism. Reality, according to its insight, is non-dual, not-two. Advaita does not profess to formulate conceptually what reality is. It is not, therefore, a system of thought, an *ism*. It is not a school among schools of philosophy. It does not reject any view of reality: it only seeks to transcend all views, since these are by their very nature, restricted, limited, and circumscribed. The various pluralisms, theistic or otherwise, imagine that they are opposed to Advaita, but Advaita is not opposed to any of the partial views of reality. An illustrious predecessor of Śaṅkara, Gauḍapāda, makes this clear when he says:

'The dualists (i.e. pluralists) are conclusively firm in regard to the status of their respective opinions. They are in conflict with one another. But, Advaita is in no conflict with them.

'*Advaita*, verily, is the supreme truth; *dvaita* (duality) is a variant thereof. For the dualists, there is duality either way (i.e. both in the Absolute and in the phenomenal manifold). With that (duality) this (non-duality) is not in conflict.'[1]

That Advaita is not opposed to any school of thought or mode of spiritual life is evident from the fact that the teachers of

[1] *Māṇḍūkya-kārikā*, iii, 17–18.

Advaita have freely adopted terms and expressions and even concepts that belong to the various philosophico-religious traditions. The resilience of Advaita is responsible for the possibility of setting forth the plenary truth. Admittedly, no language is adequate for giving expression to the non-dual reality. Even terms such as *advaita* (non-dual) and *ekam* (one) are not adequate. All language belongs to the realm of duality. That is why the first teacher of Advaita, the Lord Śiva as *Dakṣiṇāmūrti*, is said to have revealed the truth through eloquent silence—dumb exposition (*mauna-vyākhyā*). Words are to be used only where the language of silence is not understood; but even then, words are not to be taken in their express sense, but as indicators in an implied manner. Words are there to be transcended, and not to be clung on to. It is refreshing to note that a well known western philosopher ends his work which has become a near-classic with this note:

'My propositions are elucidatory in this way: he who understands me finally recognises them as senseless, when he has climbed out through them, on them, over them. (He must so to speak throw away the ladder, after he has climbed upon it.)

'He must surmount these propositions; then he sees the world rightly.

'Whereof one cannot speak, thereof one must be silent.'[1]

But, the human mind cannot be, and will not be silent; it must express itself in words; it needs must speak even of things which go beyond the reach of words and concepts. The teachers of Advaita, recognising this, use words in such a manner that they will lead to the transcendent, without the words insisting that they should go all the way, which they cannot. Paradoxical as it may seem, the teachers, while being convinced that words and concepts fail to reach the end, still use them for setting forth the truth of non-duality. In this undertaking, they freely borrow the linguistic and conceptual

[1] Ludwig Wittgenstein, *Tractatus Logico-Philosophicus* (Kegan Paul, Trench Trubner & Co. Ltd. London, 1922), p. 189.

tools which belong to the different schools of thought and religious traditions.

The illustrious Gauḍapāda, in his *Māṇḍūkya-kārikā*, makes use of Buddhist terms and concepts for teaching Advaita. Especially in the fourth chapter, *Alātasānti-prakaraṇa*, he employs Mādhyamika arguments and illustrations for showing the unreality of the world. Certain important terms in their specifically Buddhist meanings are used: e.g. *dharma* (element of existence), *saṅghata* (aggregate), *advaya* (free from the perceptible object and the percipient, or neither of the two extreme views), *adhvan* (time), *kṛtaka* (artificial), *prajñapti* (practical denomination), *saṁkleśa* (impurity), *saṁvṛti* (practical or empirical truth), *nirmitaka* (a thing made of illusion or supernatural power), *nimitta* (specific appearance which is the cause of attachment, aversion, and delusion), *dharma-dhātu* (the essence of reality), *śuddha-laukika* (pure mundane), *lokottara* (supra-mundane), *kṣānti* (patience), *nirvāṇa* (quiescence), and *tāyin* (he who shows the way). Although Gauḍapāda presses into service Buddhist terms and concepts in the course of his exposition, it is to be noted that he does not identify his view with that of either Vijñānavāda or Mādhyamika; he never loses sight of the goal of Advaita. For instance, using the terminology of Vijñānavāda, Gauḍapāda says that the world is the result of the vibration of *citta*. But what he means by *citta* is not the contentless mind which is the reality, according to the Vijñānavādin, but the non-dual Self (*Ātman*). What is worthy of note in the present context is that Gauḍapāda succeeds in conveying the truth of Advaita through Buddhist terminology and conceptual framework, in the fourth chapter, to the same extent as he does in the first three chapters, in expounding the truth in the conventional Upaniṣadic manner—i.e. through scripture (*śruti*), reasoning (*yukti*), and experience (*anubhava*).

Śaṅkara expounded Advaita not only in his well known commentaries and manuals, but also in the hymns that he composed. In a very popular hymn which begins with the words *bhaja govindam* (worship the Lord Govinda), the

Master sets forth the essential teachings of Advaita—the absolute reality of the Self, the ephemerality of the world, the means for realising the Self, etc. In the *Hymn to Dakṣiṇāmūrti* which has also become famous, Śaṅkara gives in a short compass the quintessence of Advaita. The hymn is addressed to the south-facing Śiva as the *Guru*, by whose grace one receives the teaching of non-duality. How the one reality appears as the many, how even the distinction of the teacher and the taught comes about, one cannot explain. But the basic truth of Advaita which is the Self, of the nature of consciousness, cannot be denied. Whether it is called God, *Guru*, or the Self, it is the same. The realisation of this truth is the goal of Advaita, and, Advaita is in opposition to no system of thought or mode of spiritual discipline. In order to show this, Śaṅkara employs in the hymn some of the terms and concepts peculiar to Kashmir Śaivism: e.g. the illustration of the mirrored city (*darpaṇa-dṛśyamāna-nagarī*); *spanda*, in the sense of movement; the expression *pratyabhijñā*, meaning self-recognition.

Quite a few of the outstanding teachers of Advaita after Śaṅkara have adopted theistic modes in their approach to the plenary truth: here, in this regard, any of the theistic traditions has been found to be as good as any other: Śaiva, Vaiṣṇava, or Śākta. Appayya Dīkṣita, who lived in the sixteenth century, was a great Advaitin; but at the same time he was passionately devoted to Śiva. It was, however, his Advaita conviction that made him disagree with the sectarian devotee of Śiva who pulls down Viṣṇu to the status of a finite self. Madhusūdana Sarasvatī (sixteenth century), who was a great exponent of Advaita dialectics, was an ardent devotee of Kṛṣṇa, whom he regarded as the supreme incarnation of the highest reality, *Brahman*—which, again it will be noted, is a non-sectarian view.

In their interpretative expositions of Advaita itself, the post-Śaṅkara Advaitins followed modes which reveal minor differences among themselves. These doctrinal differences, instead of detracting from Advaita, contribute to augmenting its greatness. It is a tribute to its penetrating insights that they admit of a variety of formulations. The variations range from near-subjectivism to near-realism, but these do not make any change in the basic truth of non-duality. Appayya Dīkṣita, who discusses the doctrinal differences in Advaita in his work, *Siddhāntaleśa-saṅgraha*, says in the invocatory verse that the commentary on the *Brahma-sūtra*, having for its sole purport the non-dual *Brahman*, issued from the blessed lotus-face of Bhagavatpāda Śaṅkara and got diversified a thousand fold on reaching the preceptors who expounded it after him, in the same way as the Ganges, which originating from the feet of *Viṣṇu* gets variegated on reaching different lands.

II

In contemporary times, one finds a similar phenomenon in regard to the expositions of Advaita. Some interpreters of Advaita lean heavily on realism—not mere epistemological realism, but ontological realism. According to them, the world is a real emanation, and not an illusory manifestation. *Brahman* is always characterised by *māyā* which is its real power. The causality of the origination, sustenation, and dissolution of the world, is not the qualification *per accidens* (*taṭastha-lakṣaṇa*) of *Brahman*, but its essential definition (*svarūpa-lakṣaṇa*). The external world, therefore, is not to be dismissed as a fiction of the mind, or as a fictitious projection of ignorance.

What is referred to as the Mysore school rejects outright the idea of a primal nescience (*mūlāvidyā*). It is contended that the theory of a positive ontological 'basic ignorance' put forward by the author of the *Pañcapādikā* and other post-Śaṅkara Advaitins, has no sanction in Śaṅkara or Gauḍapāda.[1] Since the notion of cause and effect is unintelligible and fictitious, and 'the entire universe is only idea or mental phenomenon', the accounts of creation that are to be found in the scriptures are 'but fairy tales or myths meant for children' and have no

[1] See Satchidananda Sarasvati's Introduction to his *Sanskrit commentary on the Naiṣkarmya-siddhi* (Adhyyātmaprākaśa-kāryālaya, Holenarāsipur, 1968), p. 21.

real significance. 'The one key to the entire system of Vedānta, the philosophy of Śaṅkara, lies in the meaning of causality', says one of the leaders of the Mysore school. 'Unless one clearly understands that no such relations as "cause" and "effect" exists as a reality one cannot, according to Śaṅkara, understand the philosophy of Vedānta'.[1] Truth is the goal of Vedānta, and will be discovered not on the strength of authority or tradition but through reasoning. Mystic attitudes and ecstatic visions are not what the seeker should aspire for. The prime source of correct knowledge is 'experience as tested by that universal touchstone of truth, namely, reason'.[2] It is claimed by this school that Gauḍapāda and Śaṅkara relied solely on reasoning, and not on a single syllable of the scriptures, in their exposition of Advaita. The truth of Advaita is to be realised through a thorough and persistent inquiry into the three states of experience, waking, dream, and deep sleep. It is by a comparative analysis of the three states, it is stated, that the central truth is established. The Vedāntic view which has been described as tribasic is considered to be the only means of transcending the veil of phenomena and arriving at Reality.[3]

Many interpreters of Advaita steer clear of near-realism and near-subjectivism, and adopt what may be called the middle-of-the-road standpoint. The world, according to them, has a grade or reality, lower only to that of the supreme Self, and should not be brushed aside characterising it as 'sound and fury signifying nothing'. 'The world is neither pure being nor pure non-being.'[4]

'The bewildering mass of phenomenal diversity must belong to reality, for there is nothing else in which it can be, and yet it is not reality. So it is said to be a phenomenon or appearance of reality'.[5] *Māyā* is the term which signifies the

[1] V. Subrahmania Iyer, *The Philosophy of Truth*, Court Press, Salem, 1955, p. 245.
[2] *Ibid.*, p. 235.
[3] See K. A. Krishnaswami Iyer, *Vedanta or the Science of Reality*, Ganesh, Madras, 1930, p. 335.
[4] S. Radhakrishnan, *Indian Philosophy*, Allen & Unwin, London, 1962, Vol. II, p. 563.
[5] *Ibid.*, p. 564.

phenomenality of the world. *Māyā* is neither real as *Brahman* nor unreal as the sky-flower. As the creative power of the eternal God, it is also eternal. One may even say that God is in need of the world of *māyā* for his own self-realisation. The view that we are at present alluding to, thus holds that it is wrong to characterise the phenomenal world as an illusion, a creation of the mind. The metaphors of rope-snake, nacre-silver, etc., should not be stretched too far. 'If the world of experience were illusory and unrelated to *Brahman*, love, wisdom, and asceticism could not prepare us for the higher life.'[1] When *Brahman* is realised, the world is not so much negated as reinterpreted. To say that the world is a phenomenon is not to say that it is a phantasm. *Brahman* is in the world though not as the world.

With regard to the question of *māyā*, the classical view, however, as set forth, for instance, by Bhāratitīrtha-Vidyāraṇya in the *Pañcadaśī*, is that one may look at it from three different standpoints: that of the man of the world, that of the sage who has realised the truth, and that of the metaphysician who inquires. From the standpoint of the unreflective man, the world is real, and the problem of *māyā* does not arise. He is satisfied with the first look of things; he does not doubt the veracity of what he sees; for him, seeing is believing. At the other extreme is the sage, for whom there is no world of plurality and, therefore, no question of its being real. With reference to his plenary experience, one could only say that *māyā* is the name for that (*yā*) which is not (*mā*). From this standpoint—if it may be called standpoint—there is no bondage, no release, no one who is bound, no one who is released, and no one who is striving for release. The sage is one who has realized that *Brahman* alone is, and nothing else: and so, for him, there is no world, no *māyā*. The third standpoint is that of the inquiring intellect. *Māyā*, from this standpoint, is a riddle. Wonder is its garment; inscrutable is its nature. *Māyā* is not real because it is sublated when self-knowledge arises; nor is it unreal because it is experienced so

[1] *Indian Philosophy*, p. 583.

long as there is delusion. *Māyā* is not both real and unreal, because contradictories cannot co-exist, and so, *māyā* is said to be indeterminable (*anirvacanīyā*).

Here, again, with regard to the status of the world of *māyā*, it is to be noted that different accounts become possible at different levels of experience. Each view falls into its place, because Advaita is all-comprehensive, accommodating as it does varying perspectives, and eventually transcending all of them.

The study of comparative philosophy is a relatively recent development. Almost the first Indian philosophical tradition to be compared with Western philosophical perspectives—the most compared tradition as well—is Advaita-Vedānta. Similarities have been noted between Śaṅkara and such modern Western philosophers as Spinoza, Kant, Schelling, Hegel, Bradley, and others. Spinoza conceives of Reality as the one substance which he identifies with Nature and God: his formula of equation is: Substance = Nature = God. God is the immanent cause of the totality of finite things that constitute the world. There is no second substance. To the one substance, the rest are related as attributes and modes: thinking and extension being the attributes, and thinking beings and extended things being the modes. Kant, in his critical philosophy, ruled out the possibility of knowing the noumenal reality. What are, and can be, known are only the phenomenal objects. The noumenon is trans-empirical, and so it is beyond the reach of sense and understanding. Schelling, who systematised pantheism, said that in intellectual intuition the identity of the subject and object is realised. The ego and the non-ego are identified in the Absolute, the Infinite World-Spirit. For Hegel, the Real is the concrete universal, which includes all differences within itself, the One which contains the many. Of the Absolute Spirit or Mind, the world is a self-expression. Bradley, it is believed, comes nearest to Śaṅkara. The Absolute, for Bradley, is not its appearances. The appearances are riddled with contradictions, and, therefore, are not real. Thought cannot comprehend reality. It sunders the 'what' from the 'that', and so is incapable of reaching the goal. Reality is sentient experience which eludes the dissection of thought. The Absolute is not a person; it does not require a phenomenal world as its perpetual object. 'The Absolute does not want I presume, to make eyes at itself in a mirror, or, like a squirrel in a cage, to revolve the circle of its own perfections.'[1]

We have referred to some of the western thinkers of the modern period and their teachings, in the context of a comparative study thereof with Śaṅkara and his Advaita. When Indian scholars who were acquainted with Western thought turned their attention to Advaita, they were naturally struck by what they considered to be close similarities between the monistic philosophers of the West and Śaṅkara, but, subsequently, a deeper study revealed significant differences between, for instance, the Substance of Spinoza, the Thing-in-itself of Kant, the World-Spirit of Schelling, the Absolute Mind of Hegel, and the sentient Experience of Bradley, on the one hand, and the *Brahman-Ātman* of Śaṅkara. But, it is significant that Śaṅkara should have provided the basis for the comparisons which eventually brought to light differences as well as identities.

Attempts are being made today, both in India and abroad, to present Advaita in contemporary idioms. Mention may be made of the adoption of the phenomenological, existentialist, and analytical approaches for interpreting the insights of Advaita. Those who make such attempts generally say that their aim is neither to defend Advaita nor to attack it, but only to promote clarification—meaning by promotion of clarification, 'explication through the application of some of the modern techniques'. Starting from the ordinary world of things, for instance, it is possible to distinguish from out of it, progressively, one's body, mental states, etc., and arrive at pure subjectivity which is never an object. The phenomenological method that is employed here is useful in exhibiting the true 'I' as the non-dual cosmic pure subjectivity, by

[1] F. H. Bradley, *Appearance and Reality*, Clarendon Press, 2nd Ed., 1897, p. 152.

extricating it from the pseudo-'I' which is the body-mind-consciousness complex.[1] To restate this in the old language, what is sought to be done is to discriminate the Self from the not-Self, to draw it out from the latter, as one would draw out the pulp from a stalk.

The endeavour to understand Advaita-Vedānta in terms of one or the other of the existentialist philosophers and vice versa is becoming quite frequent now. In spite of mutual differences, the existentialists hold in common the view that existence precedes essence, which means that we must begin from the subjective. To cite a famous utterance of Kierkegaard, the first of the existentialists, 'Truth is subjectivity'. Sartre, who is an atheistic existentialist, says that there is at least one being whose existence comes before its essence, and that being is man. Man exists first of all, and defines himself afterwards. To begin with, he is nothing, and becomes anything at all only later, and then too he will be what he makes of himself. 'Man is, indeed, a project which possesses a subjective life, instead of being a kind of moss, or a fungus, or a cauliflower. Before that projection of the self nothing exists; not even in the heaven of intelligence.' Man is thus free and not pre-determined. He chooses what he wants to be. It is in the context of responsibility and choice that expressions such as 'anguish', 'abandonment', and 'despair' are employed. Sartre's theory of human freedom follows from his conception of nothingness which is basic to his philosophy. It is through man or human consciousness that nothingness comes into the world. Nothingness is not the antithesis of being, as in Hegel; it is complementary to being, and is dependent on being in a way that being is not dependent on nothingness. What makes its appearance in nothingness is being-for-itself. It 'lies coiled in the heart of being like a worm'. The for-itself is a borrowed being, as it emerges from the in-itself through the power of negation whose source, however, is inexplicable and myster-

---

[1] See Kalidas Bhattacharyya's article 'Advaita and Western Thought', in *Indian Philosophical Annual*, Vol. vii (The Centre for Advanced Study in Philosophy, Univ. Madras, 1971), pp. 3–18.

ious. The for-itself simply finds itself *there*; it emerges as an irreducible and ultimate datum. To the question, what is it about the being of man that occasions nothingness, Sartre answers: freedom. Freedom is the 'nature' of man. There is no difference between the being of man and his being free. To be, for the for-itself, is to cancel the in-itself which it is. What Sartre calls freedom is nothing other than this cancellation. It is by this that man escapes from his being as from his essence; it is by this that he is always something other than what one can say of him, for at least he is the one who escapes from this very classification, the one who is already beyond the name one gives him, the attribute one recognises in him. It is man's freedom, as we have seen, that occasions his 'anguish', etc. Every human presence in the world is a passion, in that it is a project to lose itself in order to found being and in the same act constitute the in-itself which escapes contingency in being its own ground. It is to be observed that there is the danger in Sartre, as he himself is aware, of using common terms in uncommon senses. There is also in his philosophy a tendency to overemphasise the absurd and the abnormal, the elemental passions and the pre-reflective consciousness. In spite of the fact that Sartre conceives of human existence as consciousness and freedom, his philosophy does not exert a liberating influence, because no way is opened for a man's recognition of his infinitude as the Self—pure being, basic consciousness, and bliss. Sartre's human reality, therefore, is by nature 'an unhappy consciousness, without the possibility of surpassing its unhappy state'.[1]

Martin Heidegger invites comparison with Śaṅkara. Although there are obvious differences, one may notice in Heidegger's theory of Being and analysis of the empirical self (human existence) some identity with the Vedāntic teaching. In view of this, Heidegger's philosophy, it is thought, may serve as a 'suspension bridge' to Advaita-Vedānta. In his *Being and Time*, Heidegger says that the main purpose of his

[1] See the present writer's article, 'Jean-Paul Sartre', in *The Vedānta Kesari*, Madras, May, 1968, pp. 47–9.

inquiry is to 'raise anew the question of the meaning of Being'. 'What is Being?', 'What is what, is': this is his basic problem. All ontology, no matter how rich and firmly compacted a system of categories it has at its disposal, must first clarify the meaning of Being, and conceive this clarification as its fundamental task.[1] The method that Heidegger adopts in the task of determining the meaning of Being is 'phenomenological', and not ratiocinative or argumentative. His structural analysis aims at disclosure of what is hidden and implicit in experience. And so, Heidegger does not seek to found a system of thought. His philosophy is rather a trail blazed, a path traversed, a way taken by thought, as he calls it, toward the one goal of enshrining in language, or rather preparing to do so, the unuttered thought of Being.[2] Instead of doing any conceptual analysis, what Heidegger does is to analyse the structure of man's existence, since 'an understanding of Being is itself a feature of man's mode of being'. In order to convey the direct reference to Being constitutive of the essence of man, Heidegger uses the term *Dasein*, which means literally Being-there. Dasein's mode of being should be differentiated from that of things that are simply present in the world. The whole history of Western philosophy shows, according to Heidegger, an exclusive pre-occupation with beings, with the things that are: and so, it has gone wrong. What metaphysics has to do is to study the to-be of Being as opposed to beings. In this task, it is the preconceptual understanding of human existence that will prove to be of great value. *Dasein* in this sense, is not an I-substance, but a field, not a private self confronting a world of external objects, but an impersonal and public creature which each one of us is even before he is an I. 'We exist thus in a state of 'fallen-ness' (*Verfallenheit*), according to Heidegger, in the sense that we are as yet below the level of existence to which it is possible for us to rise. So long as we remain in the womb of this

---

[1] See Martin Heidegger, *Being and Time,* John Macquarrie & Edward Robinson (Trans.), Harper & Row, New York, 1962, p. 31.

[2] J. L. Mehta, *The Philosophy of Martin Heidegger,* Banaras Hindu Univ., Varanasi, 1967, p. 1.

externalised and public existence, we are spared the terror and the dignity of becoming a Self.'[1]

Externalised public existence is inauthentic existence: it is when one ceases to be the impersonal and social 'One among many' that one is free to become oneself, and thus comes to have authentic existence. In authentic existence, man enters the region of Being 'where subject and object no longer confront each other in murderous division'.[2] It is claimed that in so far as Heidegger conceives of Being as the non-segmented whole, favours a view which does not detach beings from Being, and counsels our letting Being be instead of trapping it in the prison-house of the intellect, he is turning in the direction of the Orient. 'When he repeats over and over again that the tradition of the West begins with the forgetting of Being, that this tradition has come to its completion in a dead end, and that we have now in our thinking to go beyond it to the source from which it sprang, one is forced to think of the other great civilisation of mankind that arose in the East.'[3] We may also point out that when Heidegger conceives of Being as the invisible and all-pervasive presence which cannot be enclosed in any mental concept, he holds a view which is similar to that of Advaita.

Analytical philosophy which is a recent arrival has still to exert its influence on Indian thought. As it is practised in India today, it mostly follows the Western models. But, if it is to become significant, its votaries must explore the allied areas of Nyāya, Mīmāṁsā, and Vedānta. Stray attempts are being made to analyse Vedāntic statements which are sometimes wrongly described as theological statements. Vedānta, especially Advaita, is not afraid of analysis, and will not shy away from it. Vedic language is not a separate language from ordinary language, there are injunctive statements as well as descriptive statements in it. The former refer to what is to be accomplished; and the latter to what already is. How the Upaniṣadic texts which are statements about reality are to be

---

[1] William Barrett, *Irrational Man, A Study in Existentialist Philosophy*, Heinemann, London, 1961, p. 196.   [2] *Ibid.*, p. 207.   [3] *Ibid.*, p. 208.

interpreted—how, in particular, the major texts which are identity statements are to be analysed—is minutely explained in Advaita. This analysis may prove to be of considerable value to linguistic philosophy.

Scientists, usually, have little time or inclination to look beyond the particular problem with which they are occupied in depth. Most of them seem to believe that metaphysics is not relevant to their particular field of study and research. But a few discerning scientists, some of them are very distinguished ones, are convinced that their quest for scientific truth cannot be detached from man's search for the ultimate. One such great scientist, a Nobel prize winner, was Erwin Schrödinger. He states his conviction thus: '. . . if we cut out all metaphysics it will be found to be vastly more difficult, indeed probably quite impossible, to give any intelligible account of even the most circumscribed area of specialisation within any specialised science you please'.[1] The metaphysics that Schrödinger finds satisfying is that of Vedānta whose basic vision is that 'the plurality that we perceive is only *an appearance; it is not real*'.[2] Support for this basic vision is adduced by pointing out particular lines of modern thought which converge upon it. One of the lines of thought pointed out by Schrödinger is that 'we can now scientifically speak of the identity of an individual's consciousness with that of one of his ancestors in much the same sense as we can of the identity of my consciousness before and after a deep sleep.'[3] The Self, he says, 'is not so much *linked* with what happened to its ancestors, it is not so much the product, and merely the product, of all that, but rather, in the strictest sense of the word, the *same thing* as all that: the strict, direct continuation of it, just as the Self aged fifty is the continuation of the Self aged forty.'[4] The Self that is conscious is non-plural: 'We never in fact have any experience anywhere of a plurality of consciousness but always and everywhere only of consciousness in the singular.'[5] The

[1] Erwin Schrödinger, *My View of the World*, Cecily Hastings (Trans.) (Cambridge Univ. Press, 1964), p. 3.
Ibid., p. 18.   [3] *Ibid.*, p. 23.   [4] *Ibid.*, p. 28.   [5] *Ibid.*, p. 34.

eschatological doctrine of the transmigration of souls does not appeal to Schrödinger, but he whole-heartedly accepts the Upaniṣadic doctrine of Identity: the lovely thought of unity, of belonging unqualifiedly together, of which, as he points out, Schopenhauer said that it was his comfort in life and would be his comfort in death.[1]

We have, so far, indicated in general how the insights of Advaita are supremely relevant to man as such, and we shall now refer to some of these insights which constitute man's invaluable legacy.

III

Consciousness

According to Advaita, consciousness or knowledge is the very nature of the Self. This should be distinguished from *consciousness-of* which pertains to a mode of the mind. The former is *svarūpa-jñāna*, essential knowledge; the latter is *vṛtti-jñāna*, knowledge which results from the operation of a mental mode. By themselves, the mind and its modes are inert, since they are the products of *prakṛti*, but since the mind is made of the *sattva* constituent of *prakṛti*, it has the ability to reflect the consciousness which is the Self. Thus far, the Sāṅkhya and Advaita agree. The one difference between them is that while for the Sāṅkhya, the mind and its parent, *prakṛti* are real, for Advaita *prakṛti* is the principle of illusion, *māyā*, and therefore not real.

The knowledge of objects is made possible by the functioning of the cognitive mode (*vṛtti*) of the mind. But the mental mode can function only as carrying the reflection of the essential consciousness which is the Self. For objective knowledge to arise, then, the mental mode and the prototype consciousness which is also described as the witness-consciousness (*sākṣi-caitanya*) are required. There are cases of knowledge where the witness alone is the revealer, and not the mental mode. The cognition, say, of a pot arises in the form 'This is a pot'. For this cognition, the instrument is the approximate cognitive mode (*vṛtti*) of the mind. But how is

[1] *My View of the World*, p. 114.

this cognition known? When I say 'I know this is a pot', how is this knownness of the pot known? The Nyāya-Vaiśeṣika view is that the first cognition is known through reflective cognition (*anuvyavasāya-jñāna*), but this will lead to infinite regress, and so the Advaita position is that the 'known-ness' of an object is revealed by the witness-consciousness. While cognitions manifest objects, it is the witness that manifests cognitions. It is not cognitive modes alone, but also all modes of the mind, such as desire, anger, pain, pleasure, etc., that are directly revealed by the witness. There is one more significant instance where there is awareness because of the witness, without the instrumentation of a cognitive mode: i.e. the awareness of the absence of objects, or the unknownness of a thing. The awareness of the absence of objects, as in deep sleep, is nonetheless awareness; the unknown-ness is also known. Here it is the witness that is the revealing principle. The witness-self is the constant and unfailing consciousness. It neither rises nor sets. It is the eternal, immutable, pure awareness (*cin-mātra*). It is on the basis of the Self that all empirical knowledge takes place, involving the distinctions of cogniser, means of cognition, and object of cognition.

Value

Consciousness which is the ultimate Reality, the Self, is also the plenary value, for Advaita.

A sense of value, although rudimentary and crude, is to be found even in animals. There does not seem to be any difference between animal behaviour and the human in pleasure–pain situations. Animals, like men, have appetition for the pleasant and aversion for the unpleasant. Cattle, for instance, seek green pastures and run away from possible dangers. Thus in regard to the instinctive seeking of value and avoidance of disvalue, the humans are not different from the animals.[1]

What distinguishes man from the animal, however, is his ability to think and reflect, to grade valuables in a hierarchy, to differentiate the good from the merely useful, and to choose

[1] Śaṅkara, *Sūtra-bhāṣya*, Introduction: *paśvadibhiaś cāviśeṣāt.*

the former in preference to the latter.[1] It is not that man exercises this ability always; but he ought to, and can. A healthy and hungry cat, for instance, cannot but eat the food that is proximate to it provided there is no visible risk involved in such eating. But a man placed in similar circumstances may prefer not to eat, if he is convinced that that course of action is good. Just as eating is not an end in itself, not eating, too, is not an end in itself. There is no virtue in absolute fasting. One has to live, and therefore eat in order to keep body and soul together, before one could seriously seek for and gain the *summum bonum*. By abstention from eating, says Śaṅkara, one would only die, and not realise the Self. Although food has no value in itself, it has subsistence value.[2]

Do we not come across cases of suicide? In such cases, it may be asked: Does life or living have any value? An analysis of suicide cases reveals that one is compelled to take the extreme step not because one is dissatisfied with oneself or with life as such, but because one finds the conditions of life intolerable and imagines that living under these circumstances is valueless. This only shows indirectly that it is for the sake of the self that living is sought to be put an end to by some. Mere living has no intrinsic value, even prolonged living. That is why the boy Naciketas, in the *Kaṭha-upaniṣad*, rejects the gift of long life, when it is offered by Yama in the place of self-knowledge. No one who is wise will delight in mere length of life.[3]

Value, then, is to be distinguished from the valuables. The valuables vary and are inconstant, while value is unvarying and constant. What is unvarying and constant in the midst of what are varying and inconstant—that is real. Judged by this test, we shall show, the self is value, the self is reality.

The realisation of values, which means being endowed with them, is clearly considered to be the human end, and not the

[1] *See* Śaṅkara, *Taittirīya-upaniṣad-bhāṣya*, ii, I. Also *Āraṇyaka*, III, ii, 3.
[2] See commentary on *Bṛhadāraṇyaka-upaniṣad*, IV, iv, 22; *bhojana-nivṛttau mṛyata eva, na ātma-vedanam.* See also Vācaspati, *Bhāmatī*, I, i, 1.
[3] *Kaṭha-upaniṣad*, I, i, 28: *atidīrghe jīvite ko rameta.* See also Śaṅkara's commentary.

so-called values themselves, such as wealth and pleasure.
When the latter are valued, it is by connecting them with the
self or by superimposing selfhood on them. The not-self
appears to gain significance only by posing as the self or as a
part thereof. Three notions of selfhood, in fact, may be
distinguished from one another: secondary self (*gauṇa*),
illusory self (*mithyā*), and principal self (*mukhyā*).[1] The
secondary selfhood belongs to persons related to oneself, such
as son, wife, and others. When the son or the wife is the
primary self, the parent or the husband, as the case may be,
becomes the subsidiary self. The selfhood of a son, for instance,
is said to be secondary because, while difference is experienced
between the son and oneself, one identifies the interests of
the son with one's own. The illusory self is the mind-body
complex. This is said to be illusory because in ordinary
empirical usage like 'I walk', 'I want', etc., no distinction is
made between body-mind and self. The principal self is the
supreme Self, the witness of all experiences; but one may
start the inquiry into its nature by identifying it with oneself.
The concept of selfhood thus, it will be seen, differs according
to the mode of empirical usage. When the son is ill, the father
says, 'I am ill'. Identifying the self with the body or mind, one
says, 'I am lean', 'I am clever', etc. One who believes in after-
life or in going to heaven through performance of religious
rites identifies the self with the transmigrating soul, and says,
'I shall be reborn as such and such', 'I shall go to the heavenly
world after death,' etc. At each level of empirical usage, the
notion of self that is pertinent thereto becomes primary,
while the other notions are subsidiary. But whatever notion of
self is primary in a given instance, that is considered to be the
supreme value. What is neither the self nor a subsidiary thereto
is either disregarded or disdained. What is clearly recognised
as unconnected with the self is not rated or valued. What is
regarded as the self or as its subsidiary—even though erron-
eously, as happens in empirical usage—becomes endowed with
value. That the self is the supreme value is declared in the

[1] Pañcadaśī, xii, 39.

Bṛhadāraṇyaka text, 'This self is dearer than the son, dearer than wealth, dearer than everything else, and is innermost.'[1] Explaining this passage, Sureśvarācārya observes,

'Dearer than wealth is the son; dearer than the son is the body; dearer than the body are the sense organs; dearer than the sense organs is the vital air; much dearer than the vital air is the self.'[2]

The rule is this: the nearer a thing is to the self, the dearer it is than the rest; the dearest is the self.

That the self is the seat of supreme love, that it is the highest value, is the teaching given by Yājñavalkya to Maitreyī. 'Not for the sake of the husband is the husband dear, but for the sake of the self is the husband dear. Not for the sake of the wife is the wife dear, but for the sake of the self is the wife dear. . . . Not for the sake of all is all dear, but for the sake of the self is all dear.'[3] The teaching herein contained does not bear any subjectivistic implication; there is no egocentric predicament involved. Even if the hearer of this teaching were to understand by the 'self', in the first instance, his own 'private' self, it would serve a useful purpose; it would serve to turn the attention of the individual from external values to internal value. Especially in the context of modern civilisation, which has externalised and instrumentalised man and considers him to be worth only as much as he produces, it is good to stress the dignity of man and to induce him to cultivate the inward vision.

The real teaching, however, is not that the individual self is the highest value, but the non-dual Self, the 'I–that' whose value-reality nature is indicated by such terms as *sat, cit, ānanda* (being, consciousness, bliss). The self is said to be 'being' not in the sense in which, say, 'Minds are' and 'Bodies are'. 'Existence', it is claimed by some philosophers like Gilbert Ryle, has a diversity of meanings (multivocalism). When we

---

[1] *Bṛhadāraṇyaka-upaniṣad*, I, iv, 8.
[2] *Bṛhad-vārtika* (Ānandāśrama ed.), p. 640.
[3] *Bṛhadāraṇyaka-upaniṣad*, II, iii, 12.

say 'There are minds and there are bodies', we use the expression 'there are' to mean different sorts of existence, so that to say 'There are minds *and* bodies' is not false but nonsense. If this be the case, then the statement 'There is the self', it is clear, does not refer to existence in either of the two senses already mentioned, and it would be nonsense to say 'There are minds, bodies *and* the self'. Existence is not a predicate of the self; the self is existence. As an Upaniṣad text puts it, the self should be known simply as 'It-Is'.[1] The self is existence without conditions. The meaning of the other terms, 'consciousness' and 'bliss', should be understood in a similar manner. It is not that the self has consciousness or is blissful; the self is consciousness-bliss. Even thus, it is not proper to regard the self's nature as constituted by three factors, being-consciousness-bliss. Language is here useful, not in describing what is real or what is value, but in drawing us away from what is non-real and what is non-value. The limitations of language even in the sphere of the empirical have become evident as a result of language-analysis. 'What we say there is' is not the same as 'What there is'. If our descriptions of even that which can be experienced are not adequate, much more inadequate should be our attempts to describe pure experience which is the self. Even ideal language, 'disinfected' language—if it is possible to accomplish this—will be inadequate. Yet, we have to use language so long as our understanding is language-bound, and language can help by pointing to the direction in which illumination is to be sought. 'What we say there is' is not altogether unconnected with 'What there is'.[2] 'What we say there is' is by way of projection; in our language, we would say, it is by way of *māyā*. But the act of projection has two aspects: concealing and revealing. While language serves to conceal the real, it also reveals, in a way. It is thus that we may fairly intelligibly talk about the self; and I may realise it because it is 'I'. That is why Śaṅkara says that the self is not altogether a non-object, because it is the object of

[1] *Kaṭha-upaniṣad*, II, iii, 12.
[2] See W. V. O. Quine, *Word and Object*, New York, Wiley, 1960.

the concept 'I', and because of the immediacy of the realisation of the inner self.[1]

What we have said regarding language will apply *mutatis mutandis* to thought or to the reasoning process. We may not 'prove' the self, as we may prove the presence of 'fire' on the strength of the *probans*, 'smoke'. It is a matter for dispute whether we can properly speak about 'proving' fire by an inference; but that apart, it is true that the self is not to be found at the fag end of a chain of syllogisms. Yet we may make use of arguments such as the following: (1) The self is different from the mental modes, because it is the witness of those modes; whatever is not different from the modes is not the witness thereof, as, e.g. a mental mode, etc. (2) The Self is real, because it is the substrate of what illusorily appears, as nacre is of the illusory silver. (3) The self is of the nature of consciousness, because it illumines what is inert, as, e.g. a pot. (4) The self is the supreme bliss, because it is the seat of absolute love; what is not the supreme bliss does not become the seat of absolute love, as, e.g. a pot. (5) The self is the *plenum*, because it is related to or is the basis of all, like ether.[2]

The self that is the reality is the supreme value in the sense that there is nothing else that can serve as the ultimate human goal (*parama-puruṣārtha*), or release (*mokṣa*).

Release

The Self is of the nature of release. *Ātman* and *mokṣa* are synonyms in Advaita. The Self is ever free; freedom is its very nature. Only this truth is not realised because of nescience. The removal of nescience alone is required for the attainment of release. The same is true about the destruction of *saṁsāra* which is bondage.

It is true that release is said to be 'attained' and bondage 'destroyed' when nescience is removed. But the expressions 'attainment' and 'destruction' should be understood in this

---

[1] *Sūtra-bhāṣya*, Introduction: na tāvad ayam ekāntenaviṣayaḥ, asmatpratyaya-viṣayatvāt, aparokṣatvāc-ca pratyagātma-prasiddeḥ.

[2] See Rāmakrṣna Paṇḍita's gloss on the *Pañcadaśī*, viii, 58.

E

context in a figurative sense. There are two kinds of attainment, and two of destruction: attainment of the unattained, and attainment of the already attained; destruction of what has not been destroyed, and destruction of the already destroyed. For the first kind in each, action is necessary; not for the second variety of attainment and destruction. Let us illustrate. For getting an ornament made of gold, action is essential. It is not enough that one procures the money, which itself involves action; one must buy the gold, and get the ornament made, or go to the smith's shop and buy the jewellery. This is a case of attaining what has not been attained. An instance of the other type is the following. A person imagines that the gold chain he is wearing round his neck is lost. The chain is right there round his neck; but he is under a delusion. He sets about searching for the chain. A passer-by, on being appraised of the situation, points out to the deluded person that the chain is there round his neck. The person clutches at the chain, jumps in elation, and cries out saying, 'I have got back my precious chain'. This is a case of attaining what is already attained. The person affected has nothing to do for 'getting back' the chain. All that he need get is the knowledge of the fact that the chain was not lost. Destruction, we said, is of two kinds. For destroying a real serpent, action, such as beating with a stick, is required. This is a case of the first kind. For destroying the rope-serpent, any amount of beating will not do; what is necessary is sufficient light. This is an instance of the second kind of destruction. Now, the 'attainment' of release and 'destruction' of bondage are in the second of the two senses, which is the figurative sense. Release is eternal, and, therefore, it is the ever-attained. On account of nescience it seems to be unattained as it were. At the dawn of knowledge its eternal nature is revealed. Similarly, bondage is not real, being nescience-caused. At the rise of knowledge, it is removed as it were, being already removed. Thus it will be seen that knowledge, and not action, is the means to the gaining of release and the destruction of bondage.

Since, according to Advaita, *Brahman* is the supreme bliss, release which is *Brahman*-realisation is of the nature of supreme bliss. In release, 'one gets firmly established in the supreme *Brahman* that is endless, of the nature of unending Heaven, i.e. happiness devoid of misery, the reality that is greater than all. Realising *Brahman* that is known through all the Vedānta texts as the Self, one attains that *Brahman* alone.'[1]

As release is the eternal nature of the Self, one need not wait for realising it until death overtakes the physical body. Even while tenanting a body one is released at the onset of knowledge. Such a one is called a *jīvanmukta*, released even while living in the body. This, again, is a precious insight of Advaita. *Mokṣa* is not an unseen fruit to be gained after death. It is not a *post mortem* experience. It can be realised here and now. A text of the *Upaniṣads* declares: 'One realises *Brahman* here'.[2] The supreme knowledge arises as dispelling ignorance. And, when this happens, release which is the eternal nature of the Self is realised. The continuance of the body is in no way incompatible with the status of release. What happens when release is gained is a change in perspective. Before release, one took the world of which the body is a part to be real; after gaining Self-knowledge one realises that the world is an illusory appearance. If the body were real, then release could come only after the destruction of the body. But, since the body is not real, its continued appearance or disappearance is of no consequence.

There is a text of the *Bṛhadāraṇyaka-upaniṣad* which says: 'If the *puruṣa* knows the self as "this am I", then desiring what and for whose desire should he suffer along with the body?'[3] Here, the reference is to the *jīvanmukta*. The one who is released while yet living has nothing more to achieve and has no more ends to gain. The satisfaction (*tṛpti*) that is his is without any limit and determination. Now that he has realised the supreme Self, all obligations have been fulfilled and all desires have been quenched. Prior to the acquiring of true knowledge man has many duties to be performed and many

[1] *Kena-upaniṣad-vākya-bhāṣya*, iv, 8.   [2] *atra brahma samaśnute.*
[3] *Bṛhadāraṇyaka*, IV, iv. 12.

desires to be satisfied. He works for the pleasures of the world and the happiness of heaven; and he strives for release from his earthly bonds. But when once he attains *Brahman*-know-ledge, there is nothing else for him to do.

Some critics of Indian thought believe that the Indian pursuit of spirituality is a selfish quest, and that the saint and the sage are concerned with only their own salvation. This criticism, however, is the result of a gross misunderstanding of the Indian ideal of spirituality. Whether from the theistic or from the absolutistic standpoint, the goal is not a selfish gain. God-realisation or Self-realisation is the state of perfection where there can be no room for even the least trace of selfishness. For the man of wisdom there is not the distinction of 'mine' and 'not-mine'. He regards the whole world as his household.[1] But what is the true help that the world could receive from the *mukta*? 'The realisation of the Self,' declares Ramana Maharshi, 'is the greatest help that can be rendered to humanity. . . . A saint helps the whole of humanity, unknown to the latter.'[2]

Such insights as the ones we have tried to explain will be found to illumine man's path to perfection. They will never be outmoded or become obsolete.

---

[1] *ayam nijaḥ paro veti gaṇanā laghu-cetasām, udāra-caritānām tu vasudhaiva kuṭum-bakam.*

[2] *Talks with Sri Ramana Maharshi*, Sri Ramanasramam, Tiruvannamalai, 1958 p. 18.

Chapter 7

INTENTIONALITY AND THE BODY–MIND PROBLEM

by

J. N. MOHANTY

Visiting Professor, Graduate Faculty, New School for Social Research, New York

In this paper I want to explore the question, how and to what extent the intentionality thesis affects the body–mind problem. This is a question about which there is considerable unclarity. Contemporary English and American philosophers who have concerned themselves with the body–mind problem have not, with few exceptions, paid much attention to the intentionality thesis, while European continental philosophers who have seriously concerned themselves with the intentionality thesis have generally neglected its implications for the traditional mind–body problem. Further, the implications of the intentionality thesis, even for those who are aware of it, are by no means clear. Professor Quine, for example, writes:

'One may accept the Brentano thesis as showing the dispensability of intentional idioms . . . and the importance of an autonomous science of Intention, or as showing the baselessness of intentional idioms and the emptiness of a science of Intention.'[1]

Of course, he chooses the latter. Karl Popper derives mentalism from the Brentano thesis,[2] whereas Chisholm does not. Quinton holds that the Brentano thesis does rule out beha-

[1] W. V. O. Quine, *Word and Object*, New York, London, 1960, p. 221.
[2] K. R. Popper, *Conjectures and Refutations*, London, 1963, p. 298.

viourism, but argues that it is compatible with a form of identity theory according to which the identity between every mental state and some brain state is not logical but contingent.[1] Price on the contrary uses the Brentano thesis to refute the identity theory.[2] Charles Taylor, however, thinks that the identity thesis may be accepted by phenomenologists, and that the idea of disembodied thoughts is not very credible to them.[3] In the face of such diversity of opinions, it is necessary and it may indeed be fruitful to look closer into the problem or problems involved.

I

The intentionality thesis, which I shall seek to expound in brief and shall not defend here,[4] as developed by philosophers from Brentano up to Merleau-Ponty may be formulated in the following theses, not all of which can be ascribed to any single philosopher.

Thesis A: Every mental state, and no non-mental state, exhibits a peculiar directedness towards an object. It is *of* or *about* something, in a sense of *of* or *about* in which no non-mental state is so. Furthermore, the object towards which a mental state is so directed need not be real, it need not exist; if the object is a proposition, it need not be true (Brentano).

Thesis B: Every mental state has its correlative *noema*, *Sinn* or meaning which is but its intentional object (i.e. the object towards which it is directed, according to thesis A) *precisely as that object is intended* in that state. Thus every mental state has a meaning or content—quite apart from the question if its intentional object is real or not (Husserl).

Thesis C: Consciousness or states of consciousness which are intentional (in the sense of thesis A) are not things having

[1] A. Quinton, 'Mind and Matter', in J. R. Smythies (Ed.), *Brain and Mind. Modern Concepts of the Nature of Mind*, New York, 1965, esp. 224–5.

[2] H. H. Price, in J. R. Smythies (Ed.), *ibid.*, esp. pp. 59–60.

[3] C. Taylor, 'Mind–Body identity, a side issue?' in C. V. Borst (Ed.), *The Mind–Brain Identity Theory*, London, Macmillan, 1970, esp. p. 240.

[4] I have attempted a defence of the intentionality thesis in Chapter 3 of Part One of my *The Concept of Intentionality*, St Louis, 1972.

the *property* of intentional directedness, not substances or states of substances. They wholly and entirely consist in, are nothing but, the sorts of directedness they exhibit. They are thus utterly empty of contents, they do not contain anything within themselves. They are in this sense modes of nothing-ness. Consciousness is, but is not a thing of some sort. Its being is just the opposite of the being of a thing. It is the negation of all things, and yet is directed towards the world of things by a sort of internal dialectics (Sartre).

Thesis D: Intentionality, contrary to thesis A, characterises not only states of consciousness but also bodily movement, in so far as bodily behaviour is directed towards the world. Basically, the directedness exhibited by bodily movement is *sui generis* and not reducible to mechanical bodily motion plus an indwelling mental intention—though sometimes, i.e. in some cases, that model may work (Merleau-Ponty).

Thesis E: Every state of consciousness, in fact every action, of man is meaningful, as in thesis B, but its meaning is not its own regarded as an isolated individual occurrence but derives from the temporal-historical horizon in which it is embedded. Intentional acts (states of consciousness, bodily behaviour as well as actions), *quâ* intentional, are not merely occurrences in objective time, concurrent with other physical events, but in fact constitute—by virtue of their retentional and expectational context dependence—an inner temporal horizon, and no isolated occurrence could be understood as detached from this context (Husserl, Merleau-Ponty).

Now all these theses are not mutually compatible, and to be made compatible each would need considerable modification. It should be apparent that thesis B and thesis C are not compatibles: one of them asserts that every state of consciousness has its own meaning, its correlative content, while the other denies any meaning or content to it and reduces it to an empty intending of an absolute other. Now the opposition between the two theses is, to some extent, mitigated by the consideration that the content, meaning or *noema* which, according to thesis B, belongs to every state of consciousness is not a real, immanent component of it but its irreal correlate. What thesis C rejects is the traditional empiricist (and possibly, also rationalist) conception of consciousness as consisting in, or containing, contents (ideas, images, and what not) within it; and this is not what thesis B wants to assert. The resulting concept of consciousness, as formulated by Aron Gurwitsch,[1] is a remarkable improvement over the classical concept of it as a one-dimensional flow of momentary states. The model that we have now is of a two-tiered structure—a series of *real* acts and a series of *irreal noemata* or contents or meanings. Temporality of consciousness, as asserted in thesis E, pertains to the former and not to the latter. Thesis D, if valid, entails a rejection of the concept of intentionality as a criterion of the mental. The Brentano thesis is therefore rejected in one of its major concerns; but really speaking it is expanded to cover the entire domain defined by the concepts of man's being-in-the-world and being-with-others.

II

Theories about body–mind relation are *metaphysical* theories. They tend to go beyond the immediate or mediate testimony of experience, beyond what may be called the phenomenological data, and use such data for the purpose of constructing a picture of man and his world, which would be theoretically (and perhaps, also practically) satisfying, which would be in accordance with either one's scientific or one's religious beliefs. Since in this paper I am exploring the bearing of the intentionality thesis on the body–mind problem, it would be fair to begin such explorations from what may be called a phenomenological point of view—for the intentionality thesis itself is founded on this point of view. The distinctive feature of this point of view is that instead of asking what the nature of a certain thing is, one asks how is it given, and precisely as

[1] A. Gurwitsch, *Studies in Phenomenology and Psychology*, Evanston, 1966, esp. p. 157.

what? There should be hardly any doubt that the latter question is prior to the former, for there seems to be no other pathway to ascertaining what the real nature of a thing is save by ascertaining how the thing under consideration is given in experience, precisely in what mode and with what characteristics. In other words, the latter is also the problem of ascertaining what the *concept* of the thing *means* in its original intuitive clarity.

Now the philosopher who looks upon intentionality as the, or as one of the distinguishing features of conscious life is really looking at consciousness from within, as it is lived through, and not observing from outside what could be called the conscious behaviour of another person. This attitude which may be called the phenomenological attitude is not quite the same as what is called 'introspection' in introspective psychology. The introspectionist looks into his own mind, searching for data immanent to it. The phenomenologist seeks, not to look within at the immanent components of mental life, but to relive, to 'reflect' upon, to capture the original pre-reflective experience in which the other was intended or meant. Thus the phenomenological attitude places one midway between the concern with the immanent of the introspectionist and the interest in the transcendent of the objectivist. One's concern is the act of intending the other, neither the other itself nor the act as an immanent occurrence in my biography.

Now if the intentionality thesis is founded on this point of view, one may as well begin one's meditations on the body—mind problem by approaching the concept of body from the same point of view. As soon as one adopts this point of view, one realises the imperative need for distinguishing between the phenomenological body and the objective body. We are in fact asking, how is my body originally given to me? The phenomenological approach assumes, quite legitimately it would seem, that for every *type* of object there is some mode of givenness that is originary—of which then there could be various modifications, but the modified modes point back to the originary. In the case of physical objects, the originary mode is sense perception to which the modified modes such as memory, imagination, phantasy and empty symbolic thinking refer back. One way of drawing a type distinction between things or entities is to show, if possible, distinctions amongst such originary modes of givenness. To begin with, my body surely is not given to me originarily in the same manner in which other physical objects are. First, save in exceptional cases where my natural bodily movements receive a jolt or are confronted with a danger, I do not perceive my body as I perceive a physical object. I do not observe it. One might say, I feel it from within. I move about with it, but do not move it as I would push a table or a shopping cart or drive a car. I see with my eyes but do not see the eyes. The eyes, as visual organs, are defined by their functions, and even if I can look at my eyeballs in the mirror or touch them with my fingers I do not then perceive them as my visual organs, i.e. as exercising that function. Having the body which I have is having certain abilities to execute various sorts of movements, my awareness of such abilities which accompanies my actual execution of some of them at every moment of my waking experience constitutes my awareness of my body. My body is also given to me through a whole set of kinaesthetic sensations, not precisely localisable, vaguely diffused—especially such sensations as feelings of well-being and tiredness. To perceive a physical object is to localise it in space, but such localisation, as has been noted by many philosophers, requires a 'zero' point of reference which is provided by my body which then itself is not localised in that system. This felt or lived body is intentional, it is not a thing but a way of existing—as the 'zero' point of one's spatial references, as temporally oriented towards what one is going to do or in the readiness of movements, as a way of being directed towards the world through the specific abilities which define it. Now one may suggest that this lived body, or what K. C. Bhattacharyya calls bodily subjectivity, forms the original basis on which the concepts of pure objectivity (of the natural sciences) and pure subjectivity (of transcendental idealism) are constituted. As a matter of fact, the latter concepts are, in an important sense, correlatives. As the lived body is objectified and the lived world transformed into the objective world (of the natural sciences), the concept of subjectivity is detached from the body (which becomes another object before its gaze) and becomes the pure transcendental subjectivity before which everything else has become an object. 'Subjectivity', writes K. C. Bhattacharyya, '. . . is rooted in body-feeling and is only imagined to be dissociable from it'.[1]

The concept of the objective body may now be regarded as an idealisation of the originally lived body. The objective body is, to begin with, the observed or perceived body, the other's body localised for me in another region of space with reference to my body as the 'zero' point. I then imagine my body likewise to be a perceived object for the others, I also imagine myself in the other's position looking at this body which is mine. Further, I might be led to observe *parts of* my body—my face in the mirror, my hand which is bandaged, my foot which hurts. But while such specific parts may be emerging as objects for my perceptual attention, they do so against the background of the felt body which tends to recede inwards, in the last resort, to the inner mass of kinaesthetic sensations. My body, then, at this level is both felt and perceived. The perceived figure emerges against the felt background. The other's body, even when it is perceived, is perceived as that which is felt by the other. A further objectification is achieved by the scientific attitude which decomposes the body to its parts, whereby the distinction between the 'inner' and the 'outer', the background and the figure, is abolished, the body consists not of 'powers' and 'abilities', but of parts—irrespective of whether the parts be conceived of as 'hardwares' or as 'soft organs', as cogs and wheels of a watch or as wires and tubes within a computer. The felt body did not include objective parts like liver and brain, it surely comprehended 'powers' and 'abilities' like the visual, tactual, auditory,

[1] K. C. Bhattacharyya, *Studies in Philosophy*, Vol. 2, Calcutta, 1958, p. 54.

locomotive and the sexual. It was a mode of existing, not an existent thing. The objective body is a thing.

A distinction similar to the foregoing may be made even in the case of our concept of the mind—a distinction, that is to say, between the lived mind and the objective mind. By 'lived mind' I mean the mental act as it is being lived through as and when it emerges into being: as such it is out and out intentional, it is exhausted by the way in which its object is being intended in it, it has not yet acquired a position along with other mental occurrences (of mine and of others) and physical events in objective time series, but carries with it its own inner time horizon; it has no content within it and in that sense is empty, and it carries about it a sort of transparence, i.e. a sort of non-positional self-awareness which does not yet amount to a self-objectification and also not being referred to an 'I' as its owner. What I am talking about is very much like what Sartre refers to as pre-reflective consciousness. A kind of objectively oriented reflection metamorphoses this living act of consciousness into 'my' mental state and at the same time locates it in objective time. If the living act of loving was a specific way of intending a person as beloved, before the objectifying gaze of reflection it becomes 'my' act of loving, belonging as it were to my mental world, directed to a person out there, and concurrent with many other public and private events: it has now a content, even if private. The original act was nothing but a mode of intending, deriving its specificity from what was given as a property of its object out there. The objectified act shows its own immanent property, it is a mental entity, and the object out there is a neutral object, in itself neither lovable nor repulsive, neither perceived nor imagined. The original act of imagining is a way of intending a thing as absent; the same act as objectified becomes an inspection of private, inner images. The original act of suffering is a way of being in the world, just as the original experience of physical pain is a way of living one's body ('the leg hurts'), whereas for objectifying reflection these become the possessions of private mental states of suffering or pain.

Now that in each case, in the case of body as well as of mind, we have introduced a distinction, phenomenologically grounded, between the lived and the objectified, we are in a position to formulate the problem of the relation between body and mind more precisely than before. For now we have at hand, instead of one, really four different relationships to be examined:

(i) The relation between the lived body and the lived mind.

(ii) The relation between the lived body and the objective mind.

(iii) The relation between the objective body and the lived mind.

(iv) The relation between the objective body and the objective mind.

It is not the purpose of this paper to try to solve these problems. It was stated at the beginning that its aim is to explore the bearing of the intentionality thesis (or theses) upon the general problem of the mind—body relation. Now that this general problem has differentiated itself into four distinct, though related problems, we have to show in each case how the intentionality thesis or theses affect or are affected by any solution that we may have to offer.

III

(i) At the level of lived experience, the lived body and the lived mind are not distinguished in a manner in which body and mind are generally taken to be. It is not the case that body is lived as something outer, and mind as something inner; or that the body is lived as something extended, and the mind as something unextended. There is only one undivided experience of existing in the world and with others, being directed towards, within the all-embracing horizon of phenomenal space and phenomenal time. Thus one could say, with reservations, that lived body and lived mind are but two different conceptualisations of one act of existing—conceptualisations that 'look back' retrospectively at this unitary act from the points of view clearly demarcated by later objectifying reflection as 'body' and 'mind'. I want to say this 'with reservations', because the fissure signified by the dualistic concepts might be taking its origin *already there* within the very texture of lived experience—to be aggravated and conceptually solidified by later objectifying reflection. What I mean is that the picture of one, undivided, existing—which is neither the just being-present of a material object, nor the pure transparency of transcendentally purified consciousness, but the reflexive, but pre-reflective, concrete existing as being intentionally oriented towards the world and the others—is too simplistic to be true of any stage of our actual human experience. It is useful though to isolate this level, for it serves to draw attention to the fact that *even prior to the theoretical positing of an identity between 'body' and 'mind' there is already a lived non-distinction between them.* However, this lived non-distinction is always disturbed by such phenomena as a frustrated intention, illusory perception, sudden shocks presenting the body with the prospect of vital danger, which tend to isolate the inner from the outer; the mind from the body, and provide objectifying reflection with the needed foothold for its idealising activity. This pre-theoretical existential identity of body and mind—or at least of some lived mental acts not with some particular isolable bodily states and processes but with the total bodily being—is not only not inconsistent with the intentionality thesis D, but is the best corroboration of that thesis. One has only to reject that restricted form of the thesis (thesis A) which wants to make intentionality a criterion of the mental.

(ii) Once the split between body and mind has occurred, any assertion of their identity has to be a *theoretical* assertion whose justification may lie either in the pre-theoretical lived non-distinction already referred to or in the overall theoretical context of a science or a metaphysics. Now there is a difference in what is achieved by the objectifying reflection in the case of the lived body and in the case of the lived mind. In the case of the former, objectification amounts to divesting the body of all intentionality and thereby to making it into a pure thing bereft of all meaning and significance. In the case of mind, however, objectification does not go so far. That is to say, even the objective mind is intentional. Even the 'inner' mental state of love, for example, is nothing if not love *of* something or someone. Even if it is not the pure directedness towards, it is nevertheless besides its 'inner' habitation in my 'soul', also directed towards something. It is a thing, but an intentional thing. Now, the intentionality of lived body which refuses to be categorised either as inner or as outer and the intentionality of objectified mind which is inner but not outer are so distinct from each other that any attempt to theoretically connect them at the same level of discourse is bound to be unsatisfactory. To look at the situation, from another side, what we have, when we think of relating the lived body and the objective mind, is a discontinuity, a *hiatus* between the two levels of experience to which the two concepts belong, the former to the pre-reflective existing, the latter to objectifying reflection. The reflection, in fact, would seem to be dialectical: *some* objective mental states both are and are not the same as some lived experiences of the body—they are the same as the latter in so far as they were, prior to objectifying reflection, non-distinguished from it; they are not the same as it in so far as, *quâ* objective mental states, they have been cut asunder from that unity and have been 'internalised'.

(iii) There is such a radical difference between the objective body which is thoroughly opaque and non-intentional and the lived mind which is reflexive and intentional, between a thing and what may be called a 'no-thing'—that, again, as before, no relation is conceivable. As in case (ii), so also here, we never have these two on the same level. The one belongs to the level of objectifying reflection, the other to pre-reflective experience. The objective body emerges as an 'externalisation' of the lived body from which the lived mind *was* non-distinguished. Thus when I live a mental act, I am not observing my body as an object (unless, of course, that act is one of observing my body as an object, in which case the relation is that of an act to its object).

(iv) The body–mind problem with which most philosophers are concerned, and to which the classical theories of dualism (parallelism, interactionism) and monism (materialism, mentalism, double-aspect theory, metaphysical behaviourism and logical behaviourism, brain-state identity theory) are various answers, concerns the relation between what is called in this paper objective body and objective mind. It is here that classical, non-phenomenological philosophies and philosophies which are oriented after the natural sciences find themselves most at ease. They may not solve the problem with a finality, but they at least know what to do with it. For here, they have the problem of correlating or identifying or distinguishing between, two identifiable things, each with its own property or properties. Here then, i.e. at this level of discourse, what I propose to do is: instead of running through all the different theories that have been proposed in the history of thought, I shall concentrate on one theory which has received considerable attention and refinement in contemporary thought and ask how this theory stands in relation to the intentionality thesis. The theory I have in mind is the so-called Identity theory, which is generally used to designate the thesis that some mental states are contingently identical with some brain state or other. However, I shall also briefly refer to 'metaphysical behaviourism' which identifies the mental with publicly observable bodily behaviour. To begin with this latter first:

(*a*) Metaphysical behaviourism identifies mental states with publicly observable bodily behaviour, and it identifies the two in the sense that one of the terms, namely the mental, should—as a consequence of this identification—be eliminated in favour of the other, i.e. bodily behaviour. It is obvious that such a thesis is fundamentally incompatible with the intentionality thesis. For, bodily behaviour, considered not only as publicly observable but also as quantifiable is entirely non-intentional, whereas a mental state—even if objectified as an inner thing—is intentional, has a content or sense, and is of an object. It would seem there is only one way of mitigating, or even eliminating, this incompatibility, and that is by a drastic revision of the behaviouristic concept of behaviour. Consider a behaviour which I observe in my friend approaching me, which for purposes of identification but freed from any mentalistic implication, let me call 'smile-behaviour' which, according to metaphysical behaviourism, is not a sign or indication of a certain type of pleasing state of mind but *is* what, in ordinary dualistic language, is referred to as that sort of mental state. Now this smile-behaviour is publicly observable precisely in the same sense in which any physical event or 'matter in motion' is, and subject to the same principle of quantification, causal explanation of the 'covering law model' as any other physical phenomenon. The basic conceptual category—a variety of the general causal model of explanation—is the S–R concept: a stimulus eliciting a response. Neither the stimulus nor the response, regarded as a publicly observable phenomenon, has any intentional feature, any 'content' or significance, any sort of directedness towards, it is not of or about anything. The mental term which is sought to be eliminated through its identification with such a physical concept *was*, by its very essential or conceptual structure, intentional.

However, let us now for the time being ask ourselves the following questions: how precisely is the other's, my friend's smile-behaviour perceived by me? How precisely is my friend himself perceiving his own behaviour? What is the nature of the stimulus which elicits this behavior? What is the nature of the response?

Do I perceive my friend's smile-behaviour as I perceive, for example, the branches of a tree swaying on a windy day? It seems to me that the answer should be 'no'. Even when freed from any mentalistic or dualistic terminology, I perceive *him smiling*. I perceive his behaviour *as* a piece of essentially *human* behaviour with human significance carrying suggestions of meaningful reference. This is how I do in fact perceive it, but in order to show how I *ought to* perceive, if the theory is to be correct, it is necessary to explain my actual manner of perceiving as a conjunction of what I, on the theory, really perceive and other elements associated with the bare perceptual data by virtue of my mentalistic cultural background. If then I perceive my friend's smile-behaviour as a human phenomenon carrying human significance, my friend himself does not perceive it as an external phenomenon at all. What he is aware of is behaving in a certain manner, of smiling, namely. To be aware of behaving in a certain manner and to be observing a certain behaviour pattern are two different things, but none of them is like perceiving a physical phenomenon. A physicalistic conception of behaviour then has no justification save within the context of a theoretical framework. Could it be said that a certain behaviour is a change elicited in an organism by the appropriate stimulus? Again, within the framework of the system that has been set up, this is a perfectly legitimate manner of speaking. But that is only a very non-significant form of legitimacy—trivial indeed, for the theory legislates what kind of talk is to be regarded as legitimate for it. Once outside the framework questions such as the following may be raised: is the stimulus *quâ* stimulus the external thing, event or occurrence out there, or is it the external thing, event or occurrence as it is given *to* the person responding? In other words, the stimulus *quâ* stimulus is the externally presented thing, event or occurrence as interpreted by the responding person. Thus the stimulus both elicits the response, and is made into the stimulus that it is by the response; they together form, in Merleau-Ponty's words, an intentional arc, embedded not in the neutral environment of the natural sciences but in the interpreted, meaningful world of the behaving person. If in accordance with these facts, the concept of behaviour be suitably modified, then behaviour becomes intentional, meaningful, directed towards the world. Such a behaviourism would be, within limits, compatible with the intentionality thesis. I say 'within limits', for it is not clear how higher-order intentionalities (intentionalities of abstract thinking and higher emotions) can be reduced to bodily behaviour in any case. But what interests us right now is compatibility or incompatibility, and not truth or falsity of a thesis as such. However, and this seems to be important, this modified concept of behaviour no longer holds good of objective body; we have in fact slid back to the phenomena of lived body.

(*b*) The mind–brain identity theory, which we now consider, has various forms, depending on interpretations of the notion of identity involved. My comments, in the present context, will be on the weaker version of the theory according to which the identity of some mental states (like sensations and pains) with brain states is not logical but contingent, and that in two senses: as with the expressions 'morning star' and 'evening star' the meanings are different while the referents are the same, so do names of mental states and names of brain states differ in meaning, although referring to the same thing; second, the identity is to be confirmed by empirical research, and does not hold good analytically or on logical grounds. The identity nevertheless is strict identity in the allegedly Leibnizian sense, i.e. in the sense that whatever predicate holds good, in an extensional context, of one also holds good of the other. The phrase 'in an extensional context' leaves room for differences in 'meaning' and also differences arising out of epistemic contexts like 'I know that . . .'.[1] Now I shall not here raise the issue whether the notion of contingent identity is not inconsistent,[2] nor shall I ask whether by interpreting the correlation statements of scientific research as identity statements one does not end up by setting up such identities as further inexplicable.[3] These two questions no doubt affect the worth of the theory considerably. However, from the specific concern of this paper, I shall raise the following questions:

[1] T. Nagel, 'Physicalism', *Philosophical Review*, 1965, pp. 339–56 (Also included in Borst, ed., *loc. cit.*)
[2] Cf. S. Kripke, 'Identity and Necessity' in Milton K. Munitz (Ed.), *Identity and Individuation*, New York, 1971, pp. 135–64.
[3] Cf. J. Kim, 'On the Psycho-Physical Identity Theory', *American Philosophical Quarterly*, 1966, pp. 227–35.

First, it is to be noted that the concept of brain state or the neuro-physiological concepts of bodily states do not belong to the level of lived body, but have their significance and validity at a higher level of theoretical objectification. If the identification under consideration, then, is a *theoretical* identification within the structure of a scientific theory, then its status will be dependent upon that of a scientific theory, and unless one believes in a naive scientific realism it cannot afford sufficient ground for a metaphysical or ontological thesis. Second, as just said above, the notion of identity that is used is formulated in terms of extensional context; by excluding all differences arising out of inserting the terms concerned into intentional contexts as not affecting the identity thesis, the identity thesis reduces itself to a triviality—for the distinctiveness of the mental, as contrasted with the bodily when considered physicalistically lies precisely in such intensional (and intentional) implications. Third, while in the case of the concept of behaviour we could find means of so transforming the concept as to be able to ascribe intentionality to it, it is not at once clear how one can likewise deal with the concept of brain states. A sophisticated model of the human brain has to be in terms of a modern computer, and in describing its internal structure as well as mode of operation one may use such concepts as 'input', 'output', 'incoming message', 'decoding message', 'storage of information',' transmitting of message', and so on. But these concepts are highly intentional, and ought not to appear in a strictly extensional context, unless their use is recognised to be metaphorical. If mental states possess intentionality in the sense of being *of* or about something, and of having meaning or significance, it would not simply do to reduce them to (according to reductive materialism), or eliminate them in favour of (according to the variety of identity thesis upheld by, for example, Rorty),[1] or identify them, within an extensional context, with brain states—unless some way is found to capture that intentional directedness or

---

[1] R. Rorty, 'Mind–body Identity, Privacy and Categories', in Borst (ed), *loc. cit.*, pp. 187–213.

meaningfulness within neurophysiological theory. Failing this, the thesis is either a defence of scientific faith at the cost of phenomena, or a poor metaphysical thesis by its own right. A better form of the identity theory, one which is more amenable to assimilation into a phenomenological philosophy, is that suggested by Thomas Nagel:[1] according to this form of the theory, what are to be identified are not, for example, a sensation and a brain state, but a person's having the sensation and his body's being in a certain physical state. This form of the thesis has greater promise, for the concept of a person's body being in a certain physical state as such, i.e. without being embedded into a rigidly physicalistic and extensionalistic framework, is compatible with an intentionalistic reading. As Nagel himself notes, this thesis 'requires a liberal conception of what constitutes a state—one which will admit relational attributes'.[2] Also if what a suitable machine, a computing machinery, can, in principle, realise is any operation which can be defined *logically*, *strictly* and *unambiguously* in a finite number of terms, for many kinds of human behaviour, thought or experience this criterion of strictly and logically unambiguous specification in terms of a finite number of discrete terms or steps is not, in principle, possible.[3] That this is not possible follows from the way their intentionalities imply each other and the way they cluster together into one nexus of intentional life (thesis E). Finally, if one aspect of the intentionality thesis be that every mental act and bodily behaviour is embedded in a temporal-historical horizon, then it is necessary to ask whether *such* temporality and historicity may be ascribed to the brain states, and if so in what sense? It would certainly seem that the specific sense in which intentional conscious life is temporal and historical does not apply to an objective succession of physical states. In the latter case, to be temporal means to be located in the objective time

---

[1] T. Nagel, *loc. cit.*

[2] Borst (ed.), *loc. cit.*, p. 225.

[3] F. J. Crosson, 'Phenomenology and Computer Simulation of Human Behavior', *Proceedings of the American Catholic Philosophical Association*, Vol. XXXVIII, 1964, pp. 128–36.

series, and to be historical means that the past physical states causally determine the later physical states through intermediate physical states. But the concept of historicity is different from the concept of a causally determined series. In such a series, each distinct state, taken by itself, has nothing historical about it. It is what it is, the causal antecedents that determine it and the future effects that it shall produce are other distinct states. A conscious state, on the contrary, is historical in the sense that it, by its own intrinsic constitution, its meaning and significance for him to whom it belongs, belongs to a historical setting. The more loosely knit it is into that setting, the more plausible is a physicalistic explanation in its case; the more tightly does it belong to that context, the less plausibility does a physicalistic explanation have.

IV

To sum up: the body–mind problem has been considered from the point of view of its phenomenological *genesis*. At the level of pre-objective, pre-reflective existing, there is a sort of felt non-distinction between (lived) body and (lived) mind— their intentionalities seem to coincide. Various elements in experience such as illusion and frustration, sudden shock and threat, tend to create a fissure in that unity, thereby 'externalising' the (lived) body and, what is correlative to it, 'internalising' the (lived) mind. Here is the basis for objectifying reflection to create the Cartesian *hiatus* between the outer and the inner, the public and the private. Attempts to relate either lived body and objective mind or objective body and lived mind fail, for in each case one member of the pair belongs to a different level of experience (and discourse) from the other. It is only through the objectification of both the terms that a meaningful philosophical problem is first posited. What stands nevertheless in the way of a satisfactory solution of the problem so posited by way of identifying the two is that although objective body has been deprived of its original intentionality, objective 'inner' mental states do possess intentionality. Metaphysical behaviourism can be maintained for at least some mental states by suitably revising and modifying the concept of behaviour (and the concepts of 'stimulus' and 'response') and the brain-state identity theory has to find some means for ascribing content, directedness and temporality to brain states which does not quite seem feasible. Abandoning 'identity with a brain state' in favour of 'identity with a state of the body' has better prospects. But in both cases—here as well as in the case of behaviourism—trying to save the theory we tend to slide back to the level of lived body with its intentional powers and abilities and movements directed towards the world.

A few points need to be separately noted at the end:

(1) First, although this has been said before in this paper, it may yet need repetition—the sort of pre-objective non-distinction which has been brought out holds good of *some* mental acts. It does *not* seem to hold good, for example, of acts of higher-order abstract thinking. But about the possible line of demarcation between the two, I am not quite sure. Even with regard to the higher-order mental acts, one can and indeed must have to distinguish between the original lived act and objectifying reflection on the act. But it does not seem to be obvious that living in the act of mathematical thinking, for example, *is* a mode of bodily existing.

(2) Scientific thinking is a kind of intentional act, and a scientific theory is an achievement of such acts historically through time. It would seem strange that a theory that is an achievement of intentionality should end up by denying any intentionality at all. In fact, however, there should be nothing strange about it. This, in fact, using Hegel's famous metaphor, is a case of the cunning of intentionality, such that it conceals itself and forgets its own role behind its achievements. That the achievement of intentionality should be posited as autonomous is in fact a constitutive sense of that achievement. The task of philosophy would be not to deny this sense, but to explore its origin. That natural science should deny inten-

tionality is neither surprising nor is it a fault of the natural sciences, but precisely constitutes part of the methodological sense of the scientific concept of 'nature' and the concept of 'natural science' (both of which are really correlative concepts). Only philosophy cannot accept this constitut*ed* sense as final; it has to go back to the constitut*ing* origins of that sense—and to rediscover the intentionality.

(3) There is an easier, more neat, kind of solution of the body–mind problem, a solution which is compatible with a restricted Brentano thesis, which I have deliberately not made use of in this paper. According to this solution, non-intentional, physical body forms the material foundation for a higher-order being, the mental, which exhibits the property of intentionality. There is as such nothing wrong in constructing such a scheme of 'strata' in which each higher stratum shows some properties which were not there in the preceding strata. The bodily states, including the brain states, form necessary conditions for the emergence of the mental, but they certainly do not provide both necessary and sufficient conditions. This kind of ontological scheme is to be found amongst the so-called emergent evolutionists; amongst those who were closer to the phenomenological movement, it is to be found in Nicolai Hartmann's doctrine of the strata of reality. Such a theory seems to do justice to the natural sciences, while limiting their explanatory power; it also keeps the line between the bodily and the mental clear and straight. The reason why I have not accepted such a solution or some modified version of it is that it misses the very important phenomenon of 'lived' body and equates the concept of body with the physicalistic concept of it. To me the concept of body is ambiguous in so far as we are prone to move back and forth from one to the other, and this ambiguity is what I have sought to incorporate into my account. The problem I have been trying to think through is not the larger metaphysical problem of the relation between matter and mind, but the restricted one of the relation between body and mind; and one already commits himself to too much by *equating* the body with a material object.

(4) It has been maintained in this paper that it is not possible to give a physical account of *how* the mental states can be *about* something, unless one covertly ascribes intentional properties to the physical system in terms of which one is giving the explanation. Perhaps the 'how' in the above sentence is misleading. If no scientific account, even an explanation of a physical occurrence, throws light on the 'how' or the 'why' but it can only establish correlations amongst events, then such an explanation of mental states need not any more explain 'how' or 'why' in order to be a good scientific explanation. This is a perfectly legitimate contention. What I am challenging is not the feasibility of scientific explanation of mental states in this restricted sense of 'explanation', but the ontological conclusions that are thought to be drawn from it. The point I was making is that once the two, the mental and the brain state, are identified then there must be some means of ascribing intentionality to the brain states. This, however, is not required by the mere thesis that mental states can be 'explained' by the natural sciences. This partly explains why Feigl considers the problem of intentionality a psycho-*logic*al problem, not a psycho-physical problem. The problem is one of logical reducibility or irreducibility of discourse involving *aboutness* to the language of the physical sciences; it is not the problem of the possibility or impossibility of physical explanation and prediction.[1] The latter is a problem immanent to the scientific endeavour, and its answer has to be in terms of that endeavour. The former which is the typically philosophical problem concerns not the mere discourse but also the phenomena of intentionality.

(5) Finally it should be mentioned that the concept of intentionality as such entails neither the transparency (or reflexivity) nor the incorrigibility of the mental.[2] However, it may be that just as there are unconscious mental states (which are intentional but not transparent), so those mental states

[1] H. Feigl, 'The "Mental" and the "Physical"', *Minnesota Studies in the Philosophy of Science*, Vol. II, Minneapolis, 1958, esp. pp. 416–19.

[2] For the concept of reflexivity, see my *The Concept of Intentionality*, Part Three, Chapter 1.

which are conscious states are transparent or reflexive (because of which they are called 'conscious' states). In this paper I have not discussed how the phenomenon of reflexivity of the conscious states bears on the body–mind problem. Also characteristic of much of our conscious life is the accompanying sense of 'I' which itself is ambiguous: it means the consciousness of the self as the *subject* of experiences, it means also the sense of *personal* identity. Arising out of this is the problem of taking these phenomena into one's reflections on the body–mind problem. I have also not dealt with this aspect of the problem, and have sought to restrict my reflections to the phenomenon of intentionality.

Chapter 8

A PERSUASION THEORY OF
MORAL LANGUAGE

by

RAJENDRA PRASAD

Indian Institute of Technology, Kanpur

It does not need any argument to say that we have, as a part of ordinary language, a class of linguistic expressions which constitute what we call moral or ethical language. Superficially speaking, we call it moral language because its key terms are moral terms, such as 'good', 'bad', 'right', 'wrong', 'virtue', 'vice', 'ought', 'obligation', etc. Moral language employs not only moral terms but many others as well, and moral terms are used not only in moral but also in many non-moral contexts. In fact, it is not the mere occurrence of a moral term in a sentence, but the function performed by the sentence, that entitles it to be called a moral sentence or judgement. On the common sense level there is no great difficulty in identifying moral judgements, or *moral* uses of moral expressions. There are certain features of moral expressions which are quite apparent and too common-sensical to become topics of philosophical disputation. For example, it needs no proof to say that moral judgements are normative, practical, public, capable of being argued about, etc. Common usage also makes a distinction between moral and factual judgements. 'You acted correctly in handing over the thief to the police' and 'You acted quickly in handing over the thief to the police' are considered as differing not only in their lexical meanings, but in some more important ways as well. To say, then, that moral judgements are normative, practical, etc., or that they are not identical with factual judgements, is not philosophical theory but plain common sense. It may not be clear at the common sense level what specific jobs they do, or wherein precisely the difference between them and factual judgements lies, but that they do some distinctive jobs and differ from the latter are undeniable facts.

Moral language shares the general characteristics of other natural languages: its terms are not well defined and precise, but vague, ambiguous, and capable of being used to do a variety of jobs. The situation is all the more complicated because of the fact that terms ordinarily called moral are also used in such contexts in which they perform functions which are normally performed by expressions ordinarily called non-moral. It is impossible to find any moral term which is always used in moral contexts. Therefore, when I call certain terms moral terms, I mean only that they are used in moral senses ordinarily and mainly, and not that they are never used in any other way.

That moral language is a natural language, sharing with it its richness, variety, and flexibility, has great significance for meta-ethical analysis. It implies that the latter must proceed by carefully observing how it functions in actual situations. It is also possible that one of its functions is considered central by one philosopher but not by another. It is, natural, then, that philosophers offer different analyses of which none is absolutely irrelevant or mistaken, but which differ only in being more or less adequate. The relative adequacy of these analyses will certainly be determined by the amount of success obtained by them in presenting a systematic account, consistent with the intuitions of common sense, of how moral language functions in concrete situations.

It is nothing more than a truism to say that a natural language performs a multiplicity of functions. This only means that it is put to various uses by its users. The same linguistic expression may be used to perform different functions not only in different contexts but even in the same context. To understand how an expression is used it is very necessary to understand the purpose or purposes for which it is used. I have found it very helpful to classify the various functions of language into cognitive and non-cognitive in terms of the primary purposes of its ordinary uses. I call an expression cognitive (or non-cognitive) if and only if the primary purpose of its ordinary use is cognitive (or non-cognitive). Its primary purpose is cognitive if it is to convey information, and non-cognitive if it is to do something else, for example, to express a decision or choice, to express or evoke an attitude or feeling, to express a proposal or resolution, to persuade someone to do something, to ask, instruct, direct, or order someone to do something, etc.

Whenever a person utters an expression to someone, he is, in virtue of uttering it, logically committed to making some further moves; similarly, not all but only some of the hearer's responses to it are considered appropriate. It is the primary purpose of uttering the expression which determines the logical commitments of the speaker and the appropriateness of the hearer's responses to it. When someone, with the primary purpose of cheering up a sick friend, tells him that he is going to be all right in a week, he is not committed to produce medical facts in support of it, but a doctor, who makes the same remark, with the primary purpose of predicting the time of his recovery, is. Similarly to respond to the social ritual 'How are you?' by narrating one's ills is inappropriate, but quite appropriate in response to a physician's 'How are you?'. This is so because the primary purpose of a social ritual is different from that of a physician's inquiry.[1]

In what follows I shall present an analysis of moral language in terms of the purposes of its use. To treat purposes as central does not imply that other factors of its use are of no importance. I centre my analysis on purposes because it seems to me that we can better explain the behaviour of moral expressions by this method than by any other.

---

[1] Prasad, Rajendra, 'A Functional Analysis of Language', in *Current Trends in Indian Philosophy*, Murty and Rao (Eds.), Asia Publ., 1972, pp. 230–42, for a detailed statement of the author's general theory of language.

Before proceeding to the actual analysis of moral judgements, let us note the *chief occasions on which we use them*. It is obvious that they are used in both personal and inter-personal contexts. By a personal context I mean one in which only a single person is involved. Here the same person is both speaker and hearer: he addresses a moral judgement to himself. This happens when one has to make a decision or choice. In the interpersonal context at least two persons are involved. One person offers a moral judgement to another either when the latter asks for some advice or guidance, or when the former himself is eager to present his moral views to the latter to convert him to his own. There are, thus, mainly speaking, three types of occasions when we make moral judgements. In the absence of a better terminology the different uses made of them on these occasions may be called *deciding* (or choosing), *advising*, and *sermonising*. It is true that all of these can be done with any kind of motives, good or bad, and which motives are to be judged morally better than which, is itself a moral question important for the moralist, but not for the meta-ethical analyst. For the latter a moral judgement made with a morally bad motive is, conceptually speaking, as good a moral judgement as one made with a morally good motive.

I shall first take up the *interpersonal uses*, namely, advising and sermonising. In both advising and sermonising, despite the fact that their contexts are different, moral judgements are used to do the same kind of job, i.e. to influence the conduct of the recipient in some particular direction. The main difference between them is that the sermoniser or preacher is more interested, eager, and desirous to make the recipient act as he wishes than is the adviser. This is so because the latter offers advice only when he is asked to. He does not have to advise, nor does he advise on his own initiative; he advises because his advice has been sought. However, he is not indifferent; he intends his advice to be followed, otherwise there is no point in offering it. The sermoniser, on the other hand, because he offers his moral principles as he himself is anxious to see people following them, is certainly much more eager than the adviser. Thus, while both moralise with the purpose that their judgements be acted upon, the context of the adviser is such that it may give the impression that he does not have any such purpose. It is a fact that the existence of a distinctive purpose to influence the recipient's conduct is more clearly seen in sermonising than in advising, but it is not absent in advising. To ask for advice is to make a request for guidance, and one who offers the advice intends that the advised course of action be adopted; of course, advice tends to influence the recipient's conduct not by coercion, but by persuasion, by making him feel that the advised course is the best course of action for him.[1]

It is quite likely that a philosopher fails to see any distinctive purpose in the use of moral judgements if he ignores their sermonising uses, or is unable to notice the distinction between sermonising and advising. The chances of his failure would be greater if, in his analysis, he does not pay sufficient attention to the non-verbal aspects of the contexts in which moral judgements are ordinarily used. It is no wonder then if he denies that they are used for any distinctive purpose, or considers all purposes for which they may be used completely irrelevant to giving an adequate analysis of the jobs they perform.

Without minimising the importance of the distinction, noted above, between the sermonising and advising uses of a moral judgement, I shall, in what follows, discuss them conjointly and not separately since in both it functions primarily and ordinarily as an attempt to influence the recipient's conduct.

A typical inter-personal situation usually consists of three factors: the man who offers the moral judgement, i.e. the speaker or writer; the recipient or addressee, i.e. the hearer or reader; and, lastly, the object judged. The object judged is always a human being, action, or institution. This fact distinguishes a moral judgement from factual judgements and

---

[1] Prasad, Rajendra, 'Non-cognitive Discourse', in *The Journal of the Indian Academy of Philosophy*, Vol. II, pp. 59–66, for the author's analysis of advising and some other non-cognitive functions of language.

non-moral value-judgements, for example, aesthetic judge-ments. Almost anything, human or non-human, can become the object of the latter, but usage does not permit the applica-tion of moral predicates to non-human subjects. However, this is quite possible, and it also very often happens, that the object judged is one of the two persons concerned, or an action by either of them. In such a case the object of the judgement is not a third thing in the sense of something other than, or unrelated to, the speaker and the hearer. But concep-tually we can still speak of three factors.

To say that there is an object judged in every moral judge-ment is to say not merely that it is always about something but also that the speaker always has in his mind some particular qualities of the object judged. When somebody says 'Bhishma was a very loyal son', his judgement is about Bhishma and he must have some quality or qualities of Bhishma in his mind, for example, his voluntarily surrendering forever his right to marry in order to keep his father happy. It is a regular feature of the use of a moral expression that it refers to some quality or qualities of the object it is applied to.[1] The qualities referred to by a speaker can be of any sort out of a whole class considered favourable or unfavourable by him. Which particular qualities he refers to in a particular situation is very often clear from the context, though not always. Therefore, a part of what a moral judgement does is to convey some information about the object judged. But this is not its main function. Its main function is practical; it is intended to be action-guiding. The primary purpose for which it is ordinarily used is not to add to the recipient's existing fund of information, but to influence his conduct. There are several means employed by man to influence or mould the conduct of his fellow human beings; moral language is one of them.

A moral judgement is an attempt to influence conduct. This is certainly a very general and vague statement. To make it

---

[1] Prasad, Rajendra, *'Evaluative, Factual and Referring Expressions'*, *The Visva-Bharati Journal of Philosophy*, Vol. V, No. 1, 1968, pp. 72–82, for the author's analysis of the referring function of evaluative expressions.

more precise, I shall distinguish between *means*, *modes*, and *levels* of exerting influence. There are so many *means* of influencing conduct and they could be linguistic or non-linguistic. One can influence somebody's conduct by using language, drugs, or even a dagger. There is also more than one mode of exerting influence. It may be exerted in the manner of gentle persuasion, or in that of compulsion which leaves no choice or a very narrow choice. There are also different levels at which it can be exerted. I shall distinguish between two levels and call them mental and behavioural. If I am trying to influence somebody and as a result of my efforts he shows a readiness or mental preparedness to act as I intend him to act, I would say that I have influenced him at the mental level. If he actually does what I want him to do, I would say that I have influenced him at the behavioural level.

In order to execute into action what he is prepared to do many other conditions, besides his preparedness, need to be fulfilled. Therefore, it is possible that he is prepared to do something which he may not be able to do even in his whole lifetime because all the necessary conditions are not fulfilled. Under necessary conditions I include everything, positive and negative, the presence and absence of which, respectively, are required to enable him to do what he is prepared to do. For example, he may be prepared to but does not join the army because of lack of appropriate opportunities or constant ill-health of his wife. If all the required conditions are satisfied and still he does not act the way he once said he was ready to, I would say that either he has changed his mind or was not sincere in expressing his readiness. It is necessary to mention all this in order to show that to have influenced anybody's conduct one does not have to make him behaviourally execute the intended course of action. It is enough if he exhibits his readiness to do so. It should be noted here that it is possible to influence a person in any mode and at any level by the use of either one, or both, of linguistic and non-linguistic means.

A moral judgement is a linguistic means of influencing conduct, and the way it works, or is intended to work, is not

F

one of coercion but persuasion, leaving the addressee free to act as it pleases him. Further, in order to be convinced that the addressee has accepted my moral judgement, what I need to be sure of is that he has been influenced at least at the mental level. In the light of these remarks it may be stated in a more precise way that *a moral judgement is an attempt to persuade the recipient to act, or at least to have the readiness or mental preparedness to act, in a particular way.*

The word 'persuade' is ambiguous in the sense that, in appropriate contexts, it can be used to mean either 'to attempt to persuade', or 'to successfully persuade'. The main distinction between the two is that the latter is an achievement expression, while the former is not. There is a similar ambiguity in the adjective 'persuasive'. It may mean 'that which actually persuades' or 'that which tends to, or is intended to be an attempt to, persuade'. In the former sense it is a contradiction to say that a persuasive expression has failed to persuade, but not at all in the latter sense. If I say that a moral judgement is persuasive I mean it in the latter sense. Therefore, it remains persuasive even if it fails in securing actual persuasion. In what follows wherever 'persuade' and 'persuasive' are used enough care will be taken to make explicit whether they are used in the achievement or non-achievement sense.

To moralise or make the attempt to influence his recipient's conduct, the moraliser just needs to make the attempt, i.e. to offer his moral judgement to him. If he succeeds, it is his good luck but he does not have to succeed in order that he can be described as having made the attempt. In fact, achieving success depends upon many other factors besides uttering a moral judgement; these factors, for example, are the psychological condition of the addressee, his relation to the speaker, the physical situation he is in, etc. Further, because a moral judgement is a piece of language, in order to make the attempt to influence the recipient's conduct by means of it, one only needs to use language, spoken or written. This point is very well expressed by the phrase 'an attempt to persuade' because the word 'persuade' is so used in ordinary language that we normally never call anything non-linguistic a means of persuasion. A moral judgement can be used with any kind of motives, good or bad. This fact is also taken care of when it is called an attempt to persuade because persuading can be attempted with any kind of motives. It seems, thus, that the phrase 'an attempt to persuade' characterises very well the various features of the use of a moral judgement. This point will be further substantiated in the subsequent discussion.

In the italicised statement on p. 162 I have used the phrase 'to act in a particular way' and this needs some clarification. I mean by it 'to act in the way intended by the speaker'. Therefore, to the question 'In which particular way is the hearer to act, or to be prepared to act?' the reply is: in the way the speaker intends him to act. This does not, however, mean that he should know in all details the course of action he is required to adopt; it is enough if he knows the general pattern of behaviour he is to adopt. Broadly speaking, human actions towards any object can be favourable, unfavourable, or indifferent. When someone offers a moral judgement to another person, his intention is to persuade him to do either something favourable or unfavourable towards the object judged. The latter is required only to know whether accepting the judgement commits him to perform a favourable or an unfavourable action. This is not a great problem because common usage is very clear as to which moral terms are used to suggest favourable and which to suggest unfavourable actions. For example, in normal uses, 'good', 'right', 'ought', etc., are used to do the former, while 'bad', 'wrong', 'ought not', etc., to do the latter. It can thus be said that the speaker's intention can very well be deciphered from his use of moral terms. In an ironical use an expression which normally suggests a favourable action may suggest an unfavourable one. This will not go against the present position because it is claimed to be true only of straightforward or ordinary uses.

It may be mentioned that there can be various ways in which one can act favourably or unfavourably, and which particular way is intended, or adopted, in a particular circumstance, greatly depends on the respective backgrounds—psychological, social, cultural, etc.—of the parties concerned. Why one intends his hearer to adopt, or himself adopts, a particular course of action out of several possible ones is an important question for the psychologist or sociologist, but not for the philosophical analyst.

As a result of the foregoing discussion the thesis, already stated, about the nature of a moral judgement, may be presented in a still more precise form: *a moral judgement is an attempt to persuade the recipient to act, or at least to show a mental preparedness to act, favourably or unfavourably as intended by the speaker, towards the object judged; the speaker's intention is ordinarily clear from the moral terms used by him and the contexts of use.*

Normally when a man offers a moral judgement to another he intends the hearer to act in the way desired by him, but he is satisfied if the latter agrees, or shows a readiness, to act that way even if he does not do so then and there. This happens when at least some of the conditions required for the actual performance of that action are lacking at the time. The production in him of such a mental preparedness to act is, thus, the minimum required to entitle a moral judgement to being considered successful. This preparedness is important in another respect as well. It is the characteristic of a moral judgement that it influences the recipient's behaviour by first producing in him willingness to act in the intended manner. As a result of his accepting the judgement he chooses to act the way he acts. The judgement becomes his own and inspires him from within. When A acts, or agrees to act, according to a moral judgement of B, it would be a genuine case of B's moral influence on him only if he does that willingly. On the other hand, if he acts accordingly but does not have the required willingness, we would say he has acted out of fear, greed, or pressure, etc., and not out of genuine moral conviction. Someone may, however, do, without the willingness to do, what a certain judgement requires him to do, in case he has the willingness to act according to another judgement to which the present one is related in such a way that it is a consequence of the former singly or together with some other judgement or judgements, or that the action intended through it by the speaker is a means to the realisation of what the former prescribes or commends.

The production of mental preparedness must not, however, be overemphasised. A moralist is satisfied with it only when there is enough justification for postponing actual action and only because it gives him the expectation of actual action in the near future. It is more than merely empirically true that men usually do the action they *sincerely* say they are ready to do. The ultimate and primary purpose of the use of a moral judgement is to make the hearer actually do the intended action and this purpose is only partially fulfilled if he shows his readiness to do that. Therefore, it is wrong to say that a moral judgement is used only or mainly to produce a mental state or evoke an attitude. It is not primarily evocative but persuasive. It is connected with human behaviour much more intimately than it would be if it were primarily evocative.

It would be worth while to note that the conceptual link a moral judgement has with producing in the recipient willingness or preparedness to do the intended action distinguishes it from an imperative. When a person offers a moral judgement to someone either as a piece of advice or as a sermon, he will not be fully satisfied if the latter acts according to it but unwillingly. In the case of an imperative also it may happen that when the recipient obeys it he has a willingness to obey it. But the presence or absence of willingness is not so important here. The issuer of the imperative is interested mainly in getting his command obeyed. He is satisfied if it is obeyed, no matter whether willingly or unwillingly. When I tell my son 'Do not beat your sister', my command will be fulfilled if he stops beating her, willingly or unwillingly; i.e. it would not matter what attitude he takes towards beating his sister. But if I tell him 'You ought not to beat your sister' I want him to stop beating her willingly, to disapprove of the practice of beating one's sister. One's acceptance of a set of moral judgements may sometimes have very extensive and far-reaching effects; it may change a whole outlook or produce a change of heart. Sometimes such an effect may even be consciously and deliberately aimed at by a moralist. But such things need not or seldom happen in the case of commands.

Moral judgements are capable of starting arguments and discussion. In some special circumstances, one may offer a moral judgement with the very intention to start a discussion in order to help someone make up his own mind. But one cannot use an imperative for this purpose for every moral judgement has a descriptive content in a more important way than an imperative has. Given the proper contextual conditions, the former does convey at least some information about the object judged in a much more direct way than the latter can. That is why it is possible to offer, what Stevenson calls, a second-pattern analysis of a moral judgement but not of an imperative. It is not merely an accident of linguistic usage that it makes sense to apply the words 'true' and 'false' to a moral judgement, but not to an imperative.

The above discussion, though very brief, clearly shows that a moral judgement is not only structurally but also functionally different from an imperative. It is hoped that it will help the reader see, provided he is willing to take pains to ascertain how it functions in its real, normal, uses, that it is wrong to hold that it is imperatival, since he will then surely notice that it is used to perform jobs which are different from those which an imperative is used to perform.

To say that a moral judgement is an attempt to persuade is certainly to treat it as non-cognitive and at the same time to distinguish it from other types of non-cognitive expressions. It performs a distinctive, non-cognitive, function; it is what it is because of its peculiar function and therefore cannot be translated into any type of expression, cognitive or non-cognitive, which does not function the way it does.

To maintain that the primary function of a moral judgement is non-cognitive is not to belittle the importance of its cognitive function. In fact, its cognitive function helps it in performing its non-cognitive function. It functions as a means of persuasion by conveying some information to the hearer about the object judged. Therefore, it is not an insignificant empirical matter that we never come across a moral judgement which functions as a purely and wholly non-cognitive expression. So far as I know, nobody has given any example of this type, either from the average man's stock or from the philosopher's study. Early Ayer and Carnap gave the impression that they considered all moral judgements to be wholly non-cognitive, but even they could not offer any concrete example. On the view presented in this paper a moral judgement always functions both cognitively and non-cognitively. One moral judgement may be cognitively richer than another, or its own cognitive behaviour may vary in richness from context to context, but it is never wholly non-cognitive. Further, the qualities referred to by it, in so far as it performs a cognitive function, may be natural (i.e. perceptible by the senses, or combinations of qualities perceptible by the senses) or metaphysical (i.e. supersensible, mystical, etc.). It may happen that in a scientifically-minded community, where people are suspicious about the existence of supersensible qualities, they always refer to natural qualities when they use a moral predicate. There may also be general epistemological objections to the belief in supersensible qualities. Yet it is a fact that there are people who do refer to such qualities by means of this or that moral predicate. It is not difficult to find very devout Hindu women who, when they say that adultery is morally bad, have such qualities in mind as its being disapproved by gods, its expected painful consequences in hell after death, etc. Therefore, it is wrong to say that the cognitive function of all moral judgements is naturalistically analysable. One who is epistemologically more enlightened may recommend to those who refer to supernatural properties that they should not do so. But this will be making an evaluative judgement about their moral judgements, and not describing their actual linguistic behaviour.

The non-cognitive function of a moral judgement is primary in the sense that the primary purpose of its ordinary uses, from the point of view of the speaker, is not to convey information but to influence the recipient's conduct. It is for this reason that I consider it non-cognitive, and not because it does not perform any cognitive function. When I say to someone 'You ought not to betray a friend's trust', in a context where we are discussing his proposed action which would result in betraying the secrets conveyed to him in confidence by a friend, the judgement would surely carry some information about him and his proposed action. But this is not the chief purpose of my making the judgement; rather, I do so, mainly, in order to persuade him not to do what he is proposing to do. This is shown from the fact that I shall not mind if he denies some of the facts but still accepts my advice and does not go ahead with the implementation of his proposal. I shall be fully satisfied with nothing less than stopping him from doing what he intended to do, and if I have the required time and will to pursue the matter, I shall continue arguing with him until I succeed or lose all hope of success. In this respect 'good', 'ought', 'right', etc., behave almost alike. This is one reason why I am not discussing their logical behaviour separately.

A good reason for not regarding the cognitive function as primary is that it is not uniform or constant. It is not the case that wherever we apply a moral predicate to an object we have the same quality or set of qualities in mind. When somebody says 'X is good', or 'X ought to be done' (when X stands for an action), it is impossible to know what qualities of X he is referring to simply by attending to his judgement. There are no rules of linguistic usage which justify saying that X has P (when P is a quality or a set of qualities) merely on the strength of 'X is good', or 'X ought to be done', or on that of any moral judgement whatsoever. Therefore, a moral judgement does not entail any factual judgement because, if it does, then what it entails can be asserted simply on the strength of asserting it. Rather, the fact is that its cognitive function varies from case to case depending on the contexts of use. Further, it is not necessary that a moral judgement uttered in a particular context must perform a particular cognitive function. What sort of cognitive function or functions it will perform does depend upon the context, but the dependence is empirical and not conceptual.

Even if one has given a complete list of qualities possessed by an object, it makes sense to ask if it is good, or morally valuable, etc. This means that no set of factual judgements can entail a moral judgement. It also shows that however exhaustive an analysis of the cognitive function of a moral judgement is given, it cannot be a complete description of all the functions it performs in human speech. It is this type of argument which is at the basis of Moore's formulation of the naturalistic fallacy which was designed to refute theories of a certain type. He thought it refuted only *some* cognitivist theories, but it refutes *all* of them.

The chief ground, therefore, on which I reject cognitivism is that the primary purpose of the use of a moral judgement is non-cognitive. So long as this claim is not proved false, the non-cognitive theory presented in this paper remains unrefuted, and so does my objection to cognitivism. Even if somebody claims to have a vision of some unique property constantly referred to by 'good', he would not refute thereby the present position regarding judgements containing 'good' unless he disproves the thesis about the primary purpose of their ordinary use.

Frankena has raised an objection which may seem to apply to any non-cognitivist analysis of moral language. He maintains that a moral judgement cannot be said to be non-cognitive and thereby distinguished from a factual judgement on the ground that it tends to influence or direct conduct because even the latter sometimes does that.[1] I admit that a factual judgement does sometimes influence, or is intended to influence, conduct, as is true of 'This is the time my husband comes' told by a woman to a person making seductive moves towards her. But I call a moral judgement non-cognitive because it is ordinarily

---

[1] Frankena, William K., 'The Concept of Universal Human Rights' in *Science, Language and Human Rights*, Philadelphia: Univ. Pennsylvania Press, 1952, pp. 189–207.

and primarily intended by the speaker to influence the hearer's conduct, while a factual judgement is not; the primary purpose of its ordinary use is to convey information. Further, the action-guiding role of a factual judgement is not, as has already been explained, as uniform as that of a moral judgement. The above factual judgement can be uttered with the intention of stopping the man from doing further seduction as well as with the (opposite) intention of encouraging him to take her to some other place. The case is different with regard to a moral judgement; it can be used to produce only one kind of action, either favourable or unfavourable. The moral judgement 'You ought not to seduce another man's wife' can be used only to dissuade a man from doing, and not to encourage him to do, seductive actions. In this respect usage is very rigid about the employment of moral terms. For example, 'right' cannot be used to dissuade, and 'wrong' to persuade. Therefore, even if a factual judgement is sometimes used to influence conduct, the distinction between it and a moral judgement, as made here, cannot be questioned.

Very often a moral judgement is used with several purposes, and some of them are decidedly cognitive. It may even happen that in some special contexts it is used only, or primarily, to do a cognitive job. The mere possibility of such purely or pre-dominantly cognitive uses of it raises a problem regarding how to characterise them. I propose to call them non-moral and to call only those which are action-guiding moral. This is purely a matter of definition. But this does not mean that the view that moral language is non-cognitive or action-guiding is also a matter of definition. I decide to call moral only the non-cognitive uses and others non-moral because the former represent normal, usual, or most frequent uses, while the latter do not. Therefore, it is quite correct to speak of moral and non-moral uses of moral terms. If somebody objects to this mode of speaking, he can very well adopt a different idiom, but so long as he acknowledges that normally a moral judgement is used non-cognitively I have nothing to quarrel with him about. I do not see anything essentially misleading in this mode of speaking; we do speak in this way even in other spheres. For example, when 'glacier' is used by a poet in a lyric, we do not find any difficulty in understanding a critic who says that the poet has made a non-geographical use of a geographical term. The word is the same, but it is used in the lyric to do a job quite different from what it does in a book of geography.

Every moral judgement can be understood or misunderstood, accepted or rejected. When A offers a moral judgement P to B, we would normally say that B has correctly understood the meaning of P if he realises that to accept it sincerely is to adopt a certain course of action or at least to show a readiness to do that. Of course, he does not need to know in detail what *specific* action he is required to do, but just whether it has to be favourable or unfavourable towards the object judged. The proper understanding of P, then, requires that (1) it is interpreted as action-guiding, and (2) action-guiding in the right direction. Misunderstanding can occur on both the points. It is misunderstood if it is taken to involve no commitment to action. It is also misunderstood if it is taken to require an unfavourable action when in fact it requires a favourable one, or vice versa. These facts are easily explained if it is admitted that A's intention in uttering P to B is to guide his action. P is intended to be action-guiding in a certain way and, therefore, it is misunderstood if it is not so understood.

Assenting to a moral judgement is not the same as understanding it. To understand P, B has to fulfil the two conditions listed above, but he can correctly understand it and yet reject it, although in order to assent to it he must understand it otherwise he might be accepting something else. Normally we say that he assents to P when he actually shows at least a readiness to act in accordance with it. He may even actually do the action required by it, but actual action is not necessary in order for him to have assented to it. But so long as he does not show the readiness to act according to it, we would not say that he has really accepted it. To express assent is to express willingness to act. That is why an expression of assent conjoined with the refusal to act is logically puzzling. Why this is so is made intelligible if we remember that A's primary purpose in offering P to B is to persuade him to act in a certain way. When this is his primary purpose, then, quite naturally, accepting, or assenting to, P, would be equivalent to agreeing to act as required by it.

Let us distinguish between a genuine or sincere and a sham assent, and between a full-fledged and a partial assent. In the above example, B's assent to P would be treated as sincere if he actually acts as intended when the required conditions for actually doing the appropriate action or actions are fulfilled. In case he does not but still continues expressing his assent to P, we would call his assent genuine only if he convinces us that some of the required conditions are lacking. Therefore, 'assenting to a moral judgement' means showing the readiness to act in the way required by it, but the criterion of a genuine assent is actual execution of the relevant action unless reasons are given to justify its postponement. What sort of reasons would be accepted as satisfactory in a particular case is an evaluative question which need not be discussed here.

A full-fledged assent to P, on the other hand, would be one which is not weakened by any conflict. P may, for example, conflict with another moral judgement Q. It may happen, then, that B tends to accept P for some reason and Q for some other reasons. Here his assent to both P and Q would be partial. He is not fully on either side, and, therefore, it would be wrong to say that he fully accepts either of the two. There may also be a conflict between P and some desire, or desires, of B. In that case, on certain considerations he may like to follow the directions given by P and on some others the lead of his desires. In any situation of conflict, whether it is between two moral judgements, or between obligation and inclination, the assent to the judgement concerned can only be partial. Readiness to act goes essentially with a full-fledged assent and not with a partial assent. In those cases in which a man seems to assent to a moral judgement but does not have the readiness to act, we can almost invariably find out some conflict in his mind.

Although assenting to a moral judgement and acting according to it are closely connected, the two notions are logically independent. This is so because one can assent to it and may not act accordingly, without being self-inconsistent, because acting accordingly requires the satisfaction of many other conditions besides assenting to it. In the life of every person there are at least some moral judgements which he has accepted but is not able to act according to them because of various reasons. By 'acting' here I mean 'acting in overt behaviour'. However, one can quite sensibly use it in a broad sense, as I did while distinguishing between the levels of action, so that 'having the preparedness to act' also means a kind of action. In fact, I then admitted it to be action at the mental level but I want to keep distinct the two notions of assenting to, and acting in accordance with, a moral judgement, and to restrict the latter to signify the actual execution of the actions required. I do so because assenting, or showing a preparedness to act, is a very meagre sort of action. In fact, in common usage we do make a distinction between assenting and acting which we shall not be able to make if we treat assenting as equivalent to full-fledged action. If it is not confusing, one can quite correctly say that assenting to a moral judgement is acting at the mental level, while acting according to it is acting at the behavioural level. The way the two notions have been distinguished here does full justice to the non-cognitive nature of moral assent, and at the time enables us to preserve and understand better the common sense distinction between moral assent and moral action (i.e. actual action done in accordance with a moral judgement).

Gilman claims that there are cases in which the purpose for which a moral judgement is used is not to influence conduct and that there are also cases in which the very question of purpose is improper.[1] I shall examine his two types of cases separately in order to see what they actually prove.

As examples of the first type he offers judgements about

---

[1] Gilman, Eric, 'The Distinctive Purpose of Moral Judgments', in *Mind*, Vol. LXI, 1952.

non-existent things. 'When one criticises past actions, or passes judgement upon the conduct of people who are dead, or of fictitious characters, he says, 'one is not persuading or advising'.[1] Let us see what happens when we pass a judgement on someone who is dead. This will in effect take care of all the three cases he mentions in the lines quoted above. 'It is (morally) right that Hitler was killed' is a judgement about the killing of Hitler who is dead, but any such judgement is addressed always to a man existing at the time or to future generations. According to the view advocated in this paper, the primary purpose of the use of a moral judgement is to influence the addressee's conduct. There is no difficulty in understanding attempting to influence the conduct of a present (or future) addressee, but the difficulty is, it may be said, that we cannot persuade (or advise) anyone to act with regard to dead persons. The difficulty is not as great as it is imagined to be. There are certain things which we can do even with regard to dead persons. We can admire or condemn them, persuade people of the present or future generation to imitate their examples, take steps to create conditions which would make it easier or more difficult for similar people to flourish, etc.

It is to be remembered that moral judgements are always implicitly, if not explicitly, general. By offering a judgement which is not overtly general, therefore, the speaker intends to persuade the hearer to act in a certain way not only with regard to the particular object referred to by the judgement but with regard to all similar ones. In the case of judgements about past objects very often the speaker's purpose is to make the hearer act in a certain way with regard to similar objects which are existent or which may exist in future. It is clear, then, that judgements concerning past, or any kind of non-existent, persons or their actions do not present any insuperable difficulty to the present or any other similar analysis. I do not want to elaborate this point as it has been very well made by several other meta-ethicists.

[1] *Ibid.*, p. 315.

As examples of the second type Gilman mentions moral judgements made by a man in private. Such judgements exhibit what I have called *personal uses of moral language.* 'In the case of the private utterances we make in deciding that . . ., or concluding that . . .,' he says, 'the first kind of question is improper.'[1] By 'the first kind of question' he means 'the question about the distinctive purpose of moral judgements'. So far I have not talked about the personal uses. Let us now turn to them.

As was pointed out in the beginning of the paper, the chief occasion to utter a moral judgement in private is provided by the context of deciding. Usually a man utters one to himself when he has to decide which course of action to adopt if more than one course is open to him. In such a situation, it can be used to perform either one of the following three functions: one can utter it to help him arrive at a decision, or to strengthen a decision which he had already arrived at but which is not sufficiently firm, or simply to express the decision he has reached. All of the three uses can even be made in a single instance.

In the first case the judgement is uttered in the very course of deliberation, and there it acts as an attempt at persuasion as it does when used in an interpersonal situation. In course of deciding whether to nurse his dying mother or to pursue his research, a young man may say to himself 'But I ought to serve my mother'. This utterance surely is intended to guide or influence his choice. When used in the second case the action-guiding role of the judgement is all the more evident. If the young man has somehow decided to nurse his mother, but still does not feel very firm in it, he may utter the above judgement to himself to confirm or strengthen his wavering decision. It is not correct, then, to say, as Gilman does, that in the context of personal decision a moral judgement is not at all used with a view to influence conduct.

In the third case the judgement is uttered at the end of the process of deliberation to express the decision arrived at. The

[1] *Ibid.,* p. 314.

young man may express his final decision by uttering to himself 'I ought to nurse my mother'. Here the latter *expresses* the success of his earlier attempts at self-persuasion. It is still action-guiding and not unconnected with persuasion. This example further shows that it can not only be used as an attempt to influence but also to express the success (or failure) of the attempt. Sometimes even in an interpersonal situation one may repeat the judgement in question to express acceptance of it.

That a moral judgement, which normally functions as an attempt to persuade someone to do something, can also, in appropriate contexts, be used to express the fact that he has been so persuaded, should not appear to be a strange phenomenon, since in such cases also its persuasive role is not completely missing. It is likely, however, that an excessive preoccupation with its expressive uses makes it difficult to notice those cases in which it obviously or prominently performs a persuasive function. It seems to me that this is the reason why Gilman (mistakenly) thinks that in its private uses it is improper to raise the question of a distinctive purpose to influence conduct.

Chapter 9

G. E. MOORE AND THE AUTONOMY OF ETHICS

by

BINAYENDRANATH RAY

Since Kant no other philosopher perhaps has sought to defend with greater zeal the autonomy of ethics than G. E. Moore. Moore has been the most uncompromising critic of the theories which tried to reduce ethics to a branch of natural science, metaphysics or theology. He saw clearly the unique nature of ethical and valuational concepts and the consequent impossibility of their reduction to empirical concepts of natural science or non-empirical concepts of metaphysics and theology. Basically different from the latter concepts, the concept of good which for him is the fundamental concept of ethics, does not just mean what is conducive to pleasure or biological survival, or what is approved by society, or what possesses some supersensible property, or what is commanded by the Divine Will. The quotation from Butler on the title page of *Principia Ethica* that 'everything is what it is, and not another thing' is significant in that it reveals his main concern, which is to demonstrate that good is good and not another thing, and that any attempt to assimilate it to any natural or even supersensible property—metaphysical or theological—is to commit the naturalistic fallacy. In Moore's ethics the 'naturalistic fallacy' plays an important role and he uses it as his main weapon in defence of the autonomy of ethics and in refuting the views which aim at equating the ethical with naturalistic, metaphysical or theological concepts.

That the concept of good is unique and irreducible can be demonstrated by a simple test. To settle the issue, let us consider each suggested definition of 'good' in naturalistic or for that matter in any other terms and see if 'good' in any of these definitions is the predicate of an analytic or synthetic proposition. That the proposed definition of good in terms of pleasure is vicious can be seen if we attentively consider what is *actually before our minds* when we ask the question, 'Is pleasure (or whatever it may be) after all good'? We can then satisfy ourselves that the question is significant, that its answer is not just a truism, and that we are not merely wondering whether pleasure is pleasant. If with each suggested definition we try this experiment we may become expert enough to *recognise* that in every case we have *before our mind* a unique object, unique property of things meant by 'good' and different from pleasure or for that matter from any other object. The question 'Is this good'? has for us a meaning clearly distinct from the question 'Is this pleasant'?, though we may not be able to spell out what precisely this difference is. Good thus is good, and not another thing—a unique kind of property and its difference from any other property, natural or supersensible is denoted by calling it *non-natural*. (G. E. Moore, *Principia Ethica*, pp. 16–17.)

The word 'non-natural' is a vague and negative word, which instead of clarifying the logical difference between 'good' and typical property words like 'yellow' makes it more confusing. Moore no doubt notices their important difference, but the terminology he used was singularly ill-adapted and completely failed to elucidate just this difference. What is a non-natural property? If there is such a property, and 'good' for Moore is such a property, then how are we to know it? Being a simple and unanalysable notion like yellow, it can be known only in direct experience: but being a non-natural property, it cannot, obviously be an object of sensible experience like 'yellow'. Its existence can be known only in some kind of non-sensuous intuition. Moore seems to admit this when he talks of 'good' as being '*actually before our minds*' and that in every case that we *recognise* its unique character as distinct from any other natural property, it is *actually before our minds*. The view that good is a non-natural property is thus established on epistemic grounds, and its cogency rests entirely on the question of the validity of intuitive knowledge.

Do we *really* have any such non-sensuous awareness of a non-natural property? If someone denies that he ever had any such intuition of a non-natural property, there is hardly any way of our proving that he ever had it. There is no agreed procedure to confirm its existence as in the case of sense perception. The meaning of a sensible property, such as yellow, can be elucidated by ostensive definition, but this method of denoting or pointing out is obviously inept for confirming the presence of a non-natural quality. If 'good' is an indefinable intuitive concept, then it is self-contradictory to say that *I know* what the word 'good' means but I cannot ever remember to have *intuited* any non-natural property of goodness, and I do not know what it would be *like* to intuit any such non-natural property. But is it at all obvious that this is a contradiction? I am quite prepared to maintain that I understand the meaning of the word 'good', but I could not remember ever intuiting the non-natural property of goodness and that I could not *imagine* what it would be *like* to do so. When I say that 'courage is good', I *know* what is meant by the predicate 'good', although it is not obvious that I intuit any non-natural property of goodness. Moore's view thus entails the paradox that a man who knows what things are good and what it is to be good, may yet not know what goodness is, since he fails to intuit any additional non-natural property. (S. E. Toulmin, *Reason in Ethics*, pp. 24–5.) To understand the meaning of good it is not necessary that we should be able to intuit any such non-natural quality. To elucidate the meaning of the word 'good' and for that matter of any other word, we have only to explain how that word is *used* in a particular context, and its usage in that context determines its meaning.

Even if we admit the possibility of intuition our difficulty

remains. Our intuition of the non-natural property of goodness is either fallible or infallible. If it is fallible, the mere
objective existence of any such property is no guarantee that
any one has apprehended it properly. However convinced I
may be of its existence and the conviction is only psychological, not logical, yet it is open to any one else to deny the
genuineness of my intuition. In the case of such denials we do
not have, as in the case of empirical properties like 'yellow',
any agreed procedure for settling the dispute. If, on the other
hand, our intuition is infallible, then disputes cannot be
genuine. Our disagreements in that event should be attributed
to one of us being either insincere or morally perverse or
blind. But this account of the matter is false, since ethical
disagreement is genuine and we allow others to be sincere and
not morally perverse when their moral views differ from our
own. In view of these considerations, it is difficult on purely
epistemic grounds to sustain our belief in the existence of a
non-natural quality of goodness. (*Vide* P. H. Nowell-Smith,
Ethics, p. 46, Pelican.)

In representing 'good' as a non-natural property, Moore
perhaps intended to mark an important difference between
'good' and natural properties such as 'yellow'. Yet precisely it
is this sort of difference which is denied by assimilating 'good'
to the class of properties, and the description of it as non-
natural, far from illuminating this difference, muddles it
completely. Despite his stressing the unique and irreducible
character of 'good', Moore does not quite succeed in carrying
the autonomy of ethics far enough, and this failure stems
mainly from his mistaken assumption that 'good' belongs to
the class of 'property'. His elucidation of the difference between 'yellow' and 'good' in terms of the natural/non-natural
dichotomy was a source of puzzlement to many and he failed
to clarify this difference because of his wrong approach to the
problem. He tried to elucidate moral discourse in terms of a
vocabulary suitable for empirical discourse. The logical
apparatus such as thing, property, relation, etc., used appro-
priately in the context of empirical discourse, is ill-suited for the

elucidation of moral discourse. Moore failed to grasp this aspect of the matter and was faced with the consequent logical difficulties which it entails. For him, ethical judgement, which for its predicate has a non-natural property, is conceived on the analogy of an empirical judgement which has for its predicate a natural property. Empirical judgements describe or refer to empirical facts and ethical judgements, analogously, are also supposed to describe or denote non-natural facts. So ethical judgements, moreover, are true or false in the same straightforward sense as empirical judgements, according as they do or do not correspond to certain non-natural facts. This way of elucidating ethical discourse in descriptive terminology borrowed from empirical discourse creates for Moore a fiction and introduces us into a strange world of non-natural facts, which, though its contents are unfamiliar and lack literal significance, has yet the same logical pattern as the familiar world of empirical facts. Ethical judgements are thus supposed to be descriptive of the so-called non-natural features of a mysterious world in the same way in which empirical judgements describe the natural characteristics of our familiar world of empirical facts.

The postulation of a world of non-natural facts to elucidate the difference between 'good' and non-natural properties, shows clearly that Moore's approach to the problem was metaphysical and not logical. The sort of difference illustrated in the natural/non-natural dichotomy is metaphysical, a difference between two kinds of facts, and not in respect of their logical status and behaviour. In postulating a realm of non-natural facts, Moore violates Occam's rule of economy which forbids multiplication of superfluous entities; and in rendering ethical judgements in descriptive terms, he commits the same sort of logical error which he so vehemently condemns in naturalistic and metaphysical theories. For Moore, then, the difference between naturalism and non-naturalism is not a logical but an ontological difference, since both analyse ethical judgements in descriptive terms. So their difference may be indicated as that between descriptive naturalism and descriptive non-naturalism. Their logical *form* is identical, but their ontological *content* is different, since they describe two different kinds of fact.

Moore's arguments against ethical theories which commit the naturalistic fallacy are quite plausible, but his formulation of this fallacy is faulty. Because of his obsession with the view that 'good' is the name of a property, he failed to see the real point of this fallacy. Naturalism is at fault not because, as Moore supposes, it analyses 'good', a non-natural property, in terms of naturalistic properties such as pleasure, but the error it commits is of a different sort—it is logical and not ontological. What is wrong with naturalism is that it overlooks the evaluative and commendatory significance of 'good' and seeks to derive ethical and evaluative judgements from factual and descriptive judgements. This leads to a curious result. In the naturalistic definition of *'good'* it is equated with some factual or descriptive predicate. To say that 'X is good' is the same thing as to say that 'X is pleasant'. If so, then it is impossible for any one to commend 'X' for being pleasant. It is possible to say only that 'X' is pleasant and nothing more. However, we may fall back upon some evaluative word other than 'good' to perform the commendatory function, although this would not help since this device will only put back the difficulty without solving it. Commendation is ruled out in consistent naturalism which, by definition, neutralises completely the commendatory force of value terms. (*Vide*, R. M. Hare, *The Language of Morals*, pp. 83–5.)

The naturalistic fallacy brings into sharp focus the logical gap between evaluative and descriptive terms and Moore's failure to see this clearly accounts for his faulty analysis of the difference between 'yellow' and 'good' in terms of the natural/ non-natural dichotomy. The uniqueness of 'good' Moore failed to see, was not due to its being a property of the non-natural kind, but due solely to its evaluative significance. It may be interesting in this connection to see how Moore elucidates the difference between 'yellow' and 'good' in terms, respectively, of natural and non-natural properties in descriptive terminology borrowed from empirical discourse. 'Good' for him, is a non-natural intrinsic property as distinct from 'yellow' which is a natural intrinsic property. Both are properties in the sense that they depend upon the intrinsic nature of the objects of which they are predicated. But whereas according to the ordinary sense of the word 'describe' a natural intrinsic property like yellow *describes* to some extent and not completely the object of which it is predicated, the non-natural intrinsic property, such as 'good' *does not describe* its object at all. But this account of the matter, Moore thinks, is vague. To make it clear, it is necessary to specify the sense of 'describe' in question; but he confesses that he is unable to do so. However, he does realise that if 'good' is the name of a characteristic at all, then there is a problem to be faced, since this sense of 'good' certainly seems to be of an importantly different *kind* from those intrinsic properties which he has called in *Principia Ethica* 'natural'. How then does he proceed to explain this difference in *kind* between the natural and non-natural intrinsic properties? 'Good' being assimilated to the class of properties, he is tied to descriptive terminology to elucidate this difference, and so, he says that he is faced with a problem and does not know his way about it. (*Philosophy of G. E. Moore*—Moore's reply.)

If good is a property word, its function like a natural property word, would be to describe the object of which it is predicated and its being non-natural does not make any difference in its logical status and function. But, at the same time, it seems obvious that if 'good' describes its object, it cannot be supposed to describe it in the sense in which a natural property like 'yellow' is said to describe its object. For Moore 'natural intrinsic properties seem to describe the intrinsic nature of what possesses them in a sense in which the predicates of value do not'. In which sense of the term 'describe' then does 'good' describe its object? The term 'describe' thus appears to have two distinct senses; one is just the ordinary sense in which it is commonly used, and the other, a special sense in which 'good' is said to '*describe*' its object. The first sense of the word 'describe' Moore rejects as vague and unclear and in this sense 'good' cannot properly be said to describe anything at all. The special sense of the word 'describe' he wishes he could specify clearly, but confesses his inability to do so. However, he does not see that this inability is due to the simple reason that 'good' is not a property word and as such its role is not to describe, but to commend and evaluate.

In elucidating the difference between natural and non-natural properties in his *Philosophical Studies*, Moore hesitates to say that good is an intrinsic property. Though both 'good' and 'yellow' depend solely upon the intrinsic nature of the objects of which they are predicated, yet good in itself *is not, like yellow, an intrinsic property*. Good is said to be intrinsic without being an intrinsic property. This seems to imply that there must be some characteristic belonging to intrinsic properties which good does not seem to possess. Moore feels that there is a very basic difference between good and yellow, but what it is he just cannot explain. He can only vaguely express the difference by saying that intrinsic properties seem to describe the intrinsic nature of what possesses them in a sense in which the predicate 'good' never does. His play upon the word 'describe' shows that Moore is having considerable difficulty in expressing the meaning of good completely in descriptive terms and such an account of its nature leaves unexplained a residual element which perhaps constitutes its most important feature. This explains his hesitation to call 'good' an intrinsic property in the full sense of the term. It may also be due to some vague awareness that good after all in its primary evaluative significance cannot be properly said to describe any property in any sense, and as such it may be misleading to call it a property. Moore, however, later on resiles from this position as inconsistent with the view of good as a property. He later characterises good as an intrinsic non-natural property, and abandons its earlier description as 'intrinsic without being an intrinsic property' as awkward and ambiguous; but this ambiguous way of characterising good is also in a sense illuminating. It reveals that, not being a property word, the primary evaluative meaning of good cannot be adequately expressed in descriptive terms without recourse to ambiguity and radical departure from its ordinary usage. Moore's use of the word 'describe' in a special sense in the context of 'good' and his description of 'good' as a non-natural property are clear violations of the rules of ordinary language. (G. E. Moore, *Philosophical Studies*, pp. 272–5. Also *Philosophy of G. E. Moore*—Moore's reply.)

Moore's entire approach to the question of the autonomy of ethics is, from the start, vitiated by his assimilation of 'good' to the class of properties and his inability to see that the logic of the word good, a value word, is essentially different from the logic of a typical property word, such as, 'yellow'. In view of this it seems worth while to settle finally the issue whether the word 'good' primarily stands for a property or not. To deal with his question satisfactorily we should have recourse to some agreed procedure which would elucidate the logical behaviour of property words, such as yellow. We shall then be in a position to see whether a value word like 'good' shares the same logical characteristics and behaves in the same way as some word or phrase which denotes a property.

How then are we to decide whether a word or a phrase stands for a property or not? It is a common mistake to assume that all adjectives name properties and their logical role is to denote or refer to something. When we say that something is laudable and sublime, these words are evidently adjectives, but they are not descriptive of any properties in the sense in which the adjective 'red' or 'yellow' describes a property of the object which possesses it. Similarly, 'good' is certainly an adjective; but to say that 'good' is an adjective is not another way of saying that 'good' is a property. It is not this triviality, but something more which it is intended to assert when it is said that 'good' is a property. One of the factors which is responsible for this mistaken notion is the similarity in the form of words used in talking of 'good' and talking of properties. In either case we express ourselves in indicative sentences, such as, 'Courage is good' and 'The rose is red'. The adjective 'red' in the sentence 'The rose is red' obviously stands for a property and from its grammatical similarity with the sentence, 'courage is good', we may be deluded into believing that the adjective 'good' also stands for a property. But this superficial similarity in their grammatical structure should not be misconstrued as likeness in their logical status and behaviour. Though similar in grammatical form, logically they express judgements of entirely different types. What then is this logical difference between 'good' and the property words like 'yellow'? In what follows we discuss this question in detail. (*Vide* P. H. Nowell-Smith, *Ethics*, pp. 63 ff. Pelican.)

The crucial question here is: how to decide whether a word or a phrase stands for a property or not? There is an agreed procedure to settle this issue, but the procedure varies in the case of properties of different types. Some properties, such as 'red' or 'green' are simple and unanalysable, but directly perceived, while there are others which though directly perceived, are complex and analysable, such as a square or a triangle. We can distinguish a red from a green object in sense perception and teach a normal person to do the same. A person who does not know the meaning of the word 'red' can be taught it ostensively or by verbally pointing out or instancing objects having that property. Verbally pointing out to him the different instances of red objects, such as a 'rose', a 'poppy' and a 'pillar box', and repeating this process several times one perhaps ultimately succeeds in explaining the meaning of the word 'red'. The success, however, would depend upon the fact that the person concerned is without any sensory defect. The meaning of complex properties, such as a 'square', is not elucidated in direct perception, but indirectly in terms of a standard routine. All that we can say at sight of a 'square' is that it is a four-sided figure; but to say precisely that it is rectangular and equilateral, we have to apply the appropriate routine, which, in the present case, is measurement. The disagreement over simple properties, such as when one person says that '*X* is red' and another says '*X* is green', arises generally from organic defect, deliberate deception or linguistic difference, whereas in the case of complex properties, the sources of disagreement include besides these also the incorrect application of the standard routine. The disagreement over simple and complex properties disappears when these sources of disagreement are clearly detected. (*Vide* S. E. Toulmin, *The Place of Reason in Ethics*, pp. 10–18.)

Does 'good' share any of these logical characteristics of simple or complex properties? Can its meaning be elucidated like that of simple properties by ostensive definition? Obviously not, since 'good' is not an object of direct perception, sensuous or non-sensuous. Nor is 'good', like 'yellow', a factual characteristic of the object of which it is predicated, and as such cannot be indicated in any instance of it simply by pointing. Its meaning also cannot, as in the case of complex qualities, be explained in terms of some standard routine. To decide whether a figure is a square or not we have some definite criteria, namely, rectangularity and having four equal sides, and also a standard routine for the application of the criteria. For the application of the term 'good' also we have, no doubt, some criteria, but we do not have here, as in the case of complex qualities, any definite routine for confirming its presence in a particular case. We may give a set of criteria or what Broad calls 'good-making characteristics', such as, honest, kind, generous, just and truthful, in support of our appraisal of Jones as a good man. These criteria, again, may be generally accepted as sufficient justification for our calling Jones a good man. Even so, it is open to any one to disagree with our appraisal on the ground that our criteria fail to mention some quality which from his point of view is essential. If he happens to be a religious man and sincerely believes in God, he perhaps would not accept any criteria of good man which do not include such belief. This brings out the fact that ethical criteria lack that inflexibility which characterises the criteria of a complex property. This is because the criteria of a complex property, such as a 'square' are its defining characteristics and the relation between the criteria and the property they define is analytic. So it is self-contradictory to affirm the criteria and deny the property defined by them. It is contradictory to say that 'X is rectangular and has four equal sides' and deny at the same time that 'X is a square'. The same, however, is not true of the relation between ethical criteria, that is to say, 'good-making characteristics' and 'good'. The relation here is not analytic and so it is not self-contradictory to affirm that 'Jones is honest, kind, generous, etc.', but deny at the same time that he is a good man. The relation obviously is not analytic, but I am not sure if it would be quite appropriate either to call it 'synthetic', though it shares the essential feature of a synthetic relation that its opposite can be affirmed without contradiction. The word 'synthetic' is generally used to express a relation between facts and hence it may be inappropriate and perhaps misleading to use it in the context of a relation in which at least one of the terms is 'good', a value term, not descriptive of any fact. It is because of this peculiar feature of the relation between ethical criteria and good, that any description of it in terms of the analytic–synthetic dichotomy seems to be far from illuminating. The parallelism between the criteria of a complex property and the ethical criteria or good-making characteristics thus finally breaks down since they are seen to differ in fundamental ways. (*Vide* S. E. Toulmin, *The Place of Reason in Ethics*, pp. 18–19.)

Further, we notice an important difference between ethical disagreement and disagreement over simple and complex properties. If all sources of disagreement over simple and complex properties, such as organic defect, deliberate deception, etc., are removed, it seems pointless to ask two persons whether they agree or disagree about the colour of an object or the shape of a figure. The same, however, is not true of ethical disagreement. Even when two persons are fully informed of the facts of the case and all sources of disagreement are removed, it would not be at all surprising to find that their ethical judgements are not the same, one of them saying 'X is good' and another, 'X is bad'. They may or may not agree and their agreement as such is only contingent and not necessary as in the case of agreement over simple and complex qualities when all sources of disagreement are removed. (*Vide* S. E. Toulmin, *The Place of Reason in Ethics*, pp. 19–21.)

That the term 'good' does not denote a property, is again evident from the fact that while the use of a property term like 'red' is sufficient to mark the factual difference between any two objects, the use of a term like 'good' is not. While it makes sense to say of any two objects that they are exactly alike in every respect except one, namely, that one is red and the other is not, it does not make any sense at all to say of any two objects that they are exactly the same with this difference only that one of them is good and the other is not so. If someone tells us that he has painted two pictures only one of which is good, we are naturally curious to ask him what the difference is between them. Suppose he said in reply, 'That just is the difference, one is good and the other is not', most people would find this answer quite puzzling. His different evaluations of the two pictures are intelligible only on the assumption that though based upon some factual differences between them, they themselves do not express or state any such factual difference. One of the pictures, let us suppose, has the descriptive features, *a, b, c,* and the other, *a, b, d,* and it is this factual difference between them that provides the reason for saying one of them is good and the other not so. If there is no factual difference there is no basis for different evaluations. The term 'good' being evaluative bears, no doubt, a close relation to descriptive properties, but is itself not a property in any sense of the term. (R. M. Hare, *The Language of Morals,* pp. 80 ff.)

The primary meaning of 'good' is non-descriptive and commendatory, and normally our evaluation of an object is based on a set of descriptive properties which are its criteria. We call an orange 'good' in virtue of its descriptive properties, such as, large, juicy, sweet, etc. But to say that it is good is not just to convey the information that it has these properties. The basic meaning of 'good' being evaluative and commendatory, it is not in this sense used for giving and getting information.

There is, however, another meaning of 'good', the descriptive meaning, in which to say that an orange is good is to do no more than convey the information that it has a definite set of properties. In this the word 'good' resembles the property word red whose sole function is to give factual information. This similarity may have led some to deny good its evaluative function and to hold that the role of good is merely descriptive and informative. To say that something is good is just another way of saying that it has a set of descriptive properties; but this position is clearly untenable. It can be shown beyond doubt that the primary meaning of 'good' is irreducible and logically independent of the criteria of its application. It is a peculiar characteristic of objects. We talk of a good man, a good piano player, a good batsman, etc., and in all these cases the primary meaning of good is common and invariant, though the criteria of its application are obviously different and vary in each case. It is one of the noticeable features of 'good' that we can use it for entirely new classes of objects that we have never called good before and about whose properties we have not the faintest idea. Suppose someone says 'X is good' and 'X' refers to a new class of objects about which I have not the slightest idea, yet I do not have any difficulty in understanding the significance of 'good'. I can see clearly that the word 'good' is being used to commend 'X' whatever 'X' may be. Lack of factual or descriptive reference is no bar to the understanding of its evaluative significance. (*Vide* R. M. Hare, *The Language of Morals*, pp. 95–7.)

It is in its primary evaluative sense that the term 'good' is autonomous and irreducible to anything else. In this sense, as we have just seen, its meaning is independent of the criteria of its application. It is interesting to notice that Moore saw this feature of 'good' which seems obvious from the way in which he analyses the relation between good and the descriptive non-ethical characteristics of the object of which it is predicated. But on account of his obsession with the view of good as property he could not make full use of its logical implications in support of his main thesis—the uniqueness and autonomy of good. That this is so will be evident from a consideration of the quotation given below.

'Whenever a thing is good its goodness depends on the presence of certain non-ethical characteristics possessed by the thing in question; I have always supposed that it did so "depend" in the sense that if a thing is good (in my sense), then that it is so *follows* from the fact that it possesses certain natural intrinsic properties, which are such that from the fact that it is good it does *not* follow conversely that it has these properties.' (*The Philosophy of G. E. Moore*—Moore's reply.)

The way in which Moore, in the above quotation, expresses the logic of the relation between 'good' and the non-ethical natural properties, brings out two very important features. *First*, the goodness of a thing depends upon its natural properties in the sense that to say that a thing is good is to say that its goodness *follows* from the fact that it possesses certain natural intrinsic properties. Moore, however, does not clarify the meaning of the relation '*follows from*' in this context. Yet it seems clear that it is not taken in the logical sense in which to say that '*q*' follows from '*p*' is to say that '*q*' is formally deducible from or entailed by '*p*'. The relation is not intended to be analytic in the sense in which '*X* is an angle' follows from or is formally deducible from '*X* is a right angle'. Nor can we suppose that it expresses just an empirical relation between a certain natural property of the object and its other natural properties, since for Moore 'good' is a non-natural property. The relation 'follows from', then, for him obtains between 'good', a non-natural property, and a natural property or a group of such properties. The relation is synthetic, but is, unlike an empirical relation, necessary. So it seems that to say that the goodness of a thing follows from the fact that it possesses certain natural properties, is to say that there is a necessary synthetic connection *in reality* between certain natural properties and an additional non-natural property of goodness which 'follows from' them. But how are we to justify that 'good', a non-natural property, 'follows from' a group of natural properties? Being necessary, the relation cannot be justified in terms of empirical observation; and being synthetic, it excludes the formal test in terms of the logic of contradiction. This peculiar necessary synthetic connection between 'good', a non-natural property, and certain natural properties, is justified ultimately, as we have seen, on epistemic grounds, that is, on the basis of non-sensuous intuition. We have already rejected this kind of justification on an intuitional basis as untenable.

Moore could have easily avoided these muddles had he clearly seen the logical difference between 'good', a value term, and property terms like yellow. He could then have also seen that the sort of logic which validates an ethical judgement is perhaps governed by rules different from those which justify deductive or inductive reasoning. To be more precise, the sort of logic which validates an ethical judgement is a sort of informal logic which does not lay down any rigid rule as in formal logic, nor does it rely on merely empirical tests as in inductive reasoning, although it does not rule out consideration of relevant non-ethical empirical facts in its support. The rules of informal logic are not abstract and inflexible. They are subject to modification in the light of a particular moral situation and are perhaps finally discovered as an end-process in course of our analysis of the relevant facts of the situation.

Second, Moore seems to be perfectly right in saying that from the fact that a thing is good it does not follow that it has certain natural properties. It is clear that in no sense of the term 'follows from' are we justified in saying 'X is pleasant' follows from 'X is good'. This is obvious for the simple reason that unlike according to naturalism, good is not here by definition equated with any natural property, such as pleasant, and so it just cannot be said that from the fact that a thing is good it follows that it is pleasant. Moore seems to think that since 'good' as a consequential non-natural property follows from certain natural properties, it cannot be the case that the natural properties on which good is supervenient should follow from good. We agree, but for a different reason. That from 'X is good' it does not follow that 'X is pleasant', is because 'good' being an evaluative term its primary commendatory meaning is independent of its application to any natural property or conjunction of such properties. Its evaluative meaning, we have seen, is as such intelligible even in the absence of any reference to the natural properties of the object. The meaning of 'good' as a term for appraisal is obvious in 'X is good', though 'X' happens to be an unknown variable. The primary evaluative meaning of 'good' is empty of descriptive content and as such cannot be supposed to convey any information of any kind. It is in this sense that 'good' is autonomous and irreducible to any factual or descriptive term, natural or non-natural. To evaluate is not to describe and to describe is not to evaluate. Logically, they are different types of activity, yet closely related to each other. No descriptive term then, natural or non-natural, can elucidate or exhaust the meaning of 'good' which is a value term. A non-natural property *logically is still a property* and as such its job should be to *describe*, if it describes anything at all in the literal sense, and not to evaluate.

G

Chapter 10

EMBODIMENT AND THE QUEST FOR KEY AESTHETIC CONCEPTS

by

SUSHIL KUMAR SAXENA
University of Delhi

I. INTRODUCTORY

I see some serious defects in the thesis of 'embodiment'. In this article I have tried to expose them—with due regard, I hope, to the theory and fact of art. Towards its close, I have proposed, quite briefly, and with but some show of reason, a new definition of art as creative invocation, with a view to setting up *presence*, in place of other words, as the key concept of aesthetics.

Reid regards 'embodiment, not expression, as the key-idea in the aesthetics of art'.[1] Now, any concept which claims to be central to aesthetics has to meet some basic requirements. It must keep close to the fact of creative art, or be a first-order word. On the other hand, it has to be of help to aesthetical theory. Is Reid's word, *embodiment*, able to meet these demands? Is it, as he believes, *preferable* to 'expression'?

Our first task, obviously, is to see what 'embodiment' means. The claim that it is 'a defining characteristic formulated after careful examination of *all* kinds of art'[2] can be weighed only later. Now, at least once, Reid directly equates embodiment with 'unity of form and content'.[3] I find he also speaks of

---

[1] L. A. Reid, *Meaning in the Arts*, Allen & Unwin, London, 1969, p. 95. (Hereafter, throughout the essay, this work is referred to as *MA*.)

[2] *Ibid.*, p. 224. (My italics.)   *Ibid.*

the one-many involvement that characterises *all* art.[1] Are we then to *identify* 'embodiment' with the form-content, one-many unities which are known features of good art? Perhaps yes; but then we miss not only what distinguishes Reid's view, but a crucial point of his disagreement with Langer. We must mark the 'special' meaning that he gives to the word 'embodiment' as the inseparable fusion (in art) of the ideal with 'materials', of 'meaning' with perceptua.

II THE RIVAL CONCEPTS: *Reid's arguments*

I may now turn to the details of Reid's arguments.

(1) The first contrast that he draws is:

'. . . "Embodiment" suggests the thing directly before us, while 'expression' has the unfortunate tendency . . . to direct our thoughts *otherwards* to feelings or ideas which are expressed.'[2]

Let us see if it is really so.

Consider the concepts, first, as meaningful words. Does 'embodiment', thus regarded, '*suggest* the thing directly before us'? It does not; for, we are here interested only in meaning, and this does not require anything to be 'directly' before us. The suggestion in question arises only when some 'seeing' in the mind's eye here surreptitiously enters, with some felt insistence on what is thus 'seen'. Otherwise, what 'embodiment' means simply is that some content or meaning is embodied in a form or medium. 'Expression' too, as a word, implies a distinction (and relation) between 'what is expressed' and 'that which expresses'. However, in both cases the distinction falls within, or rather *is* the meaning; and in the case of neither word is there any going *otherwards*.

I suspect in the extract cited a dual vitiation of argument by spatial imagery. 'Embodiment' is turned, without notice, into *an* 'embodiment' that we *find*; and 'otherwards', in the case of expression, into the spatial 'outside'.[3]

[1] *M.A.*, p. 235.   [2] *Ibid.*, pp. 77–8. (My italics.)
[3] It is only this imagined spatiality which makes the protest seem pointed.

From meaning let us now turn to fact—to 'things' that are expressive or embodiments. Consider, first, 'things' that are non-aesthetic, say, the 'seeing' of 'character in a person's face'.[1] This is, in Reid's view:

'Neither to perceive his body only nor to apprehend his character through his body, but to apprehend one single embodied person with distinguishable aspects. If I apprehend someone as sad, . . . I am not aware just of feelings or a body behaving, but of a person—sad. . . .'[2]

Now here, again, I see some confusion.

It *is* correct to say that here 'I' neither perceives the person's 'body only' nor merely his feelings. Nor is the awareness simply one of 'a body behaving'. To say, here, that 'I' 'apprehends his character through his *body*' would also be inaccurate; for the fact in question[3] is the 'seeing of character in a person's *face*'. But, I may add, to describe this 'fact' as the apprehension of 'one single embodied person with distinguish*able* aspects' would be just as wide of the mark. For, the emphasis of attention is *ex hypothesi* on the face; and its being non-identical with the body and with what it expresses is here certainly experienced, if only as felt. This is why the percipient himself would speak of the experience in some such words: 'He looked sad', or: 'I saw grief writ large on his face'. No one would here think of saying: 'I apprehended one single embodied person'.

From the outside, and quite generally, it is certainly true that the object of experience is here 'single' and undivided, but to say so is, in this case, at once to miss the specific, inner character of the experience, that is, how (or what) the object really appears to the percipient; it is merely to reduce the phenomenological to the existential.

A little more attention to words may help us in dealing with (a possible form of)[4] the objection under review *in the context*

---

[1] *MA*, p. 76. [2] *Ibid.*, p. 76. [3] As *I* have taken it.
[4] The objection is: 'expression' takes us away from the work. Its 'possible form' I here discuss is: what is expressed is pressed out of the work, and so if we say that a work is 'expressive', we (with its 'meaning') move away from the work.

of art. Ordinarily, we speak of seeing character *in* a person's face, not of apprehending it '*through* his body'. Unlike the latter—which may evoke the image of a squeeze, and make some of Reid's objections to 'expression' seem valid—the former way of speech certainly keeps close to the undivided singleness of fact. But when my look *has* lingered on a very sad face—and, here, the sadness *is* 'embodied'—would it at all appear *unnatural* if, turning a little discursive, I say that the face seemed expressive of deep, inner gloom? We must answer in the negative, unless it be assumed that *all* expression is 'expression *through*'. Such an assumption would be quite unwarranted; for, a simple meaning of 'to express' is 'to reveal'. Yet, some such supposal is clearly implicit in Reid's following protest:

'. . . feeling-import and 'surface' are . . . in aesthetic experience so *inseparably* one that in this context it sounds artificial to say that art is projecting or expressing something else—"feeling".'[1]

I disagree. What is (in fact) expressed is not necessarily *separated* from that which expresses; and the 'separation' may not even be suggested when we *say* that something is expressive. Thus, when a face strikes us as, and is said to be *expressive* of sadness, whether we take the word as 'expressive *of*' or as 'expressive *to*', there is hardly any danger of misbelieving that the 'sadness' exists apart from, or is in any way 'loosened' from the face. Why should it be otherwise in the case of works of art?

Reid, we must note, does not deny expressiveness to the 'elements' of art, but he is anxious to uphold the autonomy of the total 'work', and so he insists that the 'materials' and the 'elements' are, *in* the work, so well organised that the whole appears single and self-contained:

'Expressiveness in it melts into the wholeness of the individual form which you see. . . .'[2] It has never been suggested in this

[1] *MA*, p. 63. (My italics.)
[2] *Ibid.*, p. 109.

book that in embodiment expression is annulled—only that expression is not the key criterion of the aesthetic.'[1]

Now, I must at once say this baffles me. To hold with regard to, say, poetry that it takes up words (all of them meaningful) and weaves its wondrous magic with them, transfiguring sense into sheer verbal radiance;[2] and that yet what it produces in the end is *embodied meaning* rather than '*expressive form*'— this is, in my view, the mere issue of a fiat rather than the reasoned attainment of a truth.

Why does Reid have to speak thus? Evidently because of the fear that if meaning is 'expressed' it would, so to speak, spill its locus, making the 'work' itself self-transcendent. But the fear and the purpose it subserves are both here suspect. The autonomy of art is not the demonstrable finality of a thing's rigid outlines. It is the seeming self-completeness of a 'work' that we find satisfying. The 'autonomy' here is a fullness that is felt. There is no risk of spilling, for there is no measured extent, and expression, we have seen, is not always an *activity* of *pressing out*. In art and psycho-physical embodi-ment alike, it may well be a mere *mode or quality of being or seeming*. Where Reid protests that in the case of abstract drawing, so long as the process of creation is determined by what is found drawn[3] on the 'paper', the artist cannot be said to be 'expressing' himself, the word is used, quite properly, in the sense of an activity. But when a face is said to express sadness, the meaning simply is that the face *looks* sad, and whereas we may agree that (self-) *expression* is not (quite) adequate to the mak*ing* of a work, we may insist—without contradiction, by availing of its meaning as a seeming—on applying the word to the work as complet*ed*.

I can here refer to some of Reid's own instances. In the case of (Barbara Hepworth's) abstract drawing, determination of creative activity by the material character of lines and

---

[1]   *MA,* p. 160.

[2]   *Ibid.,* pp. 158–9. Reid openly speaks of 'the work of art' as a 'qualitative indi-vidual *charged with meaning* . . . (and as thus) able to 'reveal' in its own important way'. *Ibid.,* p. 248. (My italics.) I invite attention to: *charged with* and *reveal.*

[3]   *Ibid.,* pp. 108–9.

curves *results in* a new form 'with its own special life';[1] and of the sculptures of Moore it is just as true that they *say* something as that it is, in every case, the stone which says it.

Every work of art, I admit, is an 'embodiment' if the word be taken to mean a deep, indivisible fusion of all that is there in the work; but all this blending is, in my view, subsidiary. Though admittedly necessary, it only *makes for* the emergence of art; and if the work is finally aesthetic, it is only because of its ability to invite and hold disinterested attention; or, because of its expressiveness.

Reid may be right in insisting that music does not *express* excitement or relaxation if the word is taken to mean 'detach from the heard sounds'. But he is wrong in suggesting that (some) music simply *has* the qualities in question, if the 'having' referred to is mere containment. I am not sure if *all* good music can be said to be essentially expressive, but there *is* a kind of soulful music which does not merely have, but *seems to teem with feeling*; and to such music as contemplated[2] the word 'expressive' would be clearly apt, and 'embodiment', quite irrelevant.

It is, however, not merely cases of actual art, but some valid emphases in Reid's own view that make me question his choice of 'embodiment'. I may put the matter thus:

Our concern, here, is with *the aesthetic* in art. *This* is revealed only in actual aesthetic experience. So, Reid rightly insists, in our quest for key aesthetic concepts we have to keep close to the *fact* of direct contemplation of art. Such contemplation, or at least its 'moment of . . . achievement', is 'natural . . . absorption in the fullness of artistic meaning'.[3] But if this is so, and if it is proper, as it obviously is, to hold that the knowledge of art and 'aesthetic testing' are (or involve) a kind of 'indwelling',[4] should not art be credited with a built-in openness in relation to 'the discriminating percipient'?[5] We can only say 'yes', but then, this 'openness' must be *directly* provided for in a concept which claims to be

---

[1] *MA*, p. 108.
[2] As against our *explaining* why the music appeals.
[3] *MA*, p. 88. (My italics.)
[4] *Ibid.*, pp. 220, 234.
[5] *Ibid.*, p. 85.

pivotal in aesthetics. Does 'embodiment' do this, and is not 'expression' *in this respect* preferable?

This mere wonder, however, is hardly enough. In our critical concern with what is expressive, its relation to the percipient is not the only line of enquiry. 'Expressive *how*' and 'expressive of *what*', the manner and the content of expression, these are here just as proper approaches to thought as 'expressive *to*'. But, I must keep within the limits, and in accordance with the *present* concern of this essay (which is simply to meet one objection to 'expression') only the following may here be said about the 'content'[1] of expression:

It is true that, as Reid insists, no critical language is quite adequate to *the fact of art as directly contemplated*—a 'fact' which is complex and yet without distinctions—but this is the understood negation to which *all* critical talk about[2] art is, in principle, subject. It is no special barrier to the language of expression; and if we only bear it in mind, quite generally, as we distinguish in words the life-contents that a work 'expresses', we keep to the 'fact' in idea, even though in speech we move away from it. It is by no means very difficult to remember that whatever life-meanings 'critical' dissection now lays open to view were, in aesthetic contemplation, all 'felt' as accents in (or of) a complex, individual whole.

(2) From the viewpoint of 'content', however, there is another protest which Reid makes pointedly:

' "expression" suggests, at least in some of its uses, events which had some sort of complete existence before they were expressed and became known in expression, whereas the aesthetic meaning which is embodied has no complete existence till it is born in embodiment.'[3]

Now here too, I fear, Reid takes sides. Of embodiment he speaks in relation to its 'aesthetic meaning'; but *expression* he considers in its 'non-aesthetic' uses. Some of these uses of the

---

[1] The question as to the *manner* of expression is being wholly left out. It is, in my view, too intricate to admit of a summary account.
[2] 'About', not 'of', as Reid points out. *MA*, p. 217.   [3] *Ibid.*, p. 78.

word certainly suggest the complete existence of content even before 'expression'; but so does 'embodiment' in its everyday meanings. We speak freely of souls as embodied or of virtue made visible in action or character. But in no such case do we think embodiment *makes* content.

Alternatively, if 'expression' too is taken in its special aesthetic uses, it may not at all suggest the complete existence of any content before (its) expression. To Langer, for instance, what is expressive is an *apparition*; and of this, she insists, *all* 'elements' are created. What the expressive apparition says, *its* import, is quite new substance.

I think the only *clear* 'superiority' of 'embodiment' over 'expression' is that in meaning it is closer to materialness. *Theories* of expression do not all underrate the material in art, but expression as a *word* does not suggest concreteness as directly as the rival word does.

Does this defect of the word permeate Langer's *theory* of art as a kind of expression? Reid thinks it does, but, let us see:

(3) The protest to which we now turn aims at Langer's 'ghostly' language. Reid complains that words like 'apparition', 'virtual' and 'illusory' belie the great value of art's material bases.

Now, the question here is about the meaning of some words. So we have to see how they have been used. Reid himself refers freely to Langer's *Problems of Art*,[1] but, where his purpose is directly critical, instead of citing her words as they occur in the book he merely picks them and weaves them into his own running comments, making them appear as manifest warrant for the protest being made. Consider, for instance, what he says about 'apparition':

'The distinction of "apparition", though legitimate, is a conceptual distinction—and as conceptual must be opposed to the "material". But this does not imply that the conceptual distinctions stand for *separate* ontological objects, that the

---

[1] S. K. Langer, *Problems of Art*, Routledge & Kegan Paul, London, 1957. (In all subsequent references to this book I have used the abbreviation *PA*, instead of the full title.)

virtual image of the dance ("a display of interacting forces", etc.) is something *cut off* from the motions of the dancers ('People running around and twisting their bodies').[1]

The charge is that Langer *separates* the material from the aesthetic, from 'apparition' or the 'virtual' art-image. Her words here are given within brackets, but let us see them now in their original context:

'In watching a dance, you do not see what is physically before you—*people running around or twisting their bodies*; what you see is *a display of interacting forces* . . . forces . . . which . . . are not the physical forces of the dancer's muscles . . . A dance is an apparition of active powers, a dynamic image . . . The more perfect the dance, the less we see its actualities . . . The virtual dynamic image . . . (as) a work of art is a composition of tensions and resolutions. . . .'[2]

Now, the beginning of this passage indeed seems queer. If in watching a dance I do not see what is physically before me, what do I *watch*? What *is* a dance *without* bodily movements?

The point of such questions is, however, merely apparent. It arises by ignoring the overall sense, for the key word here is 'physically'. I get the real meaning thus:

When does a dance strike me as *mere physical movement*? Obviously, when I do not follow it as a work of art at all.[3] In such a case, all that I see is someone 'running around'. Conversely, when I respond to the dance as required—i.e. aesthetically—I do not see *mere* physical movement. This is, in my view, the simple meaning here. Langer does not say (how could she?) that in contemplating a dance as art we do not *at all* see the danseuse and her movements, but only that we do not see merely bodily movement of the everyday kind. What is seen (merely) *physically* before us is one thing; what is apprehended aesthetically is quite another. 'People running

---

[1] *MA*, p. 84. (My italics.)

[2] *PA*, pp. 5–8. (My italics.) *These* are the words around which Reid builds his protest.

[3] This really happened when I first saw a ballet. I only *saw* movement.

around or twisting their bodies' in daily life surely do not describe patterns or keep to chosen rhythm.

And what exactly do I here see aesthetically? Obviously 'a display of interacting forces'; for, this is what dancing as an art truly is. Does this 'display' exclude the dancer's bodily movements? No, it does not; and it cannot. But the turns and glides are here all so organised, transfiguring actualities,[1] and the unity worked up is itself so significant—because of the rhythmic tensions and 'resolutions' that characterise it—that movement as merely physical is nowhere seen.

But the dancer's own figure, does *it* not remain visible throughout? Certainly, it does; but never merely as it actually is. Slender, bony fingers here at once make for some effect, which may be that of a bloom or sparkle or of mere postural invitingness. In two leading forms of Indian classical dance, *Bharat Natyam* and *Orissi*, even the basic posture is markedly different from the way a person normally stands; and, what is more, it is so beautiful[2] in itself that it does not at all allow the mind to think of *any* everyday posture. Conversely, whenever the posture lapses into a purely normal bearing—say, on the breathless completion of a hectic rhythmic pattern by an average *Kathak*[3] dancer—'the work of art breaks, the creation fails'.[4] In such cases, I may add, when the pattern is *being danced*, physical power may seem directly manifest, instead of being 'used up'[5] and swallowed in the 'dance'; whereupon what remains to be seen is mere 'gymnastics and arrangements',[6] and the aesthetic at once disappears.

Langer, I conclude, does not 'cut off' the 'dance' from actual movements. She only means that here they are not seen in themselves. The 'dance' assimilates them; and in so far as (on Reid's own view) 'assimilation and transformation does

---

[1] *PA*, p. 6.
[2] 'Beautiful' certainly in the case of *Orissi*, and at least striking in our other styles.
[3] *Kathak* is the classical dance of *North* India.   [4] *PA*, p. 10.   [5] *PA*, p. 10.
[6] *Ibid*. It *is* true to say that 'the more perfect the dance, the less we see its actualities' (*Ibid*, p. 6), assuming, of course, that we make a *trained* audience. Dancers in India wear the most gorgeous dresses; yet, after the recital, the really knowledgeable in our audiences hardly remember anything about the dancer's dress if she has danced really well.

not mean annulment or elimination',[1] I fail to see any point in the 'protest'.

In relation to painting, the objection in question may be met as follows:

Considered as an art-image, a picture is an *apparition*, in the sense that it is 'a piece of purely visual space ... nothing but a vision'.[2] From this single idea, that the picture is meant only to be seen, two other concepts emerge. First, in so far as it 'exists only for perception', a picture is a *virtual* entity, quite unlike actual things which can be used for practical purposes;[3] and, second, because it is utterly different from actual space,[4] the purely visual space that a picture is may be said to be *illusory*. Langer explains:

'To call the art-image illusory is simply to say that it is not material; it is not cloth *and* paint-smooches, but space organised by balanced shapes with dynamic relations. . . .'[5]

Here, the key-word is 'and'; and the meaning simply is that a picture is not a merely additive (or 'material') unity of canvas and pigments. Langer would readily agree that a Van Gogh picture cannot be rightly contemplated unless we attend to its 'vibrant paint-smooches' too,[6] but she would hasten to add that if we regard them aesthetically we do not perceive the 'smooches' as mere marks on the canvas. Surely, 'one does not see a picture as a piece of spotted canvas'.[7] Actual space merely 'contains' things and movement. Pictorial space is, on the other hand, organic; it at once appears made by the shapes and volumes it displays, as their interactive unity. This is why pigment and canvas, as *distinguishable* materials, are not to be found in pictorial space.[8]

It should now be easy to understand the remark on music which troubles Reid:

---

[1] *MA*, p. 165. [2] *PA*, p. 28. [3] cf. *Ibid.*, p. 5.

[4] Unlike the purely visual space of a picture, actual space has real depth and acoustical properties.

[5] *PA*, p. 24. (My italics.) [6] cf. *MA*, p. 85. [7] *PA*, p. 127.

[8] The moment we distinguish them, through an effort of analytical attention, pictorial space disappears, and what remains to be seen is the merely 'additive' space of actual life. cf. *Ibid.*, p. 28.

'In artistic production, the composer's materials must be completely swallowed up *in* the illusion they create. . . .'[1]

Langer here speaks of that thorough assimilation of 'materials' in music which makes for its 'elements'—sonorous forms that *seem* to move, and are *therefore* called 'illusory'. It is true that every musical flow builds upon some actual tones and duration; and that the way we perceive these 'materials' vitally determines how we react to the music aesthetically. What is more, they can all be distinguished by an analytical effort of attention. This is the essence of the matter, if the musical flow is to seem truly aesthetic the 'materials' must all conduce to it with inextricable jointness, and directly, that is, *without at all appearing to assert themselves against the flow*. This is what it really means to say that in music its 'materials' are 'swallowed up'.[2]

It would be wrong to regard such talk as mere rhetoric. I think it is *demanded* by the question: how is the sensuous related to the aesthetic in actual contemplation of art? To say simply that the two are compresent[3] or inseparable will just not do. It would be a merely external way of speaking and take no notice at all of the deep, inner harmony of the work which may even seem *self*-active in the case of occurrent arts.[4] Nor can we say that the material here overpowers the ideal; for, the aesthetic object is no mere thing. The only way open is to say that here the aesthetic (or the virtual) *swallows up* the material; or, from the other side, that the materials disappear *in* the aesthetic. This is precisely the logic of Langer's terminology;

---

[1] *PA*, p. 39. (My italics.)

[2] Attention may here be invited to a detail of practice which sometimes disfigures North Indian classical music without outraging its grammar. The vocalist chooses to sing 'in' an excessively slow and expansive rhythm-cycle, simply to show off his ability to deal with difficult rhythm. In such cases, the exaggerated slowness at once protrudes and makes the singing seem flabby and laboured.

[3] According to Reid himself, the 'side-by-side' image would here be as improper as the 'either-or' one. (*MA*, p. 84.)

[4] As to how, in the region of North Indian classical vocal music, the suggestion of self-activation is, as a rule, actually there in good compositions, see my article: 'The Fabric of Aamad—A Study of Form and Flow in Hindustani Music' included in *Journal of the Sangit Natak Akademi* (New Delhi, No. 16, April–June 1970, pp. 38–42).

and her positive view undeniably is that the arts *use* the 'materials', 'to create something over and above what is physically there . . .'.[1] I repeat, in no case does she sever the material from the aesthetic: she urges only that it is quite transmuted in the latter.

(4) Of the remaining arguments of Reid I shall now deal with two: first with the one by which he opposes the idea that art expresses the *forms* of life-feeling, and then with that brief bout of poetic criticism which (he thinks) warrants his choice of embodiment, rather than expression, as the right word for creation *as completed*. The first is a basic, though general, objection to Langer's view; and the second seeks to illustrate how poetry is embodiment.

(*a*) The essence of the former is provided by this extract:

'If all feelings or complexes of feeling are feelings—*of*, are concrete and particular, how can their "forms" be other than concrete and particular too? And if so, how can the "form" of one kind of concrete feeling or complex of feelings, the feelings of "life", be projected into another form, the form of art?'[2]

Now, the argument is here odd. Feelings, it is true, are all of them particular, but from this it does not follow that their 'forms' too must be particular, unless by *form* we understand the mere 'shape' or givenness, the psychological occupancy of a feeling as an event in experience. The word may instead be taken to mean the direct and non-relational *manner* of experiencing *any* content or object;[3] and in this sense we may well speak of the (general) 'form' of feeling[4] without hypostatis-

___

[1] *PA*, p. 4.
[2] *MA*, p. 61.
[3] Langer too speaks of feeling 'in the broad sense of whatever is felt . . .' (S. K. Langer. *Mind—An Essay on Human Feeling*, Johns Hopkins, Baltimore, 1967, Vol. I, p. 4). This is also in accord with Reid's own view that feeling is 'the *immediate* experience of everything that occurs in conscious psycho-physical life'. (*MA*, p. 148—My italics.) I take the word 'immediate' to mean 'direct and non-discursive or non-relational'. Langer, I may add, accepts Professor Sheffer's idea of 'unlogicised' mental life. *PA*, p. 125.
[4] Or of 'how (all) feeling rises . . . tangles or sinks . . .'. S. K. Langer: *Mind—An Essay on Human Feeling, op. cit.* p. 64. Reid himself finds it useful to speak of 'dynamic elements' though, as real, they are always found 'involved in . . . reactions to life-situations'. (*MA*, p. 164.)

ing it. Thus, though every feeling is as a total fact particular, it does not seem forced to speak of the rise and fall of feeling generally.

(b) In merely seeing this, however, we are given no direct clue to what 'the *fact* of creative art'[1] really is, an expression of some kind or artistic embodiment. To this final arbiter in all such argument Reid here turns as follows:

It may be true to say that the artist, say a poet, *begins* by 'expressing' his felt awareness of things, ideas and truths in terms of words,[2] but this 'is only part of the story. The other half . . . of central importance'[3] is that such words are here used and in such a way that a rich and fresh unity is brought into being. The poem that results is 'new embodied meaning',[4] not a mere conjunction, but an interpenetration of words and what they suggest. The 'meaning', in so far as it is now inseparable from the perceptible 'weight and rhythm of sounding words',[5] acquires a concreteness which it did not have before 'embodiment', so that it is itself now really new or 'emergent'; and the words do not merely convey,[6] but seem *charged with meaning*. 'The "sound" and the "sense" are (here) aesthetically, completely inseparable.'[7] This embodied single- ness is (necessarily) belied when we say that the poem *expresses* a 'meaning'. Though initially admissible, the language of 'expression' is untrue to the net embodiment—the complete poem—and is therefore merely 'provisional and incom- plete'.[8]

The issue here involved is clear. Can 'expressiveness' somehow be regarded as the net, real character of a poem? Now the answer, I suggest, would turn on what precisely we here understand by 'a poem', an 'object' of aesthetic contem- plation *or* of critical understanding.

The *judgement* that in good poetry 'the "sound" and the "sense" are, aesthetically, completely inseparable' is a finding of critical analysis. It *is* true as analysis; but, in so far as it involves distinctions, it is not quite true—upon Reid's own

---

[1] *MA*, p. 27. (My italics.) [2] *Ibid.*, p. 98. [3] *Ibid.*, p. 98. [4] *Ibid.*, p. 98.
[5] *Ibid.*, p. 158. [6] *Ibid.*, p. 159. [7] *Ibid.*, p. 99. [8] *Ibid.*

general view—to the poem as aesthetically contemplated. I admit that *all* talk 'about' art is subject to this inadequacy; but, and this is what I here wish to emphasise, the judgement that a poem is 'embodied' meaning, in virtue of its indissoluble sound-sense unity, or an 'embodiment' in the sense of an 'object' that is directly *before* us, is not maximally close to the poem *as contemplated*, or, as Reid himself would put it, to the 'operation' of embodiment.

I may refer here to some of his own truthful remarks on the extract from *Samson Agonistes*:

'Feeling carries the imagination to the point of identity with the tragic realisation as it flows relentlessly along. . . . We know the poignancy of the situation Milton is depicting through our participating feelings as we could not know it by detached intellectual cognition alone.'[1]

Now, I ask, if the overall manner of experience is here that of feeling, and what is 'known' (as felt), the poignancy of the situation; and if, further, the focus of attention is on the *distal* feelings,[2] how exactly is it wrong to say that, as it seems to direct contemplation, *the poem* expresses[3] Samson's agony? Reid would of course object to the word 'expresses', but then, what other words shall we use? Presented 'before' us? No; Reid himself here cannot say 'yes'. For he holds, quite rightly, that 'the words do not just picture, or tell us about, Samson's agony: . . . we participate in it'. But if that is so, if the feeling that is 'shown' is at once felt by us, it is clearly truer to hold that, *as an aesthetic* object, a poem is expressive *to us* than to say that it is a sound-sense unity which is directly *before us*. What can persist in disturbing us here is only the old prejudice that all expression is a pressing-*out*.

Reid rightly insists that all talk about art has to keep close to the undivided fact of aesthetic experience. But from the viewpoint of this requirement it should be easy to see that critical

---

[1] *MA*, p. 159. [2] *Ibid.*
[3] 'Expresses' as a presentation that is felt, not as ejection from within.

admiration of the details of the way in which a poem is inly organised—say, of its sound-sense fusion—is not really *the point of transition* from embodiment as 'enjoyed' to embodiment as analysed. What comes earlier in the wake of aesthetic experience is simply the clear realisation that the work I contemplated seemed[1] imbued with some feeling, some semblance of life. Here, as remembrance, the 'fact' keeps visible; and though it is now seen (in the main) from the outside, its aroma persists, preventing the work from getting quite divided from the subject. This is what I mean by 'the point of transition'.

In our common talk about the two main forms of experience (immediate or felt and mediate or discursive) we tend to forget that the one can in fact be seen as dallying with, before actually becoming the other. Indeed, here in the *passage* from aesthetic 'indwelling' to the extraversion of theory of which I speak, we half objectify the 'fact'; and, without quitting it, just get set on the road to analysis. The work's felt charm is now on the wane, but it has not yet deserted us; and, by its very haunting recession, it fetters and feeds the 'how' of embodiment, or the urge to unravel the fabric of art.

III. EMBODIMENT AND THE ARTS

From the context of its opposition to 'expression' I now turn to consider 'embodiment' in relation to the arts and 'genuine aesthetic experience'.[2] Of the arts which elude the grasp of 'embodiment', I choose some forms (and features) of the music of India.[3] The following brief remarks should here serve:

(a) Aesthetically, the best form of our vocal music is *alāpa*.[4] Like every other kind of Indian classical music, it too

---

[1] 'Seemed' as merely 'seemed to *be*', not as implying a contrast with truth or reality.　　　　　　　　　　　　　　　　　　　　　　　[2] *MA*, p. 225.

[3] In this article, wherever I speak of Indian music, I have its *North* Indian forms in mind. Generally, however, what I have said on the subject is applicable to the entire classical music of India.

[4] *Alāpa* is effective singing (and playing too) *without* rhythmic 'accompaniment' and language.

has to conform to a *rāga* or melody type. But, as rightly contemplated, a good *alāpa* recital is (on the whole) neither 'expressive' nor a merely objective unity of form and content, but a musical atmosphere—'one intense diffusion, one serene Omnipresence'[1]—which seems so *dis*embodied from the plural details of the *rāga*, and suffuses our being with such overwhelming completeness that a conscious judgement as to the propriety and fullness of *rāga*-rendering is made only when the spell has weakened or disappeared. The best word for such an ethereal, yet compellingly effective 'apparition' is, in my view, 'presence' in Marcel's sense.

(*b*) Indian music is 'occurrent' not merely because we see it *being made* (by the artist), but because, by virtue of an inner feature of composition or rendering, it may appear to be *making itself.* The latter suggestion is, in general, thus manifest:

In small, intimate gatherings of knowledgeable listeners— where our artists, as a rule, feel freer to perform—the music does not merely occur 'before' us as a set, predictable movement, but grows directly in accordance with our response to it, which is often quite audible.[2] To say of such music that it 'embodies' significance would be only to miss its free, improvisatory character *which is here its manifest essence.*

(*c*) All this is clearer in the region of our rhythm.[3] Here, a solo recital which is not merely competent, but aesthetically admirable is one which throughout teems with suggestions of creative freedom and vitality. Thus, some patterns may end a little before *or* after the fixed location of the *sama*, the first beat of the cycle, not marking it directly—as is the common requirement[4]—but suggesting it by the very designed quality

---

[1] Shelley, *Epipsychidion.*

[2] The suggestion is not that the musician throughout performs with his eye on the audience, but only that a felt awareness of correct audience reactions vitally determines the growth and quality of his music.

[3] As to the propriety of the (Indian) view that rhythm is *an independent art*, see my article: 'Form and Content in Hindustani Rhythm' (*Sangit Natak, op. cit.*, No. 18, October–December 1970, pp. 5–19). The chief 'materials' of our rhythm are mnemonic syllables like *tā, dhā, dir, dir.* These are *never* used for any non-aesthetic purpose; in which respect, I think, rhythm excels music.

[4] Indian rhythm runs in cycles. The first beat, called *sama*, is doubly important. From it we set out, and to it we return, completing a round. The ability to come back

of the avoidance. One *can* speak of the coy, blushing quality or the ebullient self-assertiveness of such patterns, but in (or as) such 'forms of feeling' they do not *directly* appear; and though 'form' *is* here suggested by the drummer's very refusal to be merely correct,[1] the suggestion is, in the aesthetic contemplation of such patterns, throughout subject to our felt awareness of a sweet, flowing wilfulness.[2]

Even generally, in the execution of any pattern, the drummer may, with guarded abandon and distinct aesthetic gain, shorten or withhold one syllable or tarry at or displace another, against their set speed and location, without of course failing to mark or suggest the *sama*.[3] When the playing quickens, the drummer may unleash a torrent of patterns that climax at the *sama* brilliantly and are made to reach it variously. They are all themselves designed, it is true; and they keep to a measure. But the playing as it seems, directly and on the whole, is an upsurge of the very spirit of creative freedom, a flooding of embankments, as it were; and to speak of it as 'embodied meaning' would be to interject, quite wrongly, the attitude of analysis, and with it a suggestion of inertness, into the undivided dynamics of actual aesthetic experience. One might as well say of a waterfall that it 'embodies' a flow or is 'embodiment'.

IV. TOWARDS A NEW CONCEPT

Can any *new* word be chosen to cover all art as contemplated? I think it is possible. My word is: *presence*.[4] No single word, it

---

to the first beat with split second accuracy *and in a well-designed way* is a normal requirement. Avoiding it designedly makes for added beauty.

[1] cf. Stephen Spender, *World within World*, Hamilton, London, 1951, pp. 313–14.

[2] I am not sure if Langer's view is here quite transcended. 'Feeling' seems usable, but 'form' would be untrue to the experience in question.

[3] The basic rhythm-cycle and the patterns flowing along with it—or, for a brief while, away from it—but in every case appearing to manifest its vitality and measure; this is, in general, the content of a solo exposition of Indian rhythm. The overall requirement is due observance of the speed and extent of the rhythm-cycle chosen. The *way* this demand is met can, however, vary infinitely.

[4] I borrow the word from Marcel. (See Chapter IX (pp. 251–68) of the first volume, 'Reflection and Mystery', of his *The Mystery of Being*, Gateway Ed., H. R. Company, Chicago, Illinois, 1960.)

is true, can meet all the requirements of a key aesthetic concept, but, as I shall presently argue, 'presence' is preferable to both expression and embodiment. Art, I believe, is the creative invocation of (what is, in principle) a presence. But, let me explain:

A work of art is the result of creative activity. It *can* become a 'presence' if it is rightly contemplated. But in actual contemplation the work *is* a presence. Here, what is needed is just disinterested attention, no creation as ordinarily understood.

The word 'creative' here provides, by virtue of its opposition to what is merely made, three important truths: the 'emergent' quality and unity (or form) of art, and the interplay of process and product in creation. 'Invocation' suggests the transcendent, almost magical quality[1] of the work. To invoke is to call up a being or an influence that is 'higher'[2] or benevolent. Again, as in the case of invoking a deity or its blessings, what is invoked is not a mere thing: it is a *presence*, as Marcel understands it. In so far as he uses the word not only for persons, but for affections like sickness, we may take it to mean not mere objects, far or near, but what is given *and is at once a felt influence*. So, in speaking of art as a 'presence' we provide, as required, for the immediacy of the aesthetic object, without any suggestion of ghostliness; and also without turning the 'object' into something that is merely *before* us, a suggestion which infects all talk of embodiment. Again, in relation to the form of the literary arts, essentially *non-*sensuous, 'invocation' and 'presence' seem clearly superior. They do not here need the refinements of meaning which 'embodiment' clearly does.[3]

I may here make it clear why I prefer *presence* to embodiment. The word quite fits the presentational quality of the aesthetic object; is true, as analogy rather than as analysis, also

---

[1] See: *MA*, pp. 81, 88–9. Magic, we may note, is concerned with the presential side of things.

[2] The idea of invoking a *higher* being or influence goes well with some of Reid's own words here: 'ladder', 'climb', 'upper'. *Ibid.*, p. 34.

[3] Reid himself sees it clearly that, if it is to become relevant to the literary arts too, the word 'embody' has to be '*stretched* to include the whole range of what we can imagine'. (*MA*, 78—My italics.)

to the non-discursive idiom of art experience; and thus duly answers our need for a first order word. 'Embodiment', contrarily, is 'a complex analysis'[1] of the aesthetic; and so does not in truth meet Reid's own express requirement that all talk about art has to keep maximally close to the aesthetic *as revealed*. It can, of course, be here protested that 'presence' by itself does nothing to *explain what* art is. But, to this my answer would be that if, as is necessary, we offer the required explanation without ignoring *how* all art appears in actual aesthetic experience, some of the words that we use in explaining must only insist on the basic manner of all such experience; and that in the definition I have proposed, whereas 'creation' and 'invocation' suggest ideas to understanding, *presence* keeps us mindful of the experienced singleness of what in theory we must analyse. To speak of something that is at once a felt influence is surely somewhat vague; but, by its very refusal to *mark* the other term, it seems precise speech for experience which lacks distinctions.[2] Reid's own dictum is hardly *this* accurate. A distinction denied is at once made use of; and the utterance that art is embodiment as the *in*separable union of content and medium does not quite capture, though it certainly asserts, the realised undividedness of art.

A *presence*, I may add, is not 'a sort of vaporised object',[3] but an 'object' which influences us. *This* would be my answer to the protest that 'presence' is too weak a word for solid arts like sculpture and architecture; and it should serve, quite independently of such facts as the tendency in modern sculpture to look upon surface as mere skin. As for architecture, must not a palace (as art) impress us at once with its majesty; and a church, directly with its holiness?[4]

Finally, in so far as a presence is said to *radiate* influence or to *vibrate* with meaning, we at once meet the requirement that (its) 'meaning' is neither to be separated from nor kept merely confined to the work of art. Such a way of speaking implies not

---

[1] *MA*, p. 87.   [2] cf. *Ibid.*, p. 35.   [3] Marcel, *op. cit.*, p. 255.
[4] cf. Lewis Mumford's article: 'Symbol and Function in Architecture' (included in L. A. Jacobus (Ed.), *Aesthetics and the Arts*, McGraw Hill, New York, 1968, p. 265).

only that 'meaning' emanates from within the work, but that it flows freely towards those who are open and eligible. A presence is received, felt, or 'gathered to oneself'.[1] The last phrase, specially, is in one respect welcome. It tempers overemphasis, so common, on the *outgoing* character of aesthetic experience,[2] and all such words seem generally truer to art *as contemplated* than 'symbol', 'embodiment', 'meaning', 'individual', 'seizing' or 'grasping the meaning of', which all smack of things and thought. To be subject to a 'presence' is at once to be *permeable* to it. It is no active dealing with a thing or person for any practical end. Yet, as experience, it is vital and rich. In its remoteness from art theory the direct contemplation of art is indeed 'a time to be silent';[3] but, as felt from within, it is an *active* self-opening and an inward quickening. At the same time, whatever be the precise form of this 'activity'—a passage from words to feeling imagery or the indrawn sweetness of intense musicality—it is always a disinterested self-subjugation to the other.[4] It is *this*, rather than any abstract consideration of value, that makes the 'object' contemplated, Art or Nature, always seem 'higher' than the man contemplating it; and perhaps it is only as this humility of self-opening to what is felt as benign, and not merely useful, that a genuine element of the aesthetic (as revealed) may be said to permeate all true religiousness.

[1] Marcel, *op. cit.*, p. 255.   [2] cf. *MA*, p. 261.   [3] *Ibid.*, p. 89.
[4] This is communion, not mere communication. (cf. Marcel, *op. cit.*, pp. 252, 255.)

Chapter 11

VARIABLES AND QUANTIFICATION[1]

by

PRANAB KUMAR SEN
Jadavpur University

How to interpret the quantifiers—the formulas like '$(x)\,Fx$' and '$(Ex)\,Fx$'? This is a question to which philosophers have been trying hard to find a satisfactory answer during the last few years. One answer to the question has been offered by Ruth Barcan Marcus, and another, by W. V. Quine; and, ever since, they have been debating on it. Others have joined in, some supporting the one, and some, the other; and in spite of conciliatory moves taken by some moderationists, it seems unlikely that they would ever come to any agreement.

The present paper can be regarded as a contribution to this debate; but it is inspired by the idea that the debate, so far, has been somewhat ineffective due to an insufficient recognition of the simple truth that the idea of quantification is inseparably bound up with that of a variable. Thus, in this paper, I try first to be clear about what a variable is, and then try to find out what can be done with a variable by way of quantification. The most important result that I obtain is that there is no single idea of quantification for there is no single idea of a variable.

In the first part of the paper I try to develop clearly the idea of a variable as a *place marker*, and, along with it, the idea of a

[1] This paper was written during my stay in Oxford as a Commonwealth Academic Staff Fellow for the year 1972–3. I am greatly indebted to Mr J. L. Mackie with whom I had the privilege of working at Oxford. He not only encouraged me to write something on the subject, but also discussed the paper with me in all its details. (I am also grateful to the editor for inviting me to contribute to the present volume.)

sentential function as a *sentence frame*. In the second part, I try to explain how sentences could be obtained from sentence frames by quantification and some other means. In the third part, I try to show that some accepted ways of obtaining sentences from sentence frames are not really permissible. In the fourth and last part, I sum up the results, and explain their effect on the Marcus–Quine controversy as well as on the question of ontological commitment which has been supposed to be inextricably connected with it.

I am aware that there are many questions which I have not discussed. The most important of them is that of quantification in modal contexts, but I believe that the things I have said here would provide me with a firmer basis for talking about them elsewhere.

I

Sentence
We begin with the idea of a sentence as a meaningful sequence or concatenation of words as being intuitively clear. The following is a simple example of a sentence made famous by logicians:

Socrates is human.

It is a sequence or concatenation of the three words 'Socrates', 'is' and 'human', and, no doubt, it is meaningful (or significant).

Sentence Fragment
We want now to introduce the idea of a sentence fragment. Consider the following items:

(*a*) Socrates
(*b*) is
(*c*) human
(*d*) Socrates is
(*e*) is human
(*f*) Socrates human

Each of these items can be taken to be a sentence fragment—
to be a fragment of the sentence 'Socrates is human'. However,
a mere look at (*a*) is not sufficient to enable us to decide
whether or not it is a sentence fragment. It may as well be a
name occuring in a list. The same is true of (*b*). It could be
taken, for example, as an *autonomous* use of the word 'is' designed to show what a particular form of the verb 'be' (or 'to be')
is. Similarly, 'human' *could* be taken to be a name of a species,
and its occurrence might be taken to be a part of a list again.
On the other hand, (*d*), (*e*) and (*f*) are more clearly, i.e. less
ambiguously, sentence fragments.

Sentence Fragments with Place Markers
We can now introduce the idea of a sentence fragment with
place markers. If one realises that (*a*)–(*f*) are sentence fragments, one would also realise that a whole sentence—though
not necessarily the sentence 'Socrates is human'—can be
formed out of each of them by supplementation. But neither of
the sentence fragments (*a*)–(*f*) gives us any clue as to how this
supplementation is to be made. It is not however difficult to
devise a way of removing this deficiency. We may use sequences of dots and/or hyphens as follows:

(*a*1) Socrates. . . . . .
(*a*2) Socrates. . . . . .
(*a*3) Socrates. . . ---
(*b*1) . . . is . . .
(*b*2) . . . is ---
(*c*1) . . . . . . human
(*c*2) . . . --- human
(*d*1) Socrates is . . .
(*e*1) . . . is human
(*f*1) Socrates . . . human

It is clear that (*a*1)–(*f*1) give some indication as to the manner
in which supplementations are to be made to form sentences
out of the given sentence fragments. But it should be noted
also that, in this respect, some of them are more explicit or

determinate than some others. Thus (a1) does indicate that the sentence fragment is to be supplemented by adding something *after* 'Socrates', but it does not indicate anything about the number of items, i.e. words, which are to be added; for it contains just one continuous sequence of dots. This is done by (a2): it indicates that *two* words are to be added after 'Socrates' to complete the sentence. But (a2), in its turn, is vague on whether the two places are to be filled by the same word or by different words. (a3) is more suggestive in this respect. It suggests, through a sequence of dots followed by a sequence of hyphens, that the places are to be filled by different words.

In one respect, at least, all the constructions (a1)–(f1) are vague. None of them suggests *by itself* anything about the *kind* of words which are to be added to fill in the blanks, i.e. places marked by a sequence of dots or hyphens. For all that they indicate, by themselves, the blanks could be filled in by the same kind of words, or by different kinds of words. But when *we* want to form sentences out of these sentence fragments, we do not think of filling in all the blanks by the same kind of words; we clearly realise that some of them, at least, are to be filled in by different kinds of words. If, for example, the first blank in (c2) is to be filled in by a *name*, say 'Socrates', then, we realise, the second cannot be equally filled in by a name. But how do we realise it? Not by an inspection of the place markers, the sequence of dots or hyphens, but by general considerations about forming sentences as *significant* sequences of words. Once we realise that we are expected to form sentences, we are prepared to draw upon our knowledge of how sentences are to be formed. What is important to realise is that this is *not* indicated by the place markers themselves.

Nature and Function of Place Markers

At this point, it would be advisable to try to be clear about the idea of a place marker—about what a place marker is and what it is not. At the end of the last section we have said that the place markers do not indicate by themselves whether the different places marked by them are to be filled by the same kind or by different kinds of words. In fact, strictly speaking, they do not *by themselves* indicate even that they could be replaced by words to form sentences; in other words, *they do not declare themselves to be place markers*. Possibly, they do not declare anything at all in any sense; and the reason for *that* may be that they are meaningless. But *we* take them as place markers; and we do so by virtue of a *convention* which is current to the effect that a sequence of dots or hyphens should indicate a blank in a sentence.

Now, if it is the case that the sentence fragments like ($c2$) are deficient in that they are vague as to the kinds of words which are to be written in the blanks in them, then we may try to remove this deficiency by introducing *further conventions*. These further conventions would consist in (i) classifying different kinds of words, and then (ii) allocating different (styles of) place markers to them, e.g. dots to names, and hyphens to adjectives.

We may now ask whether the place markers have any meaning. Do the dots and hyphens (and any other kinds of symbols, if they are introduced) have any meaning at all? Do they have any reference? It seems not; for they are neither names, nor definite descriptions, even although some of them could be replaced by those which are. Do they have any sense? Not this either. Nor do they stand for anything in any other semantical way.

No doubt, *we* mean something by them, in the sense that we intend to indicate, by use of place markers—and of place markers of different styles—(i) that a sentence may be formed by writing words in their place, and (ii) that such and such kinds of words are to be chosen for such and such places marked by the place markers.

Are then the place markers meaningless marks? Yes and no. Yes, because *they* do not have any meaning, like the words in the sentence fragments have. No, because *we* do mean, and sometimes we mean a lot, by their use. They are not meaningless marks in the sense that they have a purpose, or better, they are used with a purpose.

One may argue that even although '. . .' does not have any meaning *all by itself*, it does have some meaning in the background of some conventions. Is it not the case that all meanings are equally convention-bound? But there is a big difference. What are the conventions regarding '. . .'? First, the conventions assign a role to '. . .' in larger expressions like '. . . is human'. Second, they are clearly to the effect that '. . .' does not have any function in isolation. Third, and most important, these conventions only set out how it is to be *eliminated or discharged, in favour of,* something (other than it) *which* is meaningful. Conventions in the case of words like 'human' are not recipes for *discharging* those words; they are designed to *confer meaning* on them. In brief, making room or marking place for something meaningful is not itself a mode for being meaningful.

Another Look at Sentence Fragments with Place Markers
If the place markers do not have any meaning then it seems the sentence fragments (together with them) are also devoid of meaning. Thus the following does not seem to have any meaning at all:

$$(e1) \ . \ . \ . \ \text{is human}$$

It is quite clear, however, that (i) something meaningful can be obtained from it, and that (ii) when we look at it, we realise, by virtue of the conventions which may be in existence, *how* this could be done (perhaps, by writing a name in place of the place marker).

The reasoning which leads one to the conclusion that $(e1)$ is devoid of meaning may be as follows: It is only a complete sentence which can be said to have any meaning (in the strict sense). But $(e1)$ is not a complete sentence. Therefore it is meaningless.

But there is something disquieting about the first premise of this argument. I am not willing to commit myself (wholeheartedly) to the (holistic) view that everything short of a sentence is devoid of meaning. So I would prefer to argue that (*e*1) does not have any meaning in a different way as follows: '. . . is human' is meaningless for the kind of reason which makes 'Toovy is heavy' meaningless. One need not argue that 'Toovy is heavy' is meaningless because it is not a complete sentence. The quite obvious reason why it is not meaningful is that it contains the meaningless word 'Toovy' (assuming that it does not have any meaning). In a similar way one may argue, plausibly, that '. . . is human' is meaningless because it contains the meaningless '. . .'. (Of course, we cannot say '. . . is human' contains a meaningless word, for '. . .' is not a *word*. But we can say that (*e*1) is meaningless because it contains a meaningless part.)

When we say that '. . . is human' is meaningless, we do not ignore the fact that it contains some meaningful parts. We only emphasise the difference between containing a meaningful part and being meaningful. If we feel a resistance to saying that '. . . is human' is meaningless, we feel so perhaps because we tend to take 'meaningless' to be synonymous with '*entirely* devoid of meaning', and this latter with 'containing *nothing* meaningful at all', and contrast '. . . is human' with, say, '. . . is labala'.

However, the question of meaningfulness is so important that I shall have to return to it later.

Some Stipulations

It would be convenient at this point to make certain stipulations about the use of some terms in connection with the ideas which we have introduced so far.

(i) Expressions like 'Socrates', 'Socrates is', 'is', 'is human,' 'Socrates human' would be called 'sentence fragments' as they have been called so far.

(ii) '. . .', '---', etc., would be called 'place markers'.

(iii) Expressions like 'Socrates . . . human', '. . . is ---', '. . . is human', i.e. sentence fragments with place markers would be called 'sentence frames'.

(iv) A sentence which can be obtained from a sentence

frame by writing words in place of place markers would be called a 'substitution instance' of that sentence frame. Obviously, the same sentence may be a substitution instance of a number of different sentence frames. 'Socrates is human' is a substitution instance of all the sentence frames from ($a1$) to ($f1$).

(v) A sentence frame, in relation to the sentences which are its substitution instances would be called a *sentence frame of* or *for* those sentences. It is obvious that a sentence frame can be a sentence frame of an indefinite number of sentences. For example, the sentence frame '. . . is human' is a sentence frame of all the following sentences:

> Socrates is human.
> Russell is human.
> Einstein is human.

It would be worth while to note that what we have called 'place markers' may also be called 'variables', and what we have called 'sentence frames' may also be called 'sentential functions' or 'open sentences'. But, as I shall try to bring out later, these are not the only ways in which the terms 'variable', 'sentential function', and 'open sentence' have been used.

Letters as Place Markers

We were trying above to be clear about the part which dot and hyphen sequences play in the construction of sentence frames. Now, we can decide to use letters from the same or differential alphabets instead of these sequences. Thus, instead of writing the sentence frame as '. . . is human', we may decide to write,

$$x \text{ is human.}$$

By this change we could get our sentence frames as follows:

($a1.1$) Socrates x	($c1.1$) x human
($a2.1$) Socrates $x\,x$	($c2.1$) $x\,y$ human
($a3.1$) Socrates $x\,y$	($d1.1$) Socrates is x
($b1.1$) x is x	($e1.1$) x is human
($b2.1$) x is y	($f1.1$) Socrates x human

Further, we can make this device of marking places by the help of letters more powerful by using different types of letters drawn either from the same or from different alphabets to mark places for different kinds of words. We may also try to be sensitive to the differences in syntactical (or semantical) category between different words. Thus we may choose lower case letters like x, y, and z to mark places for names, and capital letters like F, G, and H to mark those for adjectives.

There are some reasons for which we may opt for letters, rather than for sequences of dots or hyphens, as place markers. Some of these reasons are as follows:

(i) Different places in a sentence frame are more easily indicated by letters.

(ii) That different places in a sentence frame are to be filled by the *same* word is easily indicated by repeating the same letter.

(iii) That different places are to be, or may be, filled by different words is easily indicated by the use of different letters.

However, if we remember that there is no difference in function between, say, '. . .' and x, they being both place markers in *exactly the same sense*, we shall agree that everything said about '. . .' and other place markers is true of x, y, and all other letters used to the same effect. We shall agree *also* that there is no difference between the sentence frames from $(a1)$ to $(f1)$ and those from $(a1.1)$ to $(f1.1)$. The most important things which can thus be carried over are as follows:

(i) Letters as place markers do not have any meaning; although it is true that if we are aware of the conventions determining their use then we should be able to tell what is to be done with them.

We should remember, *in particular*, that *they are not names*, either of single objects or of categories of objects. They are not even *ambiguous* names, as Russell so often suggests them to be. Note also that this is true not only of letters which mark places for adjectives or verbs, but also of those which mark places for *names*. *A place marker for a name is not another name.*

(ii) If place markers do not have any meaning then, as we have already argued, sentence frames do not have any meaning either. This remains true whether the place markers are sequences of dots (or hyphens) or letters chosen from alphabets. So e.g. '*x* is human' does not have any meaning.

But these precisely are the points which the use of letters as place markers tend to obscure. Letters look like words, particularly, like names (Mr *X*). So the use of letters may gradually lead a logician to hold views about place markers and sentence frames (perhaps under the more usual names of 'variables' and 'sentential functions') which he would never dream of accepting if he used only dots and hyphens as place markers. These remarks are made only to underline the importance of remembering the platitude that by merely opting for letters we do not, and cannot, confer any new character on place markers.

Illustrative Symbols

It will be instructive, at this point, to put the use of letters as place markers, or as variables in that sense, in contrast with another use of letters with which it can and, I believe, has been confused. This is the use of letters as *illustrative symbols*, to borrow a term from W. E. Johnson.[1]

Consider the following:

Let *p* stand for any proposition whatever.
Then either *p* is true or *p* is false.

Here *p* can be treated as a name, and possibly an ambiguous or generic name; and, as a consequence, the expression 'either *p* is true or *p* is false', with the foregoing stipulation 'Let *p*

[1] W. E. Johnson, *Logic*, Cambridge, 1921, Part II, Chapter III.
The letters which are used to denote 'arbitrarily selected individuals' in one particular application of the rule of Universal Instantiation, dubbed 'UI (arb.)' by Mackie, may be regarded as illustrative symbols in this sense. For this point, and for the whole subject of the use of different kinds of letters in logic see J. L. Mackie's excellent discussion in 'The Symbolising of Natural Deduction' (*Analysis*, Vol. XX, December, 1959).

stand for any proposition', can be regarded as a sentence rather than a sentence frame. As a sentence, it seems to express a truth, and indeed to be a possible formulation of the law of excluded middle.

To anticipate some of the points which we shall have to consider in detail later, one very important characteristic of an illustrative symbol, if what has been said is right, is that there cannot be any quantification over it. So, in contradistinction from what goes above, the following is not permissible:

Let p stand for any proposition whatever.
Then, *for all p*, either p is true or p is false.

One of the ways in which we may try to argue that this is not permissible is that, *when the stipulation is made*, p is already universally quantified, and so it does not make any sense to quantify it over again. But this way of putting the matter is not quite satisfactory, for it presupposes the use of p as a variable, while it is doubtful whether p has, in this context, any such use at all.

It seems, in fact, that the stipulation does not have the effect of quantifying over a variable but conferring (a peculiar kind of) namehood to a letter. So a more satisfactory way of arguing the point that quantification over illustrative symbols is not possible is this: Illustrative symbols *are* basically names, although a peculiar kind of names; so they are not variables, and *a fortiori* not free variables. As such, they are not available for quantification.

Thus it should be borne in mind that those who want to have variables for quantification cannot, at the same time, treat them as illustrative symbols. Possibly they are treating them as such when they are treating them as names, or, more cautiously, as ambiguous names.

Types of Place Markers
One important consequence of the idea of a place marker, as it has been expounded so far, is that there is *absolutely* no limit to the number of kinds or types of place markers that we may

H

have. There would be as many types of place markers as there are types of words. If the types of words, or, more philosophically, syntactical or semantical categories are limited to a certain number (for some reason or other) then there would be the same number of types of place markers. If it is not necessary (to give one example) to have both verbs and adjectives for a certain purpose at hand, it is not necessary, *for that purpose*, to have one style of place markers for verbs and another for adjectives. Obviously, the notion of a place marker is parasitic on the notion of a syntactical (or semantical) category.

Sentence Frames and Sentence Frames

So far, we have considered only one class of sentence frames, *viz.* sentence frames for simple sentences, and only one class of place markers, *viz.* place markers for constituents of simple sentences. But we also have sentence frames for compound sentences containing place markers for sentences, simple or complex. Such sentence frames would be convenient to have when a sentence occurs in a context in which it behaves as a whole as a single unit, i.e. in a context which is indifferent to the inner structure of the sentence. So we may have the sentence frame:

$$\text{If } S \text{ then } T$$

of which all the following are (may be treated as) substitution instances:

(i) If Socrates is human then Socrates is mortal.
(ii) If iron is heated then it expands.
(iii) If $10 \times 5 = 50$ then $10 = 50/5$

Such sentence frames (which we may call complex or compound sentence frames) are entirely on a par with other sentence frames, as far as the points noted above are concerned. Likewise, the place markers which occur in these sentence frames, i.e. place markers for sentences, are on a par with the place markers we encountered earlier.

II

How to Get Sentences from Sentence Frames

In the first part of the paper I tried to be clear about the idea of a place marker and the associated idea of a sentence frame. In this part I shall try, principally, to be clear about the different ways in which we can get sentences from sentence frames, as well as to be clear about their implications. I do not claim to have made a complete inventory of all these ways; but the number of ways of obtaining sentences from sentence frames which I have succeeded clearly to distinguish will be large enough to keep us busy.

(i) Sentence frames are sentence fragments with place markers marking places in which words or whole sentences can be written for obtaining sentences. So, that gives us a straightforward, and, in a sense, the most primitive way of getting sentences from sentence frames. Thus given the sentence frame

... is human

we can obtain the sentence

Socrates is human

by writing 'Socrates' in the place marked by '. . .'; and given the sentence frame

Socrates *F*

we can get, in a similar way, the sentence

Socrates speaks;

and given the sentence frame

If *S* then *T*

we can get the sentence

If real numbers are non-denumerably infinite then the substitutional view of quantification is wrong.

A sentence which is obtained by replacing or *substituting* place markers in a sentence frame by appropriate expressions (names, sentences, verbs, adjectives, etc.) has been called a substitution instance of that sentence frame. This way of obtaining a sentence may now be called *obtaining by substitution*.

(ii) Though, possibly, substitution is the most primitive way of getting sentences from sentence frames, it is not the only way of getting sentences from them.

Take the sentence frame:

$$x \text{ is human}$$

It is not a sentence, but, as we have just said, a sentence frame. But if that be so, we can obtain at least two sentences from the sentence frame without having recourse to substitution. They are:

(S_1) x is human is not a sentence.
(S_2) x is human is a sentence frame.

It is clear that while 'x is human' is not a sentence, (S_1) and (S_2) are sentences, and, furthermore, both of them are true. It is also clear the neither (S_1) nor (S_2) is obtained by substitution. But, no doubt, they are obtained from 'x is human'. We can say that they are obtained from the sentence frame by *characterisation*, in the first case as not being a sentence, and, in the second case as being a sentence frame.

It is true that as examples sentences, (S_1) and (S_2) are of very little interest and are nearly trivial. But we should not suppose that all sentences which can be obtained by sentence frame characterisation will be equally devoid of interest. Sentences which are obtained from sentence frames in fundamentally the same way may be of great importance. We shall consider in what follows a series of sentences which will clearly bring out this point.

Let us take again the sentence frame 'x is human'. We can obtain from it

(A) There is a (or at least one) name such that when the name is written in place of the place marker x in the sentence frame 'x is human', the result is a sentence (i.e. a significant sequence of words).

(B) There is a (or at least one) name such that .... is a sentence which is true (or expresses something true).

Obviously, both (A) and (B) are sentences and, as we may note in passing, both express something true. The following sentences also can be obtained from the same sentence frame:

(C) There is an individual (or at least one individual) such that, when the name of that individual is written in place of the place marker x in the sentence frame 'x is human', the result is a sentence.

(D) .... the result is a sentence which is true (or expresses something true).

There is no doubt again that both (C) and (D), like (A) and (B), are sentences (and that both express something true). Again, given the sentence frame

$$\text{If } S \text{ then } S,$$

(which, by the way, contains the same place marker in two places), we can obtain

(E) The result of writing any sentence in place of the place marker S in the sentence frame 'If S then S' is a sentence.

As well as

(F) The result of .... is a sentence which is true (or expresses something true).

Undoubtedly, both (E) and (F) are sentences, and they express truths. Indeed, one can treat (F) as a possible formulation of the law of identity.

Let us pause for a while, at this point, to consider what kinds of assertions are made by the sentences (A)–(D). We can perhaps say that (A) asserts a (four place?) relation among a name, a place marker, a sentence frame and a sentence; that (B) asserts a (five place?) relation among all these and what makes a sentence or what it expresses true (if it is at all possible to say this without making any very strong commitment to any particular theory of truth); that (C) asserts a (five place?) relation among an individual, a name, a place marker, a sentence frame, and a sentence; and that (D) asserts a (six place?) relation among all these and what makes a sentence or what it expresses true (if, again, it is possible to say that in a more or less non-committal way). However, all this talk of many place relations is not essential for what we have in mind. The important points are as follows:

(*a*) The sentence (A) is exclusively about linguistic entities.

(*b*) The sentence (B) is not exclusively about linguistic entities for it involves the concept of *truth*. But it is like (A) in the respect that it does not make any *direct* reference to any entity which is not linguistic.

(*c*) The sentences (C) and (D) make direct reference to extra-linguistic entities, viz. *individuals* which are bearers of names.

(*d*) So we can say, possibly, that (A) and (B) are *only about* linguistic entities (surely (A) is), but (C) and (D) are not only about linguistic but also about extra-linguistic entities.

(*e*) There is at least a *prima facie* temptation to say that, in spite of the differences noted above, the sentences (A) and (C), as well as the sentences (B) and (D), are logically equivalent for they have the same truth conditions. It would be a matter of great importance to consider whether this was the case.

Some Conventions and Remarks

(i) When a name is written in place of the place marker x in the sentence frame 'x is human' we get a sentence; and this sentence, according to the terminology introduced earlier, is a substitution instance of the sentence frame 'x is human'. This makes available to us a more compact mode of expressing what we wanted to express by the sentences (A) and (B). Instead of writing (A), we could write

(A_1) There is a (or, at least one) substitution instance of the sentence frame 'x is human' which is a sentence.

And, instead of writing (B), we could write

(B_1) There is a (or, at least one) substitution instance of the sentence frame 'x is human' which is a sentence that is true (or expresses something true).

(ii) It may be noted that (A_1), in contrast with (B_1), as also (A) in contrast with (B), is trivial; for a substitution instance of 'x is human' cannot fail to be a sentence, while it can fail to be true. Since we have stipulated that it is only a *sentence*, that can be obtained from a sentence frame by writing words in places marked by place markers, which will be called a substitution instance of the sentence frame, it is trivial to say of any substitution instance of a sentence frame that it is a sentence.

(iii) It would be instructive to consider now whether the convention (of compactly expressing, what we want to express, in terms of substitution instances) introduced in (i) can be extended to (C) and (D). That is, can we say that (C) means the same as

(C_1) There is a (at least one) substitution instance of the sentence frame 'x is human' which is a sentence,

and (D) means the same as

(D_1) There is ....
...... which is true (or expresses something true)?

This is doubtful. A look at (C_1) and (D_1) reveals that they are not at all different from (AI) and (BI), respectively. So, if we want to maintain that (C) means the same as (C_1) and (D) means the same as (D)$_1$, we shall have to grant that (A) means the same as (C) and (B) means the same as (D): and it is doubtful whether *this* can be granted at all. In fact, it can be doubted whether (A) and (C) or (B) and (D) would even be logically equivalent. It seems that they would be logically equivalent if and only if it is logically true that (α) for every individual there is a name, and (β) for every name there is an individual. Both (α) and (β) are, however, doubtful examples of logical (or even necessary) truths. We could possibly amend (α) a little to give it the appearance of necessary truth: we can say that (α_1) for every individual there is an *actual or possible* name, and that this is sufficient for our purpose. But there is greater difficulty with (β), for notoriously, there are empty names.

However, the matter is extremely complicated, and we cannot hope to solve all the problems involved. But we shall return to it later.

(iv) We have distinguished so far two ways of obtaining sentences from sentence frames. The first is by way of substitution, and the second, by way of characterisation. The second mode of getting a sentence is called characterisation because it consists in saying that the sentence frame from which it is obtained is of a certain sort. This is the reason why in every sentence which is obtained from a sentence frame in this way the sentence frame occurs within quotes. And this fact brings out clearly that, in these cases of obtaining sentences from sentence frames, the sentence frames in question are not used, but they are only mentioned.

The Sentence Frame 'If S then S'

We have considered so far only how sentences could be obtained by characterisation from the sentence frame 'x is human'. But of course, we can obtain sentences by characterisation from other sentence frames as well. To illustrate this, we can now take the sentence frame

If S then S.

Given this sentence frame, we can obtain the sentences:

(E) The result of writing any sentence in place of the place marker S in the sentence frame 'If S then S' is a sentence.

(F) The result of writing .... is a sentence which is true (or expresses something true).

For (A) and (B) we have partially extra-linguistic 'versions', respectively, in (C) and (D). Let us ask now whether such partially extra-linguistic versions for (E) and (F) are available at all.

A little reflection shows that what enables us to get (partially) extra-linguistic versions of (A) and (B), in (C) and (D), is that we have a general term for things which are nameable by names which can be written in place of the place marker x. So, it is clear that if we have a general term related to the place marker S in the sentence frame 'If S then S' in the way in which the general term 'individual' is related to the place marker x in 'x is human', then we should be able to get extra-linguistic versions of (E) and (F). Let us see, therefore, whether we can find such a term.

Note, to begin with, what *type* of place marker S is; i.e. what kind of linguistic items could be written in its place. S is a place marker for sentences, and, to make explicit one assumption made throughout our discussion, it is a place marker for *indicative or declarative* sentences, i.e. for the kind of sentences which can be used for the purpose of making statements or stating *facts*. And *that* gives us the idea: the term which we are in search of is 'fact'. So we may try to formulate a (partially) non-linguistic version of (E) as follows:

(G_1) Every *fact* is such that, when a sentence by which we can state that fact is written in place of the place marker S in the sentence frame 'If S then S', the result is a sentence.

And we may try to formulate a (partially) extra-linguistic version of (F) as follows:

(H₁) Every *fact* is such that, when a sentence . . . .
. . . . the result is
a sentence which is true (or expresses something true).

However, there is something wrong about this formulation. The term 'fact' does not really suit our purpose; for neither does every sentence express a *fact* (i.e. an *existing* state of affairs) nor is it necessary that a sentence for such a fact should be written in place of *S* in order to obtain a sentence or a truth. So we require a weaker and wider term to suit the purpose of non-veridical as well as veridical sentences. The term which naturally suggests itself is 'state of affairs'. A corresponding replacement of the verb 'state' may also seem advisable, for it is arguable that it is only a *fact* which can be stated. So let us replace it by the term 'express'. Thus, it is not implausible to suggest that the correct extra-linguistic versions of (E) and (F) will respectively be:

(G) Every *state of affairs* is such that, when a sentence expressing that state of affairs is written in place of the place marker *S* in the sentence frame 'If *S* then *S*', the result is a sentence.

(H) Every *state of affairs* is such that, when a sentence . . . ., the result is a true sentence (or, expresses something true).

It is clear that whatever is said above about the sentences (A)–(F) can be said, *mutatis mutandis*, about the sentences (G) and (H) with equal propriety.

We may now consider the possibility of more compact expressions of (E), (F), (G) and (H) in terms of substitution instances.

First take (E). Since the result of writing a sentence in place of the marker *S* in the sentence frame 'If *S* then *S*' is a substitution instance of that sentence frame, we can give (E) the more compact form:

(E1) Every substitution instance of the sentence frame 'If *S* then *S*' is a sentence.

For the same reason, a similar compact form of (F) would be

(Fı) Every substitution instance of the sentence frame 'If *S* then *S*' is a sentence which is true (or expresses something true).

Could we have similar formulations of (G) and (H) in terms of substitution instances? We could have, only if for every sentence there were a state of affairs which the sentence expressed, and for every state of affairs there were a sentence which expressed that state of affairs. Although this seems more likely than a correlation between names and individuals, one cannot be quite certain about this. For there can be at least two kinds of sentences for which it seems difficult to find any state of affairs at all. These are contradictory and paradoxical sentences.

Some Other Sentence Frames
(i) Let us take now the sentence frame

Socrates *F*

Obtaining a sentence by substitution being obvious, we ask how a sentence could be obtained by characterisation from this sentence frame. (From now on, we shall not formulate the kind of trivial characterisations exemplified by (A), (C), (E), and (G) above.) By characterisation, we may have

(I) There is a predicate (taking the term 'predicate' in the widest grammatical sense) (or at least one predicate) such that, when it is written in place of the place marker *F* in the sentence frame 'Socrates *F*', the result is a true sentence (or expresses something true).

Is it possible to have an extra-linguistic version or counterpart of (I)? We know that for such a counterpart we require an appropriate general term for the things which are expressed by *all* predicates. The term which suggests itself is indeed 'property'. So the following may be accepted as a (partially) extra-linguistic version of (I):

(J) There is a property (or, at least one property) such that, when a predicate expressing that property is written in place of the place marker F in the sentence frame 'Socrates F', the result is a true sentence (or expresses something true).

(ii) It would be instructive to consider now a sentence frame which is in some ways fundamentally different from the sentence frames we have considered so far. Take the sentence frame

Socrates is mortal . . . Socrates is human

of which all the following sentences can be regarded as substitution instances:

(a) Socrates is mortal *and* Socrates is human.
(b) Socrates is mortal *if* Socrates is human.
(c) Socrates is mortal *or* Socrates is human.
(d) Socrates is mortal *if and only if* Socrates is human.

If we want, we may use the letter C instead of '. . .' to serve as the place marker and have our sentence frame as follows:

Socrates is mortal C Socrates is human.

For the sake of convenience, we can use the letter 'M' as an *abbreviation* of the sentence 'Socrates is mortal', and the letter 'H' as an abbreviation of 'Socrates is human', and write the sentence frame more simply as

M C H.

The sentence frame M C H is different from the sentence frames we have discussed earlier in that it contains a place marker for what are called '*logical* words' ('and', 'if', etc.), while they contain place markers for non-logical words.

It is obvious that we can obtain sentences from this sentence frame by substitution. All the sentences (a)–(d) above are so obtained. But can we obtain sentences from this sentence frame by characterisation? A sentence involving no direct reference to extra-linguistic entities is not difficult to find. The following may be one:

(K) There is a (or at least one) logical word such that when that logical word is written in place of the place marker *C* in the sentence frame M *C* H, the result is a sentence which is true (or expresses something true).

But can we have an extra-linguistic counterpart of (K)? We know that the possibility of having such a counterpart of (K) depends upon whether or not we have a general term for the thing or kind of things which are expressed by all logical words, or, at least those logical words which can replace *C*. But it is doubtful whether we have any such term, for it is doubtful whether there is a thing at all of which a general term could be said to be a term for it. But supposing we have such a term in the term 'logical constant', the extra-linguistic counterpart of (K) could be as follows:

(L) There is a (or at least one) logical constant such that, when a logical word expressing that constant is written in place of the place marker *C* in the sentence frame M *C* H, the result is a true sentence (or expresses something true).

We may point out also that we have a more compact expression of (K) in

(K1) There is a (or at least one) substitution instance of the sentence frame M *C* H which is a true sentence (or expresses something true).

Whether or not we can have a similar compact form of (L) apparently depends on whether or not we have a logical constant for every logical word and a logical word for every logical constant. But that is a question which I find extremely difficult to answer; and so I leave the matter at that.

Quantification

Characterisation of a sentence frame, as we have found, sometimes consists in asserting that some or all substitution instances of the sentence frame are true. Characterisation of this kind can be called 'quantification'; and there is no doubt that what logicians have called quantification is best interpreted as characterisation of this kind *at least* in some cases. It is advisable to remember that, in a quantification in this sense the sentence frame on which the quantification is made is *mentioned*, and *not* used. This fact is made evident by the occurrence of the sentence frame inside quotation marks.

III

Some Restrictions on Getting Sentences from Sentence frames

In the previous part of this paper we tried to describe some of the ways in which it is possible to obtain a sentence from a given sentence frame. In the present part, I shall try to describe, as clearly as I can, some of the ways in which it is *not* possible to obtain sentences from sentence frames, as well as some other ways with which they may be confused.

Two ways of getting sentences from sentence frames have been considered so far. They have been called (*a*) substitution, and (*b*) characterisation. In the former, we *eliminate* the sentence frame by completion; in the latter, we *mention* it by using some name or referring expression for it. In none of them do we *use* the sentence frame to obtain a sentence. But could we obtain a sentence from a sentence frame in *this* way? Let us try.

Consider the following:

(M) For all x, x is human.

Is (M) a sentence? A careful consideration, especially with reference to the manner in which place markers and sentence frames have been introduced, reveals that it is not. In fact, it does not mean anything at all, if we do not confuse having meaning and having meaningful parts. 'x is human' is devoid of meaning, and so is 'for all x', and the obvious conclusion is that (M) itself is meaningless. This becomes obvious when we recall that (M) is only a way of writing

(M_1) For all . . ., . . . is human.

The latter is at best a sentence frame, having a possible substitution instance in

(N) For all Indians, Indians are human.

In contradistinction both from (M) and from (M_1), (N) seems to make sense and to be a sentence. So those who have supposed that (M) makes sense, and it is a sentence, must *not* have taken x as a *place marker*. In what way could they have taken x in that case? The question is very difficult to answer, but the following is a distinct possibility.

A phrase of the form 'for all . . .' makes sense if, and *only if*, the blank is filled by a *general term*, as in (N). A phrase of the form 'all . . .' itself would make sense, it appears, only if the blank is filled in by a general substantive term. Thus 'all men', 'all Indians', 'all philosophers', 'all acrobats' make perfect sense, and, possibly 'for all men', 'for all philosophers', etc., also do. So those who have taken (M) to be a significant sentence might have taken x to be a general term, indeed as a very generic term like 'individual' or 'thing'. So (M), i.e. 'For all x, x is human', might have been taken by them to be the same as

(O) For all *thing*, the *thing* is human,

or

(P) For all *individual*, the individual is human.

But if they *have* done so, they have *not* treated x as a place marker, and they have *not* treated 'x is human' as a sentence frame.

Now, what is true of (M) is also true of

(Q) For some x, x is human.

If x is taken as a place marker, and 'x is human' as a sentence frame, then (Q) does not make any sense; and if (Q) does make some sense, then (possibly) we take x as a generic term like *thing* or *individual*.

It would be instructive to pause for a while and consider what 'x is human' would in fact be, if x is taken as a generic name. The answer, I suppose, is not very difficult to find. Let us take a look at

(P) For all individual, the individual is human.

To ask what 'x is human' is like, under this interpretation of x, is to ask what 'the individual is human' means, or is like. It is, in fact, an *indeterminate* sentence, a sentence which could be used on occasion to make indeterminate statements. It is like 'he is honest', which is indeterminate, and remains indeterminate, so long as the person to whom the reference is made by the pronoun is not specified or indicated by the context.

But one may say that 'x is human', even when it is used as a genuine sentence frame, means the same as 'he is human'. But that would be a mistake. After all 'he is human' is a sentence, though an indeterminate one. It is *not* a sentence frame. 'x is human' and 'he (she, it) is human' are not afflicted by the same kind of deficiency. *Indeterminacy of meaning is not the same as absence of meaning.*

And this brings out another important point. Those who give x a *pronominal*[1] function do not, because they cannot, treat it as a place marker. I would suggest that they treat it *more* like a generic name, though I am not sure whether treating it as a pronoun and treating it as a generic name are exactly the same way of treating it. I am inclined to believe that they are not.

Illustrative Symbols Again
Whatever has been said so far about 'For all x, x is human' and 'For some x, x is human' can be said with equal justification about the following:

(M₁) For every x, x is human.
(M₂) For any x, x is human.

[1] For example, Quine. See especially his *Mathematical Logic*, Rev. Ed., Cambridge, Mass., Harvard Univ. Press, 1951, §§ 12 & 13.

(M_3) All (every) x is such that, x is human.
(Q_1) For at least one x, x is human.
(Q_2) There is at least one x such that, x is human.
(Q_3) There is an x such that, x is human.
(Q_4) There exists an x (or at least one x) such that, x is human.

But the case of

(R)   Whatever x may be, x is human

seems to be a little different. It can, no doubt, be taken to be a variant of (M)–(M_3), as they are variants of each other. In that case it would be either a construction like

(M_4) Whatever . . . may be, . . . is human,

and be vulnerable in exactly the same way in which all of (M)–(M_3) are, or else be a sentence of the kind

(S)   Whatever man it (he) is, the man becomes aggressive when it (he) is frustrated.

But it is possible to treat (R) in a different manner, which may even seem more natural. (R) may be taken to mean the same as

(T)   Whatever individual x may stand for, x is human.

Under this interpretation, (R) compares very well with

(U)   Let x stand for any individual. Then, x is human.

In (U), clearly, we are making an *illustrative* symbol of x. The first part makes a stipulation bestowing the status of an illustrative symbol on x, and the second part exploits this status.

(U), by itself, is quite unexceptionable. But we are to remember that we are neither using x as a place marker nor using 'x is human' as a sentence frame.

Another Re-interpretation

Before proceeding further to consider some other attempts at getting sentences from sentence frames, I should like to consider another possible interpretation of such constructions as 'For all x, x is human'.

Let us, for this purpose, take again one of the permissible ways of forming sentences out of sentence frames, viz.,

(D) There is an individual such that, when the name of that individual is written in place of the place marker x in the sentence frame 'x is human', the result is a sentence which is true (or, expresses something true).

Now, is it possible to treat 'For some x, x is human' to be just an abbreviation of this? Yes, it is possible. Only we are not to take this which is nothing but an abbreviation of a sentence formed out of a sentence frame by *characterisation* to be a sentence formed in a different way. We are to remember in particular that the sentence frame 'x is human' is not still *used*, even though the absence of quotation marks conceals the fact that it is only mentioned (for the purpose of characterisation) in the construction. In this interpretation, locutions like 'For all x, . . .' and 'For some x, . . .' are to be taken as exemplifying a *quotation-absorbing device* of language, comparable to the device exploited in the following sentence:

Giorgione was so called because of his size.

Experiments with Some Other Sentence Frames
In the last section, we considered the possibility of constructing sentences out of sentence frames in ways other than substitution and characterisation. We have considered in particular the claim of such constructions as 'For all x, x is human' and 'For some x, x is human'. We have also found that their claim cannot be sustained, unless they are taken in some way in which they were not originally intended to be taken. But these constructions are all on the sentence frame 'x is human'. Could we meet with greater success with other sentence frames?

(i) Let us take first

Socrates F,

where F is a place marker for a predicate. Could we have a sentence like

(V₁) For all F, Socrates F.

or

(V₂) For some F, Socrates F?

Once again, none of them is a sentence, if F is a place marker, and 'Socrates F' is a sentence frame.

Is it possible to interpret them by taking F to be a generic name? Though, as we have seen earlier, such a generic name interpretation is possible in the case of 'For all x, x is human', a little reflection shows that it is *not* possible in the present case. To make sense of a phrase of the form 'all . . .' or 'for all . . .', we are to fill in the blank, as we have pointed out earlier, by a general *substantive* term. Now, while it is clear that we have a general substantive (name-like) term for all things which are expressed by predicates in general, it is no less clear that the term cannot be used to fill both the places marked by the place marker '. . .' in the sentence frame

For all . . ., Socrates . . .

For what can be written in the first place is a *substantive term*, but what can be written in the second is a *predicate*. The general term to which we allude is, of course, 'property'; and let us try to write it in both the places in the sentence frame. The result will be

(V₃) For all property, Socrates property.

This is irremediable nonsense. It suffers from a kind of sense-lessness which cannot be remedied by the (merely) idiomatic adjustments which were sufficient in the case of a possible filling in of the sentence frame 'For all x, x is human'.

So it seems that, if we are to make any sense at all of the constructions (V₁) and (V₂), we are to interpret them either (*a*) as quotation absorbing devices of briefly formulating sentence frame characterizations, or (*b*) in terms of illustrative symbols.

(ii) Consider now the sentence frame

$$\text{If } S \text{ then } S,$$

where S is a place marker for a sentence. Could we have a sentence like

(W_1) For all S, if S then S?

We know that (WI) is no different from

(W_2) For all . . ., if . . . then . . .,

and, consequently, it is not a sentence either. It is at best a sentence frame. The same remarks seem to apply, for example, to

(W_3) For some S, and some T, if S then T,

where T is another place marker for a sentence.

There is no doubt that we can try to salvage (W_1) and (W_3) by interpreting them as abbreviations of sentence frame characterisations. But it is doubtful whether it is possible to give it a generic name interpretation which is available for 'For some x, x is human'. (Has Prior tried to do something like this with his neologisms such as 'somewhether'? See his *Objects of Thought*, Chapter 3.) It is doubtful, for such an interpretation would demand that we have an expression which is *both a (generic) name of what sentences in general express and is a sentence itself*—a sentence which could be written in the blanks in the sentence frame 'if . . . then . . .'. It seems *impossible* to have any such expression. To repeat a well established truism, what is a sentence is not a name, and what is a name is not a sentence. So we can also add, perhaps, that those who take the possibility of a generic name interpretation of (W_1) or (W_3) for granted do confuse names and sentences.

It can be pointed out, finally, that an illustrative symbol interpretation is again possible here. For

(W_4) Let S stand for any sentence. Then if S then S

is perfectly all right.

(iii) Then consider the sentence frame

M C H

in which C is a place marker for whatever it is necessary to write in between the sentences M and H to form a further sentence. All remarks which were made about the immediately preceding case seem equally justifiable about the following attempt:

(X_1) For all C, M C H

or

(X_2) For some C, M C H

A straightforward interpretation of (X_1) or (X_2) makes it nonsense, an abbreviative interpretation seems to be possible, and a generic name interpretation seems to be equally out of place. The generic name interpretation seems bound to fail because we cannot have any expression for all things which logical words (or connectives) in general express (if they express anything in this way at all) and which can at the same time function as the kind of connective required for filling in the sentence frame M C H. In other words, there is *no* expression which can take both the positions marked by the place marker in 'For all . . ., M . . . H' or in 'For some . . ., M . . .H'. This fact is connected with—indeed one and the same as—another truism, viz. names are not connectives.

To round up our discussion of the construction (X_1) and (X_2) we may add that, once again, an illustrative symbol interpretation of these constructions is possible. We *can* have sentences like:

(X_3) Let C stand for any logical constant. Then, M C H.

Another Ambiguity

So far, we have talked as though there were only one interpretation, of constructions such as 'For all x, x is human', in terms of the idea of illustrative symbols. This, however, is not the case. Consider the following constructions:

(i) Let x stand for any *individual;* then, if x is human then x is human.

(ii) Let x stand for any *name;* then, if x is human then x is human.

(i) and (ii) are really two distinct variations on the illustrative symbol interpretation. They obviously differ, as well as the respective senses in which the phrase 'stand for' is taken in (i) and (ii).

It is obvious that this ambiguity affects constructions involving *all* kinds of place markers.

IV

In this part of the paper I first sum up the results of our investigation, then relate these results to the controversy over two opposing interpretations of quantification, and finally try to see whether these findings throw any light on the question of the ontological commitment supposed to be involved in the choice of variables.

A Summing Up

Starting from the idea of sentence we gradually developed the ideas of a sentence fragment, a place marker, and a sentence frame. The idea of a place marker which we developed can be regarded as an explication of one particular notion of a variable, and the idea of a sentence frame can be regarded as an explication of one particular notion of a sentential function or open sentence. Along with the development of these two ideas, we also tried to distinguish clearly the different types of place markers and the different types of sentence frames associated with them. Then we asked how sentences could be obtained from sentence frames. We found that, if we adhere consistently to the idea of a sentence frame we have developed (or to the idea of a sentential function or open sentence in *that* sense), there can be *only* two ways of getting sentences from sentence frames. They are: (i) substitution, and (ii) characterisation. Then we distinguished varieties of characterisation, starting from the most trivial and uncontroversial, and going up to the more and more important and controversial varieties. Some of these characterisations take the form of the claim that some or all substitution instances of a given sentence frame are true.

The idea of a characterisation of *this* type can well be regarded as an explication of *one* notion of quantification. In a sense, all (quantificative) characterisations involve some extra-linguistic reference, for they invoke the concept of truth and a *purely* linguistic concept of truth, i.e. a concept of truth which does not make *any* extra-linguistic reference at all, seems impossible, if not absurd. But some of these quantificative characterisations seem to be more extra-linguistic in significance than others, for they involve reference to, *as well as use of the idea of,* entities of different categories, e.g. individuals, properties, and states of affairs. Other quantificative characterisations do not involve any extra-linguistic reference in this way.

After having described the *legitimate* ways of constructing sentences out of sentential functions or open sentences, in the sense of sentence frames, we considered some futile, because illegitimate, attempts at constructing sentences out of them. The most important of them consists in prefixing the phrase 'for all ...' or the phrase 'for some ...' to a sentence frame. We argued that this prefixing device does not yield any sentence— that constructions like 'For all x, x is human' are not sentences. We argued also that these constructions do not seem to make any sense at all. They are at best sentence frames. There are, however, some ways in which one may try to salvage this prefixing device. First, it may be regarded as a way of abbreviating sentence frame characterisation. Second, it may be regarded as a way of using very generic (name-like) terms such as 'individual' and 'thing' for the purpose of making general statements. Third, it can be reinterpreted as a way of making *and* using illustrative symbols for the same purpose. But what we found to be most important about these attempts at salvaging the prefixing device is that in none of them can it be regarded as a quantification over a sentential function or open sentence with respect to one or more variables, if by sentential function or open sentence we mean a sentence frame. For, in the first, it remains a characterisation which is *not* prefixing; in the second, the variable is no longer a place marker and sentential function is only an indeterminate sentence; and, in the third, there is neither a place marker nor a sentence frame. These results are unfavourable to some views of quantification, e.g. Quine's, which maintain *both* that variables are place markers (and, consequently, sentential functions or open sentences are sentence frames) *and* that quantification is nothing but a prefixing device. It is *not* possible to obtain sentences from sentence frames by prefixing.

An important thing which is borne out by our discussion is that the idea of quantification depends essentially upon that of a variable, and that, since there are at least three different ideas, viz. a place marker, a generic name and an illustrative symbol, which are covered by the same term 'variable', there are at least three different ideas covered by the term 'quantification'. However, to repeat, none of these ideas corresponds to what Quine calls 'quantification', for none of them consists in prefixing expressions like 'for all . . .' and 'for some . . .' to expressions like '. . . is human'. The only thing which all ideas of quantification have in common is that in each of them quantification is a way of expressing generality.

About the different ways of getting sentences from sentence frames, we have found that (i) substitution is universally valid, if analytically so, that (ii) a merely linguistic or syntactical characterisation, i.e. characterisation in terms of names, predicates, etc., is also universally valid and above all controversy, and that (iii) characterisation in terms of individuals, properties, etc., is not equally uncontroversially valid. About the prefixing device, we have found the following: (i) If it is only an abbreviation of some sentence frame characterisations, it is valid to the extent the sentence frame characterisations which it abbreviates are themselves valid. (ii) If it is given illustrative symbol interpretation, and if the illustrative symbol interpretation itself is taken in its purely linguistic form, i.e. taken to make stipulations of the form 'Let x stand for any *name*', then it is universally valid for we can make an illustrative symbol for *all* kinds of linguistic items. (iii) If the illustrative symbol interpretation of the prefixing device is, on the other hand, taken in terms of stipulations of the form 'Let

x stand for any *individual*', then it is open to questions to which characterisations with reference to individuals, properties, etc., were said to be open. (iv) If the prefixing device is given the generic name interpretation then it is valid as far as it goes. But it does not go far, for it is restricted exclusively to only one kind of case, viz. to the case in which only generic names (or 'variables') for *things*, as distinguished from properties, states of affairs, etc., occur.

This last point, I think, brings out very clearly the strength of Quine's position. What Quine has argued indefatigably for years is that there can be variables of only one kind, viz. the individual, or, as we may call it, thing name, variables. But he has done so because he takes the variable as a kind of generic name ('thing', 'individual') which can fill both the blanks in the sentence frame 'for all . . ., . . . is human'. If a variable *is* a generic name of this kind, there can be no other kind of variable than the individual, and consequently, there can be no other kind of quantification than the first order. But this also brings out very clearly the great weakness of Quine's position. For, *if* a variable is a kind of generic name, then as we have shown, it cannot be at the same time a place marker. But the idea of a variable as a place marker is perfectly respectable, and, as far as I know, it owes its existence more to Quine himself than to anybody else. In so far as Quine's own view of a variable is that it is a place marker, Quine has been inconsistent in treating variables as generic names of a sort required for the kind of prefixing he calls quantification, as well as in ruling out all quantifications beyond the first order. We can indeed say that Ruth Barcan Marcus, or S. Lesniewski, as Quine[1] reports, were more faithful to the idea of a variable as a place marker in their view of quantification. It can be added that there is another respect in which Marcus and Lesniewski are right. If variables are place markers and quantification is characterisation of sentence frames involving such place markers, then there is at least one kind of quantification which is valid for all levels of generalisation. There can be all kinds of variables, and

[1] W. V. Quine, *Ontological Commitment*, p. 63.

all kinds of quantifications with respect to them; quantification need not be restricted to the level of individuals as Quine wishes it to be. Neither is it necessary that it should be confined to the so called transparent contexts. However, one should be more careful about concluding that this or that contending party in the dispute is right. For a more correct assessment of the situation seems to be that the contending parties are at cross purposes, because they work with different conceptions of a sentential function or open sentence.

Objectual and Substitutional Quantification

We can now turn to the conflict between two rival interpretations of quantification—of formulae like (E*x*) F*x* and (*x*) F*x*. The first of these two interpretations, which is called objectual or object-oriented, is favoured by Quine, and the second, called substitutional, is favoured by Marcus. These two interpretations of quantification are, roughly, as follows:

(A) The objectual interpretation.
    (i) (*x*) F*x*=df. For all *x*, F*x*.
    (ii) (E*x*) F*x*=df. For some *x*, F*x*.
(B) The Substitutional Interpretation.
    (i) (*x*) F*x*=df. Every substitution instance of F*x* is true.
    (ii) (E*x*) F*x*=df. At least one substitution instance of F*x* is true.

It could not have escaped the notice of a careful reader that our discussion has revolved a great deal round the opposition between these conflicting views of quantification. In fact, there is very little to add to what we have already said about it in the course of our discussion. However, we can record here the more salient points which have emerged. *First*, the opposition between objectual and substitutional interpretations is not really absolute. There are at least two reasons why it is not so. One reason is that even the substitutional quantification invokes the concept of truth, and, consequently, must have some reference to *objects*, unless, of course, we want to have a purely syntactical (e.g. the coherence) account of truth. Another reason is that the substitutions themselves, as we pointed out quite early, can be objectually understood, as they can be understood in terms of individuals, properties, etc. But it must be admitted that Marcus herself was aware of the difficulty with the concept of truth[1]—and it may be that the objective reference which is involved in the concept of truth is not really the point at issue. It should also be admitted that substitutions *can* be understood in terms of purely linguistic categories, such as names, predicates, etc., and it is open to Marcus uniformly to take substitution in this way. *Second*, the exact significance of what *Quine* calls objectual quantification is not brought out by formulae like 'For all x, x is human' for these formulae themselves are ambiguous. This significance is brought out in taking the 'variable' x as a kind of generic name, i.e. as equivalent with the term 'thing' or 'individual'. *Third*, if we want to have a theory of quantification which is powerful enough to cope with all levels of generality, we shall have to take the substitutional view, for the Quinian type of quantification, as he is no doubt right in holding, is possible only at the level of individuals.

Ontological Commitment

We shall conclude with a few remarks on the question of ontological commitment. There is no doubt that no ontological commitment is made in the use of variables if variables are taken only as place markers; and there is no ontological commitment made in quantification if quantification is made in terms of substitution and substitution is taken in a purely syntactical manner. So there will be ontological commitment either if we take variables to be generic names of a sort and make non-substitutional quantification over such variables, or if we interpret substitution in terms of such ontological categories as individuals, properties, etc., within the framework of substitutional quantification. If we exclude the second possibility as uninteresting then we are left with the kind of

[1] See her 'Interpreting Quantification' (*Inquiry*, Vol. 5, 1962).

quantification of which Quine speaks, and it does seem that Quine is right in maintaining that quantification of this sort does make ontological commitment. But there is still something to be said against this conclusion.

Even although we have been using the two terms 'individual' and 'thing' interchangeably, there is a sense in which they are not altogether such. The term 'individual' *is* a category word: it is difficult to imagine a use of the term which does not involve allocation to some ontological category *in contradistinction from* others. But that is *not* the case with the term 'thing'. There is indeed a use of the term in which it is synonymous with the term 'individual', when, for example, we distinguish a *thing* from its *properties*. But this is not the only use of the term. We can have a wider use of the term in which we can say, for example, that both an individual and its properties are things. Now, the variable x *can* be used as a short form for the term 'thing' in *this* sense. If it is so used, and quantification is made by its help, the quantification, we can say, *is* devoid of ontological commitment for it does not involve allocation to any ontological category in *contradistinction* from others. We *can* make such allocation to some distinct ontological category within the framework of such quantification if we want, but in order to do so we shall have to take help of some *additional* clause within the scope of the quantification. It will not be achieved by the mere mechanism of quantification. Take the quantification:

(i) For all x, x is human.

It can be taken to mean

(ii) For all thing (*to whatever ontological category it may belong*), the thing is human.

And, if the claim made in this quantification seems to be extravagant, and if we want to make a more realistic claim in (i), we can write, instead,

(iii) For all x, if x is an individual then x is human,
or, in the more spelt out form,

(iv) For all thing (to whatever ontological category it may belong), *if the thing is an individual,* then the thing is human.

So, it seems to me that even within the framework of the Quinian type of quantification it is possible to avoid making ontological commitment. We may however equate having ontological commitment with having objective commitment, i.e. commitment to the existence of *objects in general*; and in that case this type of quantification will have some ontological commitment. But to say that quantification involves onto-logical commitment in *this* sense is not to say anything which is either controversial or philosophically important.

Bibliography

BOOKS

From a Logical Point of View, W. V. Quine, Harper & Row, New York, 1961, 2nd ed., Essays I & VI.

'Interpretation of Quantifiers', D. Føllesdal, in *Logic, Methodology and Philosophy of Science,* van Rootselaar and Staal (Eds), North Holland, Amsterdam, 1968.

'Modalities and Intensional Languages', R. B. Marcus, in *Boston Studies in the Philosophy of Science,* M. W. Wartofsky (Ed.), Dodrecht, Holland, 1963.

Objects of Thought, A. N. Prior (P. T. Geach & J. P. Kenny (Eds)), Clarendon Press, Oxford, 1971, Chapter 3.

Ontological Relativity and Other Essays, W. V. Quine, Columbia Univ. Press., New York, London, 1969, Essays 2 & 4.

Ways of Paradox and Other Essays, W. V. Quine, Random House, New York, 1966, Essay 14.

ARTICLES

'Quantification and Ontology', R. B. Marcus, *Noûs,* Vol. VI, 1972.

'Quantification Theory and the Problem of Identifying Objects of Reference', P. T. Geach, *Acta Philosophica Fennica,* 1963.

'The Substitution Interpretation of Quantification', J. M. Dunn & N. D. Belnap, Jr., *Noûs,* Vol. II, 1968.

'Two Concepts of Quantification', Leonard Linsky, *Noûs,* Vol. VI, 1972.

Chapter 12

KNOWING THAT

by

SIBAJIBAN
University of Burdwan

Contemporary philosophers have studied the use of 'know' in various contexts in order to solve or dissolve many problems about the nature of knowledge. For example, some have held that 'know', when used in the first person singular in the present indicative tense and active voice, has a merely performative function; some have held that 'know' is a capacity verb and has only a dispositional use; still others have held that it has an episodic use. In the present paper we propose to examine these theories.

I

The view that 'know' in such contexts as 'I know that . . .' has a merely performative use was originally put forward by Austin.[1] Chisholm,[2] however, states:

'Austin did not provide a clear definition of the concept (of performative utterance), but I think that "performative utterances" might be described as follows:

'There are certain acts—e.g. requesting, ordering, guaranteeing, baptizing—which have this characteristic: When the circumstances are right, then to perform the act it is *enough* to make an utterance containing words which the speaker commonly uses to designate such an act.'

---

[1] J. L. Austin, 'Other Minds', in J. O. Urmson & G. J. Warnock (Eds.), *Philosophical Papers*, Oxford, 1961, Chapter 3.
[2] Roderick M. Chisholm, *Theory of Knowledge*, Prentice-Hall, 1966, p. 16.

This is what Chisholm calls 'the strict sense of performative utterance'; he further contends that according to Austin 'I know' is a performative utterance in this strict sense, 'It looks very much as though Austin was assuming mistakenly that "I know" is performative in the strict sense . . .'.[1] Thus on Chisholm's interpretation, Austin's theory is that to perform an act of knowing it is enough merely to say 'I know' (in suitable circumstances).

If we accept Chisholm's interpretation of Austin as substantially correct, we may wonder how determining the conditions of saying 'I know' can, in any way, throw light on the nature of the act of knowing for performing which it is *not necessary*, but *only sufficient*, to say 'I know'. Thus there seem to be two ways of knowing: (i) knowing by saying 'I know', and (ii) knowing in some other way. Now if it is possible to know without making any performative utterance, but by performing some other act, then is it not *possible* that we are performing *that* act even when we do say 'I know'? This possibility cannot be ruled out unless we can show that performing that other act and saying 'I know' are incompatible acts. We now examine Austin's theory in some detail to see how far, if at all, he has succeeded in eliminating this possibility.

We begin by noting that none of the acts of seeing, judging, recognising, remembering, inferring, analysing, comparing, distinguishing, etc., is an act which can be performed by making any performative utterance. 'Know' seems to be only a general term for these (and other) more specific acts. It will be strange if I can know merely by saying 'I know', yet cannot perform any specific act of knowing in this way. A general word denotes every member of a class of similar things, but the specific acts of knowing do not seem to resemble each other as acts which can be performed by making performative utterances, for none of them seems to be such an act. So let us see if seeing, etc., is knowing according to Austin. We here compare and contrast Ayer's theory with Austin's.

[1] *Ibid.*, p. 17.

According to Austin, saying 'I know' is not saying I have 'performed a specially striking feat of cognition, superior, in the same scale as believing, and being sure, even to being nearly quite sure: for there *is* nothing in that scale superior to being quite sure ... when I say 'I know', *I give others my word: I give others my authority* for saying that '*S* is *P*'.[1]

'When I have said only that I am sure, and proved to have been mistaken, I am not liable to be rounded on by others in the same way as when I have said "I know". I am sure *for my part*, you can take it or leave it. ... But I do not know "for my part", and when I say 'I know' I don't mean you can take it or leave it. . . . If I have said I know or I promise, you will insult me in a special way by refusing to accept it . . . and so, where someone has said to me, "I know", I am entitled to say *I* know too, at second hand. The right to say "I know" is transmissible, in the sort of way that other authority is transmissible. Hence, if I say it lightly, I may be *responsible* for getting *you* into trouble.'[2]

Ayer, however, seems to differ from Austin on the exact meaning of 'I know'. According to him 'I know that *p*' implies only 'I *have* the right to be sure that *p*'. If the right to say 'I know' is transmissible, in the sort of way that other authority is transmissible, then there must be a *prior* process which confers on me the authority which I can then transmit to others by saying 'I know', for I cannot transmit a right which does not vest in me. The question 'How do you know?' is a demand to know how I have myself acquired the authority which I am now seeking to transmit to others by saying 'I know'. So we may ask whether knowing should be identified with acquiring this authority or right, or also with its transmission to others. Austin seems to accept the latter alternative while Ayer accepts the former. This difference in their views leads to some further differences. For example, in Ayer's sense of 'know' seeing is also knowing, for if I see that the table is brown, then I have the right to be sure that it is so. But

---

[1] Austin, *op. cit.*, p. 67. [2] *Ibid.*, p. 68.

if knowing, i.e. saying 'I know', is also to transmit this right to others, then seeing is not knowing, for I do not by simply seeing that the table is brown, transmit to others the right which seeing confers on me.

If we understand literally Austin's remark that the right to say 'I know' is transmissible 'in the sort of way that *other authority* is transmissible' then no one can transmit it to a minor; for, this right to say 'I know' cannot be held in trust by guardians (natural or *ad litem*) until the minor comes of age. Thus Austin seems to be very severe with minors whom he debars from knowing anything from others, 'at second hand'. Not merely that; on Austin's theory a one year old child, for example, cannot be said to know anything at all, for he is hardly a person who can realise his responsibility to others. He does not ordinarily say 'I know' when he knows, and is also not able to assume any responsibility for what he says or does. He cannot have any duty, and if right implies duty, then he cannot even *have* any right at all. This shows that neither Austin nor Ayer is considering cases of knowing by children, they are considering cases only of adults. But Austin, holding a stronger theory, is excluding cases of a type of adults too. Consider, for example, the case of a person known to be a liar. His 'crying wolf' will not be taken seriously by others even when he is serious. Even when on a particular occasion he speaks the truth and intends to transmit his authority for saying 'I know' to others, he fails, for he has forfeited his social right to transmit his authority.

We note here some other consequences of Austin's theory. (1) There seems to be a considerable amount of agreement among philosophers that 'I know that *p*' implies that *p* is true.[1] Yet on Austin's theory this implication cannot hold. If I know that *p* by merely saying that I know that *p*, and 'it is naturally *always* possible ("humanly" possible) that I may be mistaken' (but that by itself is no bar against using the expres-

---

[1] It would generally be agreed that no expression of the form "*X* knows that *p*" is true unless *p* is true. (Griffiths, A. Phillips, *Knowledge and Belief*, Oxford, 1967, Introduction.)

I

sion 'I know'), then from 'I know that *p*' it cannot logically follow that *p* is true. Thus on Austin's theory we can *never* use 'know' in a sense in which knowing that *p* implies that *p* is true; knowing that *p* cannot mean more than that 'reasonable precautions only are taken' against the possibility of error. (2) Austin further restricts the sense of 'know'. 'And, further, it is overlooked that the conditions which must be satisfied if I am to show that a thing is within my cognisance or within my power are conditions, not about the future, but about *the present and the past;* it is not demanded that I do more than *believe* about the future'.[1] He elucidates this point by an example. 'If "Figs never grow on thistles" is taken to mean "None ever have and none ever will" then it is implied that I *know* that none ever have, but only that I *believe* that none ever will".[2] It is not clear what *special* difficulty there is in my *knowing* that figs will never grow on thistles, if there is no difficulty in my knowing that figs have never grown on thistles. How are conditions about the past, as in this example about an indefinite past, in any way easier for me to satisfy than conditions about the future? If a thing in the past was actually experienced then this certainly gives me the right to say that I know it, but surely I could never verify a statement about all past figs although they are past. How am I to satisfy the conditions about the past if I am to say that I know that the moon separated from the earth so many million years ago?

Thus if we accept Austin's theory we can never say: (i) that seeing, etc., is knowing; (ii) that children, etc., can ever know anything; (iii) that to know that *p* implies that *p* is true; and (iv) that we can ever know, even in principle, anything about the future.

II

We now propose to discuss a type of theory according to which '*X* knows that *p*' implies that *p* is true. The theories of Ayer[3] and Chisholm,[4] although differing in important respects,

[1] Austin, *op. cit.*, p. 69.   [2] *Ibid.*
[3] A. J. Ayer, *The Problem of Knowledge*, Pelican, 1957, Chapter 1.
[4] Chisholm, *op. cit.*, Chapter 1.

have this point in common. For examination we state here a version given by Gettier:[1]

X knows that p = Df.   (i) p is true,
                      (ii) X believes that p, and
                     (iii) X is justified in believing that p.

In a definition of this type the definiens is a conjunction of several sentences which are, of course, intended to be logically independent of one another. That 'p is true' is one of them shows that it cannot be deduced from the rest. Its addition to them looks very much like an *ad hoc* measure only to ensure the truth of p if known. To see why it has to be there we have to note how the problem of defining knowledge has been posed in this type of theory. The problem is formulated as being one of finding out what factor, if any, is necessary (and sufficient) to turn a *true* belief into a state of knowledge. The problem stated in some such form has been traced to Plato's *Theaetetus;* yet, as we shall try to show here, it seems an improper formulation of the problem, making it in principle insoluble.

'X believes truly that p' is analysed into the conjunction 'X believes that p and p is a true proposition'. That is, in believing truly that p, X does no more than simply believe that p, the rest is left to chance, a factor wholly beyond his control. Believing truly, unlike, for example, believing firmly, is not a special type of believing, difficult to achieve; it is just believing. The truth of p which makes his belief true *has to remain unknown to him* if he is *merely to believe* truly that p. 'X believes truly that p' is a judgement about X's belief which can be made only by *someone else* who *knows* that p is true but never by X himself. This situation may be compared with Descartes' *cogito.* The sentence 'I am unconscious' is quite in order and is often true, for it may be a fact that I am unconscious. Yet I can never make the true statement 'I am unconscious' for, if I am unconscious, I cannot make this or *any other* statement; and

[1] Edmund L. Gettier, 'Is Justified True Belief Knowledge', in A. P. Griffiths (Ed.), *Knowledge and Belief*, Oxford, 1967, p. 144.

the fact that I make it implies that I am not unconscious.[1] That is, the fact which I state by saying truly 'I am unconscious' comes into conflict with what is obviously implied by the fact that I say it. So also when I say 'I (merely) believe truly that *p*' what is implied by the fact that I say it comes into conflict with what I say; for what I say is that I *merely* believe that *p*, although truly, that therefore I do not know that *p*, yet my saying implies that I do know that *p*. If it is a fact that I (merely) believe truly that *p*, then I can never state that fact.

But are there any circumstances in which I can say truly 'I believe truly that *p*'? It would appear that I can say truly 'I believe truly that *p*' if I know that *p*; for on the given definition of 'knowing that', from 'I know that *p*' it will follow logically that I believe truly that *p* (which is the conjunction of (i) and (ii) of the definiens). Although from the fact that I believe truly that *p*, it will not follow that I know that *p*, yet if I say (truly) 'I believe truly that *p*' then from the fact that I say it, it will follow that I know that *p*. Thus I can say (truly) 'I believe truly that *p*' if and only if I know that *p*. The sentence form 'I believe truly that *p*' is odd because saying this truly *presupposes* that I know that *p*, so that 'I believe truly that *p*' will necessarily be an understatement which however cannot be an understatement. If I say 'I believe truly that *p*' then my saying this implies that I know that *p*, and this implication is obvious to everyone including myself; it is puzzling why I say this not in so many words, but only by way of an unnecessary implication. Surely, to say 'I believe truly that *p*' is not a subtle way of saying 'I know that *p*'.

If what we have said so far is correct, then 'I know that *p*' cannot be defined by 'I believe truly that *p*' even when supplemented by other sentences purporting to determine further the nature of the belief. For when 'I know that *p*' is defined in this way, then to know that *p*, I can no more than hold a justified belief which happens to be true. Whether *p* is a true proposi-

---

[1] For a detailed discussion of this point see Sibajiban ('Descartes' Doubt', in *Philosophy and Phenomenological Research*, Vol. XXIV, No. 1).

tion or not is a matter of chance; so when I hold a justified belief that p, it is an accident which turns my believing into knowing that p.

This is the reason why Gettier[1] could construct his two examples to show that the definiens is not a sufficient condition of the definiendum. In the two examples he has constructed the chance element which turns the propositions into true propositions has been highlighted. In the first example, he says 'but imagine, further, that *unknown to Smith*, he himself, not Jones, will get the job. And, also *unknown to Smith*, he himself has ten coins in his pocket'.[2] In the second example, he says, 'And secondly, by the *sheerest coincidence, and entirely unknown to Smith*, the place mentioned in proposition (h) happens really to be the place where Brown is'.[3]

Michael Clark's attempt to remedy this defect is misdirected. For he thinks that by adding one more condition to the three already listed he can solve this problem. We shall try to show here that Clark has failed because the difficulty is not amenable to this type of cure.

Clark begins by slightly altering the second example of Gettier to show that even if S's belief is not merely true and justified but also the grounds on which he holds his belief are true, even then S may not have knowledge. 'Yet Brown's wild guess can hardly be regarded as providing Smith with knowledge merely because it happens to be right. In this case, then, the grounds on which Smith believes (i) (i.e. Jones owns a Ford) are true, but the grounds on which he accepts these grounds, viz. *that Brown knows them;* are false'.[4] Thus it appears that according to Clark in order for Smith to know that Jones owns a Ford under the conditions specified, he has to assume that someone else, viz. Brown, knows something else, and this assumption which is Smith's second-order ground for believing that Jones owns a Ford *has to be true*. This is not solving the problem, but is very much like 'passing

[1] Gettier, *op. cit.*   [2] *Ibid.*, p. 145. (My italics.)   [3] *Ibid.*, p. 146. (My italics.)
[4] Michael Clark, 'Knowledge and Grounds: A Comment on Mr Gettier's Paper', in *Analysis*, Vol. 24, No. 2, p. 47. (My italics.)

the buck', for if the definition of 'S knows that *p*' essentially involves '*R* knows that *q*' then the definition becomes obviously logically defective. Perhaps an awareness of this difficulty has led Brown to rephrase the grounds on which Smith believes that Jones owns a Ford when he later on gives an analysis of the higher-order grounds. Thus although Clark has initially stated that the ground of the ground of Smith's belief is that 'Brown *knows* them', yet later on when he enumerates these grounds he changes it radically to read 'What are your *grounds for claiming* Brown knows this?', and nowhere in the list of the successive grounds 'Brown knows this' occurs. Thus Clark is not sure if the grounds on which Smith accepts the grounds on which he believes that Jones owns a Ford are 'Brown knows them' or 'Smith claims that Brown knows them'. But these are entirely different propositions and need different sorts of justification. As a matter of fact, Clark's analysis of the chain of grounds is not correct, and needs to be modified in the following manner:

(2) What are your grounds for saying Jones owns a Ford?

(3) Brown told me he always has owned one.

(4) What are your grounds for claiming Brown knows this?

At this stage the logical answer which Clark omits will be:

(5) Brown himself claimed that he knew this.

Here there are two ways in which we can proceed. (A) We can ask:

(6) What are the grounds on which Brown bases *his* claim?

and this procedure is what I have dubbed as 'passing the buck' for, here, the reply will be 'Ask Brown' and we shall have to begin anew with Brown. (B) The second way is to proceed as Clark does, and ask:

(6) What are *your grounds* for accepting Brown's claim?

But if the reply to this is, as Clark suggests, viz.

(7) He is generally reliable and honest

then this will not prove that Brown knows what he claims to know in the particular case; for Brown's general reliability is not inconsistent with his making a mistake in a particular instance and being *by chance* right, as in Gettier's examples. But then can we say that Smith knows it either, as he bases his knowledge on what Brown tells him? The answer seems to be obviously in the negative. This shows that Clark's attempt to salvage the definition from Gettier's attack has not succeeded. The reason for this is that Clark's modification of the Ayer-type definition suffers from the same defect as the original definition, viz. that although S believes that p, and is justified in believing that p, and his belief is well grounded in the sense of Clark, yet all these do not imply that p is true which is therefore retained as a separate and independent condition. Thus the possibility always remains that although S's belief is justified and also well grounded, yet it may be false and that if it is ever true, it is only by chance that it is true. Gettier explicitly states '*It is* possible for a person to be justified in believing a proposition that is in fact false';[1] Clark's modification does not eliminate this possibility and we can say that it is possible for a person to hold a belief which is both justified and well grounded and which is yet false.

We now show that Austin's definition, too, suffers from this fundamental defect. We do not avoid the element of chance in knowing simply by giving up the theory that knowing that p implies the truth of p. Austin, as we have already seen, does not accept this implication; yet he too allows chance to play a vital role in knowledge. According to Austin although there is *always a possibility* of p being false, still *actually p* is true often, most of the time, if I know that p. In order to be able to say 'I know that p', all I can do is to take 'reasonable precautions only' against error; I do my duty well if I take such precautions. But whatever I may do will not eliminate the *possibility* of error, and p may be false. Now, if in spite of my best efforts, I may be wrong, then it is just by chance that I am right when I happen to be right. There is no

[1] Gettier, *op. cit.*, p. 145.

reason why I shall ever be, and *the fact* that I am often, most of the time, right, is inexplicable.

This was the occasion for Descartes to bring in the veracity of God, and on that ground assert that it is inconceivable that ideas known clearly and distinctly may yet fail to be true. Leibnitz introduced the principle of pre-established harmony for the same reason. Although Austin, Ayer, Chisholm and other supporters of this type of theory do not seem to be aware of it, their theory depends entirely on providence for the coincidence of the truth of a proposition and its being known, which coincidence seems to be the rule proved by the exceptions.

The reason for this impasse is that 'p is true' is made logically independent of the process of knowing that p. If the process by which I come to know that p has got nothing to do with the truth value of p, then there will be an insoluble mystery if p turns out to be true even once on the occasion of being known. True belief and knowledge have to be conceived as *different in kind;* true belief is belief which happens to be true; the credit for this, if any, does not belong to him who believes, he is just *lucky.* But if I know that p, then the credit for this belongs to me; it is an achievement on my part. If knowledge be merely a variety of true belief, justified true belief, then how am I to answer 'How do you know?'. For I can then only reply that all I have done is to be careful to see that my belief is justified, and depended on luck to do the rest. The coincidence which has turned my justified belief into knowledge is not due to anything which I could have done as a knowing subject. So if I can answer 'How do you know?' in a way different from the way I answer 'Why do you believe?', then that shows that knowledge is not a justified belief which happens to be true. We are then led to the view that the way in which I come to know that p—the careful, cautious, safe, proven procedure which I have followed—does guarantee that p is true. That is, the function of the Cartesian God has to be taken over by the very impersonal and still very mysterious procedures acknowledged as procedures of knowing.

III

We now discuss only one point of difference between the definitions of Ayer and Chisholm. This difference is that of meanings which the authors give to 'know'. Ayer, in defining knowledge, uses the term 'know' in the dispositional sense; although he does not deny that the disposition can be actualised, yet he does not think that the actualisation has anything to do with the nature of knowing. Chisholm, on the other hand, uses 'know' in the episodic sense in his definition. He not merely holds that 'there *is* a state, after all, that may be described or reported by means of the word "know" ',[1] but wants to clarify only the episodic sense of 'know' by his definition. Thus, instead of Ayer's definiendum, viz. '*X* knows that *p*', Chisholm has '*X* knows at *t* that *p*'. In the definiens this difference is reflected in the difference between '*X* believes that *p*' and '*X* believes *at t* that *p*'. If 'know' or 'believe' is used in a dispositional sense, then 'knows at *t*' or 'believes at *t*' (i.e. at a particular point of time) will not make sense.

It may be argued here that the mere reference to a particular time does not prove that knowledge or belief is not a disposition. For dispositions also change from time to time, and it will be not merely natural but also necessary to mention the time element in referring to a disposition. Thus a lump of clay is plastic, but when it is dry it *becomes* hard. Similarly when a belief is cancelled by a contrary or a contradictory belief, an old disposition is destroyed and a new disposition is formed. So the mere reference to time does not prove that Chisholm is not discussing knowing as a disposition.

But this argument does not seem to be valid. For a knowledge cannot be destroyed by a later knowledge, so if knowledge is a disposition, then this disposition is a permanent acquisition and cannot be cancelled at all. Moreover, even if dispositions change in time they are not momentary, nor do they last only for a few moments in the way mental acts do. That Chisholm is using 'know' in the episodic sense becomes

---

[1] Chisholm, *op. cit.*, p. 18.

clear in the footnote to his definition of knowledge where, *inter alia*, he says, 'for any subject and any time, if *e* is evident to that subject at that time then *h* is evident to that subject at that time'[1] and when he talks of being evident to a subject at a particular time he cannot be talking about a disposition. So Chisholm is defining 'know' only as an actual mental state. Moreover, as we shall see later, there is a sense in which *mental* dispositions are permanent and cannot change or be modified.

Now let us see what are the consequences of this difference. We begin by examining some statements of Arthur Pap[2] and Eric Toms[3] who use 'believe at *t*' and 'believe', but in an altogether different context. Pap declares:

'Thus explicitly self-contradictory sentences do not express anything that could possibly be believed; that there are round squares, for example, is not something that could possibly be believed; and the impossibility in question is not just *psychological*. That somebody should believe both (and at the same time) *p* and not-*p* is itself a contradictory supposition. The frequent claim that people, alas, are capable of holding self-contradictory beliefs notwithstanding, the statement "*X* believes at *t* that *p* and not-*p*" is self-contradictory. It entails "*X* believes at *t* that *p* and *X* believes at *t* that not-*p*" . . . the conjunction "*X* believes at *t* that *p* and *X* believes at *t* that not-*p*" is self-contradictory, though not formally so.'[4]

Eric Toms, on the other hand, asserts: 'That an object may be said or even believed both to have and not to have a certain property, every one knows to be possible, alas'.[5] The problem here seems to be whether it is logically possible for one and the same person to believe that *p* and believe that not-*p*.[6] Pap is using 'believe at *t*' while Toms is using 'believe',

[1] Chisholm, *op. cit.*, p. 23.
[2] Arthur Pap, *Semantics and Necessary Truths*, New Haven, 1958.
[3] Eric Toms, *Being, Negation and Logic*, Basil Blackwell, Oxford, 1962.
[4] Pap. *op. cit.*, p. 173.   [5] Toms, *op. cit.*, p. 3.
[6] For a different approach to this problem see Sibajiban, 'The Self-contradictory and the inconceivable', in *Analysis*, Vol. 24 (Suppl.), No. 2.

i.e. Pap is using 'believe' in the episodic, and Toms in the dispositional, sense.

To resolve this controversy it is not necessary, as we shall try to show, to take sides, to reject one view or the other; both the views can be accepted as true if we distinguish between the episodic sense (Pap) and the dispositional sense (Toms) of 'believe'. To resolve the controversy in this way, we have to understand the nature of acts and dispositions.

We may begin with a remark which Professor Ryle makes in explaining the position of those who accept introspection as a higher order act directed towards a lower order act. We shall, however, generalise Ryle's remark to make it applicable to *different* acts, not necessarily to acts of *different order*. Ryle[1] says: 'He can, in principle, never catch more than the coat-tails of the object of his pursuit. . . . He is always a day late for the fair, but everyday he reaches the place of yesterday's fair. He never succeeds in jumping on to the shadow of his own head, yet he is never more than one jump behind'.

An analysis of this remark of Ryle reveals the following points: (1) the two acts cannot be simultaneous; and (2) if introspection is to be possible, then the introspective act must follow *immediately* upon the object act, i.e. must not be more than *one* jump behind. To understand clearly what Ryle suggests by metaphors we have to formulate a theory more or less in the following way.

The acts of believing, doubting, supposing, judging, knowing, etc., have three moments or *phases:* (a) a moment of origination; (b) a moment of duration, and (c) a moment of cessation leaving behind a trace which forms a disposition. If we have thus acquired a disposition, then it may again be stirred up, activised to result in a conscious act. (This is a causal theory of disposition which may, or may not, be accepted for our present purpose.) Now Ryle's first point is that two acts cannot *originate* at the same time. An act originating at *t* will *prevent every other act* from originating at *t;* this is because of the psychological law that we cannot attend to

[1] Gilbert Ryle, *The Concept of Mind,* Barnes & Noble, New York, 1960, p. 196.

more than one thing at a time. Thus we have a general law about conscious acts—two conscious acts cannot originate, hence, more generally, be in the same phase, at the same time.

We now try to understand what it is for one act to be 'one jump behind' another act. We explain this in the following way. Although two acts cannot originate at the same time, still one act can, and if introspection is to be possible, must, originate, i.e. be in its first phase, when a prior act endures, i.e. is in *its second* phase. It is not necessary to assume that all acts take the same time to originate, or to lapse into a disposition, or that all acts endure equally long—i.e. moments, here, need not be understood as, atoms, or equal lengths, of time. Now it is necessary to assume that a higher order act can originate while the object act endures if only to be able to catch the coat-tails of the object act. This, we claim, is what Ryle expresses as the introspective act's being *just one jump behind* the object act.

Now we return to an analysis of Pap's view. Pap seems to have confused two different forms of believing. He thinks 'X believes at t that p and not-p' and 'X believes at t that p and X believes at t that not-p' are the same. Yet, if what we have said earlier about acts and their origination be true, then it is not *psychologically* possible to have two acts of believing originating or enduring at the same time, t. It is psychologically impossible that an act of believing that p, and a different act of believing a different proposition, be both at t. Thus 'X believes at t that p and X believes at t that not-p' is impossible psychologically, not because p and not-p are contradictories, but because no two acts can be at the same phase at the same time. But then Pap asserts that 'X believes at t that p and X believes at t that not-p' is 'self-contradictory though not formally so'. Let us see if we can understand the point that Pap is trying to make.

We have already argued that a second act can originate when a prior act endures, so that if we symbolise by t' the time when the first act endures and by t the time of its origination, then we can say that it is psychologically possible that 'X

believes at t that p and X believes at t' that q'. The point which Pap is trying to make then can be expressed in the following way. We can never say truly 'X believes at t that p and X believes at t' that not-p'; i.e. so long as X *continues* to believe that p, he cannot *start* believing that not-p. So long as the belief that p *endures* as a conscious act, the other act of believing that not-p *cannot even originate*. This impossibility has got nothing to do with the psychological mechanism of the origination of acts, but is completely determined by the logical relation between p and not-p. But if the belief that p has lapsed into a mere disposition and is no longer a conscious act, if it is forgotten and not remembered at that moment, then the mere disposition will not prevent the same person from believing that not-p. This explains the sense in which Toms's statement is correct.

Thus we have come to the first point of difference between disposition and act. A conscious act of believing that p so long as it remains a conscious act will prevent a person from consciously believing that not-p; but if the belief is a mere disposition and is not recalled, then the same person can believe that p and also that not-p, and *one* of the beliefs can become also actualised; i.e. a person can believe that not-p, only so long as he does not *realise* that he also believes that p. A person cannot, *consciously*, *knowingly*, hold self-contradictory beliefs; but unknowingly, without realising that he does so, a person can hold beliefs which may not be consistent. As a matter of fact the law of contradiction has been formulated differently from different points of view.[1] The statement of the law as 'A cannot be both B and not-B' is that of the law as a law of reality. As a law of thought it is stated as 'A cannot be *thought* to be both B and not-B' where thought has to be understood, if our suggestion is correct, as conscious thought, i.e. as the *act of* judging.

Now let us return to the definitions of knowledge as given by Ayer and Chisholm. If 'know' is used only in a disposi-

---

[1] For a detailed discussion of the law of contradiction see Sibajiban (*Analysis, op. cit.*)

tional sense, then from 'X knows that p' it will follow that 'X believes that p' where 'believe', too, will have only a dispositional sense. But then it will be quite possible for a person to know that p, and yet not *realise* that he does so. He may even forget that he knows that p, and hence may also come to believe that not-p, that is, in the dispositional sense of 'know', 'X knows that p, but has forgotten that he knows that p' will make sense, and may even be true, especially if p is a trivial proposition. But, then forgetting seems to create insuperable problems for a dispositional theory of knowing. Does the disposition which is knowing that p remain when a person has forgotten that he knows that p? Forgetting admits of degrees; a person may be reminded of what he has forgotten more or less easily, or not at all. If he can remember or be made to remember, even in hypnosis, the presence of the disposition is proved. But if a person cannot remember at all, if he has forgotten totally and completely, can we then say that he knows that p? He may have to relearn or know anew what he had known before. The problem here is: Shall we say, in such a case, that the person knows that p? That he still retains the disposition can be inferred from the comparative ease with which he relearns it without ever realising that he is learning anew what he already knew. The difficulty seems to be due to the ambiguity of 'disposition'. Disposition, which is knowing, may be: (i) a disposition to remember at will, to answer a specific question unhesitatingly and promptly; (ii) a disposition to respond correctly only after some prompting; or (iii) the disposition only to relearn a thing more easily than at the first time. If the Freudian theory that nothing which ever enters the unconscious is ever lost, is accepted, then to know once is to know for ever, if 'know' is used in a dispositional sense. A disposition, then can never be destroyed, i.e. totally erased from the mind.

But, then, it may be asked, how can any one give up a belief when he realises that it is a false or unjustified belief? If the disposition which is the belief cannot be destroyed, then how can a person give up a belief? The answer is: the disposition which is the false or unjustified belief remains, but is rendered ineffective only by a conscious act—the realisation that the belief is false or unjustified. A false or unjustified belief is given up only in the sense that it is cancelled in the *conscious mind;* i.e. so long as the person is fully conscious, he does not allow the cancelled belief from operating; he withdraws his assent to the belief and this withdrawal is a deliberate act to begin with. It may become well-established and automatic by repetition or by other means. But, even then, in a fit of absent-mindedness, the person may be acting from the cancelled belief, which may manifest itself in dream or even in other abnormal behaviour. Thus according to Freudian psychology, cancellation, in the sense of total destruction, of false, unjustified or irrational belief by the knowledge of truth is not possible. The psycho-analytic technique of resolving inner conflicts is merely to make the subject *conscious* of what is at the root of the conflicts, to make them *ineffective,* but not to rid the mind of their presence. What goes into the mind, conscious, sub-conscious or unconscious, stays in the mind for ever.

If dispositions are sub-conscious or unconscious, then conflicting dispositions can, and do, remain side by side. A person who knows that p, and therefore, believes that p, may also believe that not-p. Thus 'X knows that p and believes that not-p' will not be self-contradictory if 'know' and 'believe' are used in the dispositional sense. The paradox may be resolved by adding that although X knows that p, he has forgotten that he knows that p and mistakenly believes that not-p; still forgetting creates difficulties which may be difficult, if not impossible, to solve. Chisholm, while defining knowledge only as an act, avoids these difficulties. Hintikka too while developing his logic of knowledge and belief, explicitly states: 'The notion of forgetting is not applicable within the limits of an occasion'.[1]

Now, this explains why Hintikka can, and Ryle cannot, hold that to know is to know that one knows. As Ryle is using the

[1] Jaakke Hintikka, *Knowledge and Belief,* Cornell, 1962, p. 7.

term 'know' in the dispositional sense, a person can know, i.e. have the disposition, without being conscious that he has it; i.e. to have a disposition is not necessarily to be aware of it. So in order to know that one knows, it is necessary to have a disposition directed towards another disposition, and it is not at all necessary that every disposition has another disposition directed towards it. So to know, and to know that one knows, are two entirely different dispositions. But if 'know' is used in the sense in which Hintikka is using it, i.e. not merely in the sense of a short-lived, if not momentary, mental act, but also in the sense in which one cannot be said to know if he has forgotten it, then it is possible to prove the equivalence of 'X knows that p' and 'X knows that X knows that p' from specially chosen axioms. But even these axioms would not have been of any avail to Hintikka if he used 'know' in Ryle's sense.

Thus we find that if 'know' is used only in the dispositional sense, then (1) knowledge will not be open to introspection; (2) 'X knows that p but has forgotten that he knows that p' will be meaningful; and (3) 'X knows that p and believes that not-p' will not be self-contradictory.

Chapter 13

THE EXPERIENCE OF NOTHINGNESS
IN BUDDHISM AND EXISTENTIALISM

by

RAMAKANT SINARI

SIES College, University of Bombay

NOTHINGNESS AS THE LIMIT OF ĀTMALOGY

Among the concepts that have always been taken to represent
the uniquely ego-exploring attitude of philosophy in the
Orient, probably the most penetrating is the concept of
Nothingness. The ego-exploring technique in certain Indian
philosophies I have elsewhere described as ātmalogy.[1] The
function of ātmalogy is to direct consciousness toward itself,
to intensify its self-transcending process, and to put it in a
position to observe its own 'roots'. It is an extremely rigorous
inward-seeing discipline which Indian philosophers since the
times of the *Upaniṣads* (c. 1000 BC) have accepted generally as
the method for philosophy. Several schools of philosophy in
India, such as Jainism, Buddhism, Sāṃkhya, Yoga, and
Vedānta, remain totally committed to ātmalogy as a way of
attaining other-worldly salvation (*mokṣa*). However, apart from
its basically ethical intentions in Indian religions and life
theories which I do not want to examine in the present article,
ātmalogy is an epistemology promising to discover the ontological ground of our world-experience.

In a concentrated ego-exploring technique there comes a
stage when consciousness appears to move away from all

[1] See my *The Structure of Indian Thought*, Illinois, Charles C. Thomas, 1970,
pp. 11–12.

positivity of the empirical experience. One of the aims of ātmalogy has always been to delineate this movement, the movement of consciousness from an ordinary to a fundamental state, from immanence to transcendence, from the reflective domain to the pre-reflective. It is perhaps logical that a method which tries to reach the background of our experiencing self should allude to an area verging on Nothingness. It is a metaphysical area, the depth of the ego where Being and Nothingness telescope into each other or rather Being fades out into Nothing. The Buddhists have referred to this area as *śūnyatā*, *tathatā*, or *nirvāṇa*; the existentialists of our own time have called it *Sein*, *Nichts*, and *Néant*.

The ego-exploring discipline in some of the systems of philosophy in India greatly resembles the method of phenomenological reduction central to the schools of phenomenology and existentialism.[1] The discipline, which is partly psychological but essentially epistemological, consists in withdrawing one's consciousness from the empirically given and concentrating it on its own primordial acts and contents. One of the remarkable points of closeness between this discipline and the phenomenological reduction is that they regard the domain of one's own subjectivity as the foundation of one's world-experience and therefore as the only sphere which philosophy must investigate. For instance, the followers of the phenomenological reduction such as Heidegger, Karl Jaspers, Merleau-Ponty, and Sartre, like the ātmalogists, have analysed the human ego and probed deep into its horizontal and vertical expanse to bring out what can be called its tie with the external world and its continuation backwards into an undecipherable ontological region. The originality of both these disciplines lies in their operating 'subterraneously', that is in going behind the given as such, in studying the happenings in the field of consciousness, in trying to reach the fringe of awareness where our very sense of being present in the

[1] For a study of the phenomenological elements in Yoga and Advaita Vedānta, see my 'The Method of Phenomenological Reduction and Yoga', in *Philosophy East and West*, Vol. 15, Nos. 3 & 4, pp. 217–18; and 'The Phenomenological Attitude in the Saṁkara Vedānta', in *Philosophy East and West*, Vol. 22, No. 3, pp. 281–90.

world arises. It must be repeated, however, that while the final goal of the whole ego-exploring technique in India's philosophies, and in Oriental philosophies for that matter, if one takes into account the Chinese and the Japanese schools of Buddhism, is the achievement of liberation (*mokṣa*) from the world of suffering, the method of phenomenological reduction is purely epistemologically oriented.

Among the philosophies of the Orient, the one which carried on its ego-exploring process to its farthest limit (that is, Nothingness) is *śūnyavāda*.[1] One could state, in an analogous manner, that among the phenomenological and existentialist tendencies in the West it is in the atheistic existentialism of Heidegger and Sartre that the phenomenological reduction has been stretched to its extreme point, viz. Nothingness. The purpose of this paper is to reflect on the points of similarity between the concepts of Nothingness in these two highly influential Oriental and Western systems of thought.

THE TRANSCENDENTAL WISDOM

Śūnyavāda, or the Nothingness doctrine, was founded by a brilliant Buddhist dialectician, Nāgārjuna, in c. AD 150, that is about 600 years after the death of Gautama the Buddha (Buddha means the enlightened). Basically it is a body of interpretations of the original conceptions of the Buddha regarding the nature of Reality, the transcendental experience, and the meaning of human life. As a philosophical view within Mahāyāna (one of the two main sects, Mahāyāna and Hīnayāna, into which Buddhism bifurcated after the Buddha's death) *śūnyavāda* must have been present before Nāgārjuna. In any case, the famous theory of *tathatā*, or suchness, propounded by Aśvaghoṣa, the first systematic expounder of Mahāyāna, is a potential statement of the Nothingness doctrine.

[1] In fact, the inward attitude which is central to Zen today is associated with the ego-exploring process in *śūnyavāda*. There is *śūnyatā* or emptiness at the heart of Zen. See, for a discussion of Nothingness in Oriental philosophy, Masao Abe, 'Zen and Western Thought', in *International Philosophical Quarterly*, Vol. 10, No. 4, pp. 501–39.

Aśvaghoṣa says that the fundamental character of things cannot be explained by means of thought and words.[1] It is something elusive, 'beyond the range of perception', 'possesses absolute sameness', and undergoes neither change nor destruction. Our ordinary experience, that is the experience of the relatedness of phenomena, of factors conditioning them, of the subject–object duality, of the many diverse beings, etc., is governed by naïveté. On the other hand, the essence of things, i.e. their *tathatā*, whose knowledge the enlightened alone can claim is the Reality, calm, blissful, and self-shining. Thus *tathatā* is the ontological ground of the world and of our being in it. To comprehend it is to be enlightened.

Aśvaghoṣa repudiates intellect and explains it as a finite manifestation of suchness. However, he does not alienate the world perceived by intellect from suchness and call it non-existent or false. He is not interested in proving whether the world which we find to be 'there' is ultimately real or illusory, but rather that when we acquire wisdom (*bodhi*) we would have *the* true view of its foundation. Being a monist, he tends to reduce the plurality of the human selves to one eternal reality. But why does *tathatā* become a variety of selves and things? Aśvaghoṣa attributes to our ignorance, to our lack of insight, the reason of pure *tathatā* being perceived as individual egos and particular phenomena. But where does the ignorance arise from? Although suchness originally transcends everything, ignorance breaks into it like a flash and individuates it.

What Aśvaghoṣa's philosophy aims at is the exposition of an attitude of mind by which one would realise the 'essence of wisdom' (*bodhisattva*). Our ego-sense, he says, is a hindrance in the process of this realisation. *Tathatā* is the awareness of pure Being, of that immaculate form of things where contingency and distinctions which necessarily control our empirical experience cease to continue. The purpose of human life is to intuit the source of the very phenomenon of 'isness',

[1] D. T. Suzuki, *Aśvaghoṣa's Discourse on the Awakening of Faith in the Mahāyāna*, Chicago, Open Court, 1900, p. 112.

and it is in our grasp of *tathatā* that the disclosure of this source lies.

It is believed that Aśvaghoṣa and Nāgārjuna were contemporaries. It is understandable, therefore, why the directions of thought of the two Mahāyāna philosophers should have so much in common. However, while Aśvaghoṣa is a confirmed philosopher of Being, Nāgārjuna appears to be a skeptic and a nihilist. Nāgārjuna's intellectual position is perhaps the most complex in the history of Buddhism and he eventually figures as the support of tendencies as distinct as Śaṅkara's Advaita Vedānta and the modern Zen. It is necessary to see first what precise problem or problems Nāgārjuna has tried to grapple with.

Nāgārjuna's most comprehensive work is the *Mahā-prajñāpāramitā-śāstra* (the method of transcendental wisdom), which is a commentary on the old Buddhist text called the *Prajñāpāramitā-sūtra*. It is in this work and in the *Mādhyamika-śāstra* that he presents his *śūnyavāda*. Generally known as Mādhyamika because of its preaching a philosophy of the middle way between affirmation and negation, *śūnyavāda* is undoubtedly one of the greatest achievements in the history of philosophy in the world.

By any modern standard, Nāgārjuna is an accomplished metaphysician. In lucidity and in the searching quality of his thought he can be found to have a great affinity with thinkers like Bradley, Edmund Husserl, Heidegger, and Sartre. In fact, he approaches different questions regarding knowledge and Reality like a rigorous phenomenologist without, at the same time, confining himself to simply methodological inquiry. Also, although he shows himself constantly to be a subjectivist of the Bishop Berkeley variety (this is possibly due to the influence on him of the subjectivist school of Buddhism, called Vijñānavāda or Yogācāra, that must have made its beginning in his time), in his view of the essence of our world-experience he clearly goes beyond subjectivism. There is no proposition which Nāgārjuna does not doubt; and even when he knows that behind the act of doubting he is only *śūnya*, or Nothing.

Nāgārjuna's distrust of the capacity of our intellect to know the truth about existence is complete.[1] What intellect is able to reach in its contact with the world is *nāma* and *lakṣaṇa*, or the word and the sign. *Nāma* and *lakṣaṇa* go to form thought-structures, concepts and their contents, the outer characteristics by which things can be distinguished and classified, or, in short, be determinate being. To be limited in one's knowledge to the determinate, Nāgārjuna says, is to be in the realm of ignorance. Ultimate truth lies beyond the determinate.

Intellectually cognised beings constitute determinate reality. It is a reality that engages us as common sense minds and holds our mundane interests. Take, for instance, the subject–object relation in any finite knowledge situation and analyse it. This relation is reducible on one hand to the object, which is a bunch of qualities, and on the other to the subject knowing this bunch. The subject participating in the knowledge situation is necessarily categorially governed. Causes, conditions, motion, time, space, beginning, end, etc., according to Nāgārjuna, are categories which alone make our empirical knowledge possible. Besides, behind every object that we perceive we posit a substance (*svabhāva*), an unseen support of the qualities actually sensed. Thus every knowledge situation is a determinate situation. It is conditioned by the categorial assumptions innate to the very functioning of intellect.

Now none of the factors determining our knowledge of objects is adequately explainable. And when we embark upon explaining them we run into embarrassing paradoxes. Nāgārjuna points out a number of such paradoxes. The paradoxes arise because of what is perhaps the basic paradox of all, viz. although what is given to our intellect is determinate or relative we take it to be indeterminate or absolute. For Nāgārjuna the sphere of intellectually controlled knowledge is the sphere of ignorance (*avidyā*) or naivete. Further, it is this ignorance that is at the root of all afflictions (*kleśas*) in human life.

---

[1] K. Venkata Ramanan, *Nāgārjuna's Philosophy* (As Presented in the Mahā-Prajñāpāramitā-Śāstra), Rutland, Tokyo, Charles Tuttle, 1966, pp. 127 ff.

The chief design of Nāgārjuna's philosophy is to establish that the ultimate ground of the determinate is a reality for whose realisation we must know the authentic nature of our own being. For so long as we mistake our mundane experiences for the transcendental, our finite being for pure Being, the categorial features of our reasoning for the constituents of our transcendental consciousness, we stay buried in ignorance and are thus deprived of wisdom (*prajñā*). The Buddhists look upon man's life as a journey through ignorance, but having for its destination the state of wisdom. It is due to ignorance that we seize wrong impressions about the world, have a tendency to cling to false expectations, and consequently invite suffering and frustration. The Buddha, Nāgārjuna says, wanted us to know the distinction between the transcendental and the mundane, the absolute and the relative, the permanent and the transitory. To know this distinction is to be on the 'way of the perfection of wisdom' (*prajñāpāramitā*).

It must be seen that the movement of Nāgārjuna's thought from the rejection of determinate experience as ignorance to the confirmation of indeterminate experience as true knowledge is essentially phenomenological. Like Descartes and Husserl, one the precursor and the other the founder of phenomenology, Nāgārjuna doubts our empirical knowledge and proceeds to seek the essential basis of the knowing consciousness itself. While Descartes claimed to have discovered this basis in the *cogito*, which, he argued, moulds the beginning of our existential experience, Husserl, being more critical, carries on his method of reflection further down into the self until he lands on that 'region of pure consciousness', or 'transcendental ego', which is its own evidence and whose knowledge is impregnably apodeictic.[1] The rigour of Husserl can be found in Nāgārjuna's self-exploration method.

There is something peculiar about Husserl's phenomenological philosophy. Its interests are strictly epistemological. It doubts and suspends the world disclosed to us by our ordinary

[1] Edmund Husserl, *Ideas*, W. R. Boyce Gibson (Trans.), New York, Collier, 1962, p. 137.

perceptual and conceptual powers because it is unable to 'see' anything necessary regarding the constitution of this world. It has no aim in respect of determining the ethical ideal of man. Besides, the phenomenological reduction is so tacit in its knowledge-defining objective that once we attain by its practice the primordial state of our world-experience it would require us to use our insight towards the re-constitution of our entire intellectual picture of the universe. To Nāgārjuna, on the other hand, the very *raison d'être* of our reflection—and by reflection he means the preparation of one's self for a break-through from the domain of intellect to the realisation of the ultimate truth (*prajñā*)—is to put an end to the mind's clinging to mundane things, a clinging which produces despair (*kleśas*). However, so far as the trans-categorial and trans-phenomenal motivation of their thought is concerned, both Husserl and Nāgārjuna have much in common.

THE NATURE OF *ŚŪNYATĀ*

When the Buddha was reflecting on the sorrowful condition of mankind, the first and foremost truth that struck him was that the individual consciousness is momentary. Momentariness is consistent with the contiguity of experienceable point-instants, and so to ascribe it to the self is to imply that the self is an eternally enduring flux without any permanent substance or identity underneath. That the Buddha was mystified by the Upaniṣadic idea of an unchangeable *ātman*, or self, and the idea of God, and that therefore he refused to commit himself to any characterisation in definitive terms of what the ultimate ground of existence is is well known.

Buddha's curiosity about the constantly fleeting experiences of the psyche was so dominant that he could not be drawn to the view that something stagnant and invariable need be postulated behind these experiences. Everything in the universe, the Buddha said, is changing. Things come into being and pass away. They never are; they always become. They are without any essence or substance or Being. Instability, disintegration, impermanence, succession, and transitoriness characterise all existence. The self of man, the Buddha said, is an uninterrupted flow of moments.

Thus, when Nāgārjuna directed his observation and transcendentally unrestrained quest toward the inner expanse of his being, which he describes as *śūnyatā*, what he ostensibly contributed to the spirit of Buddhism is a philosophy of existence that did not in any way deviate from the Buddha's thought and yet proved to be extremely subjectivist and voidist.

The term *śūnyatā* signifies emptiness or void or Nothingness and is used by Nāgārjuna to denote that germinal experience which cannot be adequately described by means of intellectual configurations. Nāgārjuna tries to show that the indeterminate ground of all that is given to consciousness as present is not only of the nature of absence but also identical with pure and self-effacing trans-phenomenality. The knowledge of this ground dawns when one has controlled one's awareness of the empirical world and achieved a total breakthrough from intellect—called by Nāgārjuna *prajñā*.

As a matter of fact, *śūnyatā* and *prajñā* are two aspects of the same thing, one ontological and the other ontic. In *śūnyavāda*, *śūnyatā* is the essence of the universe, the root of everything that is, rather the basic unreality of things, and hence renders any positive or logical statement that is made about it as superficial. All the differentiating and discriminating agencies cease to operate in the domain of *śūnyatā*, which is an experience of total and indescribable negation. Therefore we must not look upon *śūnyatā* as something existent, that is as an area regarding which meaningful assertions can be made. For Buddhists, it is through *prajñā*—an all-comprehensive and exclusively non-clinging vision of the whole transcendental field—that one can realise *śūnyatā*. Although on many an occasion Nāgārjuna does say that Nothingness is a state different from both Being and non-Being, it *is* and *is not*, he is reluctant to confer on it the amplitude one comes across in Parmenides's *is*, Spinoza's *causa sui*, Bergson's *élan vital*,

Josiah Royce's *Absolute,* or even in the ātmalogists' *Brahman* or *ātman.* Nāgārjuna's *śūnyatā* is a cipher, indeterminable, unutterable, and occult to the entire range of actual and possible knowledge.

The central metaphysical problem with which Buddhism is preoccupied is the ultimate end of human life redeemed from all relativity and contingency. Buddhism is the search for an elementary and independent reality which incomprehensibly descends to the level of empirical existence and becomes the subject of perspectives, purposes, and interests. As Stcherbatsky explains, nothing short of the full totality of all relations, 'the Universe itself viewed as a Unity', the transphenomenal ground of all phenomena, could be regarded by Buddhism as the ultimate reality.[1] But since the quest for such a reality has to start from one's being in the spatio-temporal domain, Nāgārjuna does not hesitate to characterise Nothingness as the abode of the worldly and yet as beyond the worldly, as the fleeting stream of momentary flashes and yet as no-Self or no-Substance. Nothingness as the ontological basis of all experience is for *śūnyavāda* an intellectually unidentifiable realm, solidifying so to say before our ordinary consciousness as the mundane world.

No wonder, therefore, recognising that the indeterminable and amorphous ultimate substratum of existence is beyond the grasp of mortals if they do not exercise a peculiar inward-seeing discipline, the Buddha after his enlightenment chose to preach to others the way of the profoundest silence of the soul with the noble aim of enabling them to hear their own 'inner voice'. *Śūnyatā* and *tathatā* transcend all statements, all views, all opinions. Even to state that *Śūnyatā* is beyond affirmation and negation, Nāgārjuna remarks, is to speak of something so vague and so unqualifiable that it cannot but stay remote from what is really meant by that word. Thus what words and thoughts aim at expressing futilely, so far as the language of metaphysics is concerned, is the element of the elements (*dharmadhātu*), absolute calmness (*śāntatā*), *nirvāṇa* (that

---

[1] Th. Stcherbatsky, *Buddhist Logic,* Vol. 1, New York, Dover, 1962, pp. 7–8.

which cannot be apprehended by any process other than the trans-intellectual insight).

The terms *tathatā*, *śūnyatā*, and *nirvāṇa* indicate a sphere of experience unlike any of the spheres logical thought can define. In this sphere of experience, the individual conscious-ness places itself into a state of complete self-containment and self-consummation (quite suggestively, the word *nirvāṇa*, like the word *śūnyatā*, means the death of clinging). Thus to a person who has concentrated his mind on the fundamental meaning of human life, the everyday world, or *samsāra*, consists of innumerable impressions floating on an absolute expanse of Nothingness. To 'feel' this Nothingness—this original hollowness at the root of Being—is to get to the innermost reason of one's sense of presence. So despite different propositions describing the experience of Nothing-ness in the *śūnyavāda* writings what one is finally led to intuit by them all is the void underneath the phenomenal reality, the no-Self central to the Self, the vast hollow space at the bottom of the positive reals.

Now, sometimes Nāgārjuna and his followers warn us against equating *śūnyatā* with sheer vacuity.[1] The very name 'Mādhyamika', used to typify the *śūnyavāda* doctrine of the middle course between positivity and negativity, hints at the peculiarly ineffable sense behind the conception of *śūnyatā*. *Śūnyatā*, Nāgārjuna says, is the result of the deepening of understanding. When the understanding is deepened our awareness of that is not totally destroyed but transformed into something slipping through thought. What Nāgārjuna might have meant to suggest by the positive element in *śūnyatā*, therefore, is the possibility of this ontological reality's being the subject of our assertions. The fact that statements are made about *śūnyatā* even by those who have attained a direct intuition of it suggests that it can figure as a logical and grammatical subject like *Brahman* or pure Being. Any intel-ligible reference to *śūnyatā* would necessarily confer on it an affirmative status, a 'hard' positivity. However, when *śūnyatā*

[1] K. Venkata Ramanan, *Nāgārjuna's Philosophy*, pp. 168–9.

qua *śūnyatā* is intended, as something intellectually inexpressible, it indicates the negative Universal, the dissolution of the ego-sense, the ultimate non-substantiality of consciousness and the world.

Nothingness in the *śūnyavāda* philosophy represents the climax of a strict and ontologically unrestrained ātmalogy. From the eternal pervasiveness of Nothingness spring up instants of positivity, the flashes of Being, which constitute our self- and world-experience. To re-trace all positivity to this Nothingness is for Buddhists the sole way of fulfilling life's commitment.

THE EXISTENTIALIST SENSIBILITY

Man's realization that he is weary of his mundane existence and his fear of being alienated from his authentic self, both condensed in the Nothingness doctrine in Buddhism, characterise the temper of a thought 2,500 years distant from and yet so similar to the existentialist mood of our own time. Whatever the historical forces that might account for philosophers' *Weltanschauungen*, there is no doubt that both Buddhists and existentialists, notwithstanding their situations and periods, have shared a common sensibility, a sensibility capable of feeling the basic concern of man *vis-à-vis* the world. Like Buddhism, existentialism provides a view of man founded on the insights of an inward-seeing. This inward-seeing generated in the Buddha and his followers a conviction about the inevitable restlessness of man in the world, his afflictions in different situations to which he cannot but cling as long as he is a bundle of desires, and about the metaphysical 'inanity' (or *nirvāṇa*) into which our world-consciousness finally dissolves. The existentialists look upon human consciousness as a self-transcending and self-fulfilling act, a reality 'fallen' in the world but forever 'open' toward God, Being, or Nothing.

To existentialists, man is related to the world differently from any other being. Man, or *Dasein*, Heidegger says, is 'thrown' into the world.[1] But unlike inanimate and inert objects which also fill the world man 'runs' beyond his world-situation. He *is* there in space and time, surrounded by objects, but is aware of his imminent non-existence through death. There is not a single thing which enjoys 'solid' being in presence of man. Because man tends toward his final extinction, everything around him is deprived of its fixedness and stability so to say, everything whirls away from positivity. Conscious of this self-effacement potentiality at its heart, human reality can hardly function in the world as something full or wholesome. Not only is it incomplete and finite and lacking in an absolute foundation in the world, but because of a spontaneous recognition of this fact it also lies all the time in the grip of anguish. One of the existential experiences most realistically portrayed by Kierkegaard, the father of existentialism, Heidegger, and Sartre is the experience of anguish.

Tradition tells us that the sudden realisation that the whole creation is absurd and full of ennui dawned on the Buddha at an early age, when he witnessed the misery of human life. Born and brought up in a royal family, Buddha had a 'healthy' mind until he ran into the spectacle of an old man, a diseased man, and a corpse. The spectacle so deeply shocked his conception of life that it was enough to spark off in him a devouring weariness, a sense of the grotesqueness of all existence, and plunge him into an inquiry into the ultimate destiny of man.

Nāgārjuna also is said to have felt the trauma of existence when as a child he was abandoned by his parents, who could not stand the idea of seeing their son die prematurely as foretold by the astrologers. Nāgārjuna survived the astrologers' prophecy but grew to become a different personality.

Like the Buddha and Nāgārjuna, Kierkegaard underwent an overwhelming experience of 'sickness unto death'. Buddha pronounces the immediate ground of his afflictions (*kleśas*, *duḥkha*) in his advice to his disciples, when he warns them that 'decay is inherent in all component things'. Our desires and cravings for objects in the world, he teaches, are pregnant with

[1] See my *Reason in Existentialism*, Bombay, Popular Prakashan, 1966, pp. 40-1.

sorrow and frustration. And Kierkegaard explains the terror of living the life of an aesthete, the helplessness and desolation such a life entails, the false exaltation, boredom and anguish of sensuality.[1] At a time when the traditional Christian faith wanted one to believe that human life, in spite of its culmination in death, involved divine bliss and was therefore precious, Blaise Pascal wrote about his sinking in pathos at the dreadful feeling that he was 'abandoned' in the world, 'engulfed in the infinite immensity of spaces'.[2] In almost the same cultural climate, though 200 years later, Kierkegaard spoke of being overrun by a metaphysical loneliness, a 'despair of everything'.[3] What the Danish philosopher discovered while passing through this despair is the essence of his life, of his movement toward Being as the centre of unknown possibilities.

Both Buddhists and existentialists express an intense awareness of the unique potentiality of man in the world. The former have viewed man's life, from which death is inseparable, as his bondage; the latter have found in this phenomenon man's 'thrownness'. They all emphasise that man is naïve in failing to see his dislocation from the eternal and imperishable Being. This naïveté, or, as existentialists would describe it, this inauthentic way of life is most feelingly explained by the Buddha in his *Nikāyas*,[4] by Nāgārjuna in the *Mahā-prajñā-pāramitā-śāstra*, by Kierkegaard in *The Sickness unto Death* and *Fear and Trembling*, by Heidegger in *Being and Time*, by Sartre in *Being and Nothingness*, and by Albert Camus in his *The Myth of Sisyphus*. To the existentialist sensibility, the final end toward which man is moving is Nothing. Man is confronted by Nothingness, which is his central possibility. Considering this possibility, therefore, a philosopher's vision about the destiny of man cannot but be voidist.

[1] S. Kierkegaard, *Stages on Life's Way*, Walter Lowrie (Trans.), Princeton, Princeton Univ. Press, 1945, pp. 9–10.

[2] Blaise Pascal, *Pascal's Pensées*, G. B. Rawlings (Ed. & Trans.), 1956, p. 36.

[3] S. Kierkegaard, *Fear and Trembling* and *The Sickness Unto Death*, Walter Lowrie (Trans.), New York, Doubleday Anchor, 1954, pp. 146 ff.

[4] The *Nikāyas* are five collections containing the utterances of the Buddha himself.

THE ONTOLOGY OF NOTHING

Among existentialist philosophers it is Heidegger and Sartre and not so much Nietzsche or Karl Jaspers or Albert Camus that have developed, as *śūnyavāda* Buddhism has done, a voidist ontology out of their observation of man's condition in the world. For *śūnyavāda* there is an opposition between the ordinary life of man—which Buddhists characterise as the life of naïveté or *avidyā*, and of clingings or *prapañca*—and the state of *tathatā-*, *śūnya-* or *nirvāṇa*-realisation. A similar opposition is maintained by Heidegger too. He says that our routine oblivion of the fact that we are mortal, that our existence in the world is aiming at non-existence, constitutes the inauthenticity of our life; however, when we attain an insight into the truth of our Being, into our Dasein, and know that we are 'there' in the world but project toward the future which we have chosen at the very moment when we are born, we ascend to an authentic state. Heidegger and Sartre interpret human reality as a tendency toward the unfolding of Being, which itself signifies its 'fallenness' on the one hand and its transcendence and freedom on the other. Existentialists emphasise the dynamic nature of human reality, which, according to them, is reflected in the endeavours and plans, the creativity and yearnings in which people engage themselves. Man is a 'lack', writes Sartre, 'a useless passion', a craving for the re-establishment of himself. To Buddhists, man is a thirst (*tṛṣṇā*).

The fundamental assumption of Heidegger's philosophy is that the question of Nothingness, however alien to science, is the main question our search for the ultimate truth should be preoccupied with. Heidegger says that one can intuit Nothingness at the basis of every form of logical negation. Nothingness is not in opposition to Being: it is rooted in the very ontology of Being. Heidegger suggests that it is because of the primordial status of Nothing that the 'revelation of what-is as such' takes place.[1] Again, we cannot obtain Nothing by cancelling 'what-is'. Nothingness posits itself as the ontological ground

[1] Martin Heidegger, *Existence and Being*, with Introduction by Werner Brock, London, Vision, 1949, p. 361.

288 CONTEMPORARY INDIAN PHILOSOPHY *Series 2*

of all that is. Heidegger, like Nāgārjuna, repudiates the logical approach to the question of the ultimate truth, and shows that with him the whole problem of seeking the genesis of positivity has met with a re-definition.

All existentialists, in an open revolt against rationalists, maintain that our awareness of being in a worldly situation is prior to our thinking act. Man's discovery that he is in a spatio-temporal universe, they say, is not something that can be adequately analysed. The scientist's manner of explaining logically different factors constituting human life inevitably ignores the vast and empty source, the trans-empirical Nothing, from which man's sense of being present in the world has emerged. While Kierkegaard defines human existence as a reality alienated from its metaphysical footing, viz. Being or God, Heidegger thinks of it as something floating in a void. It is the endeavour of Heidegger, much as it is for Nāgārjuna, to bring under the focus of his attention the complete negative field on which our awareness of positivity is founded.

Existentialists, in general, reject the commonly accepted authority of the logical method to discuss the nature of onto-logical reality. Since their principal concern is to grasp reality by means of an ego-exploring process, a metaphysics of subjectivity, they propound a view of the inwardness of man not unlike the Buddhist idea of 'be a light unto thyself (*ātma-dīpo bhava*)'. It is this idea that underlies Heidegger's theory in *What is Metaphysics?*—that Nothingness is the finality of man's (*Dasein*') inquiry into his own origin and goal. Heidegger has opposed all rationalist philosophies before him as Nāgārjuna opposed the Upaniṣadic tradition of stressing the absolute positivity of *Brahman*. For Heidegger, as for Nāgārjuna in particular and the whole Mādhyamika school in general, Nothingness takes the place of Being. Being 'conceals itself' within the truth of Nothing, Being dissolves in Nothing. The possibility of a direct intuition of Nothingness as the outcome of the inward-seeing, of the authentic way of 'existing', is the nucleus around which Heidegger's existentialism and *śūn-yavāda* Buddhism are constructed.

The concept of Nothingness, in Heidegger's philosophy, is intended to explain what he observes to be the key mood of man-in-the-world, viz. dread or anguish (*Angst*). The entire universe of our positive experience is so to say unable to hold on to itself, he remarks, and 'slips away' into a limitless empty field.[1] One is in dread because one feels the unavoidable fate of death hanging over one's head, the impending Nothingness of one's self in death, and this speaks of the utter baselessness of everything. The feeling of anguish puts one on the course toward a transcendental vacuum. The fading away of what-is becomes so imminent in face of the ultimate Nothingness of all existence that while one is alive one passes through a shadow of emptiness. For Heidegger, this happens as an indication of the supreme 'nihilation' at the very heart of Being. 'Only in the clear night of dread's Nothingness,' he says, 'is what-is as such revealed in all its original overtness. . . .'[2]

Heidegger's Nothingness, like Nāgārjuna's *śūnyatā*, cannot submit itself to any satisfactory articulation. It does not suggest any reference to objects standing 'solidly' in the perceptible world. It is a domain at the background of these objects and experienceable as the ontological foundation of all positivity and totality. As for the essences of things of our ordinary perception, they run into this Nothingness so that their meaning appears to rarefy and become flexible. It is interesting to note that Chandrakirti (c. AD 700) a commentator on Nāgārjuna and whom Stcherbatsky describes as 'the great champion' of the Mādhyamika school, argued that the vacuous bottom of all existence cannot be comprehended by logical categories. He held that the world, or *saṁsāra*, is the false image of Nothing, which can be encompassed only in a 'mystic intuition'. Intellect, Chandrakirti said, gives us the account of what happens in common life, of our contact with others, of our enjoyment of objects. But on establishing a rapport with what lies behind the veil of objects, their transcendental source, we must reject what is empirically given.[3]

---

[1] *Existence and Being*, pp. 368–9.   [2] *Ibid.*, pp. 375–6.
[3] Th. Stcherbatsky, *Buddhist Logic*, Vol. 1, p. 45.

K

And Heidegger, like Chandrakirti, observes that although whenever we turn to what-is we ignore the region of Nothing nullity does not really cease to thrust itself on the world, almost as its resting-place.

Heidegger strongly condemns the objectivity-oriented functioning of science and logic. Such a condemnation is quite consistent with his systematic attempt to show that all objective statements in respect of what is *essentially* real or true notably miss the anguish and Nothingness at the bottom of objectivity. In this condemnation, Nāgārjuna would join hands with him. Moreover, in so far as Nāgārjuna's anti-intellectualist passion for the pursuit of life's meaning is concerned, he can be easily regarded as a worthy precursor of the whole movement of existentialist ontology. But his motivation, that is the securing of an exit for man from the bondage and afflictions of the worldly life, is uniquely Oriental and does not compare well with the largely descriptive procedure of existentialism.

When considered as a quasi-epistemological and quasi-psychological concept, *śūnyatā* would imply Being and Nothingness, yes and no, existence and non-existence, at the same time. Complete *śūnyatā*, which means total indeterminateness, Nāgārjuna points out, is the characteristic of the ultimate truth of things. In this sense, *śūnyatā* is called *svabhāva-śūnyatā* or essential Nothingness.[1] However, this Nothingness is perceived by us as Being in our relative, mundane experience. So within the heart of every phenomenon, or at the basis of our reflective (*citta*) consciousness, there is Nothing—the pre-reflective unfathomable flux, which, when seen as the inward extremity of our world-awareness, appears to circumscribe Being. If looked at in this way, the Mādhyamika idea of *śūnyatā* comes extremely close to Jean-Paul Sartre's Nothingness.

Sartre contends that man's intrinsic disposition toward Being is the same as his transcendental movement toward Nothingness. Being and Nothingness, he says, are so immersed

[1] K. Venkata Ramanan, *Nāgārjuna's Philosophy*, pp. 172–3.

in each other that neither of them is intelligible without the other. Nothingness need not be posited as something logically prior to Being, nor is it derivable from a negation of Being. Nothingness as an entity referred to in thought, is undoubtedly a positivity. But this positivity is not an amplitude that disallows Nothingness outside or inside it. Human consciousness acts so to say in a twofold manner: it posits things and thereby creates the world of Being, and also tends toward, purely pre-reflectively, the possibility of their non-being. That is why Nothingness is not given to consciousness either before or after Being but rather along with or at the background of Being.

In one of the most penetrating chapters of his *Being and Nothingness* Sartre examines the various psychical processes that represent Nothing. For instance, our activities like questioning, judging, and destroying reveal, according to him, negation—the metaphysical *négatité*. This *négatité* indeed varies in its intensity in accordance with the nature of the phenomenon or situation we encounter. Thus, Being is not a full, solid sphere of experience. Emptiness creeps into Being, whenever the latter is confronted by human reality. Perhaps there is a trans-phenomenal 'lack' concealed in the very sense of presence human consciousness enjoys in the world. It is only an object (*être-en-soi*), Sartre remarks, that is compact and free from negativity. But the moment the *être-en-soi* is brought in relation to the subject (*être-pour-soi*), Nothingness appears on the scene.[1] Sartre metaphorically says: 'Nothingness lies coiled in the heart of Being . . . like a worm'.[2]

MAN: THE ETERNAL QUEST

Now while theistic existentialists (that is, existentialists with an adherence to the Christian faith) have not extended the ego-exploring method to elicit from man's despaired existence in

---

[1] Jean-Paul Sartre, *Being and Nothingness*, Hazel E. Barnes (Trans.), New York, Philosophical Library, 1956, p. 23.

[2] *Ibid.*, p. 21.

K*

the world what can be called the theory of transcendental absence, but have restrained it by conceiving Being or God as the absolute end, the atheistic existentialists have followed the method with the outcome of establishing the mystery of Nothingness. Just as Nāgārjuna sees no difference between *tathatā* and *śūnyatā*, or suchness and Nothing, Heidegger and Sartre look upon the transcendental vastness of Being as a void. This void, both for the *śūnyavādin* and the atheistic existentialist, is not an isolated ontological reality unrelated to the phenomenal world perceived by us. Every encounter of human consciousness with its object is pregnant with a possibility of cancellation or 'nihilation'. The cancellability of a phenomenon is due to its origin in Nothingness—a sphere which is, unlike anything that is given in the determinate experience, mysterious and indescribable. To Merleau-Ponty, this area is the 'pre-human flux'. Zen Buddhism describes it as the 'timeless moment' or 'awareness-itself'.

The most unique characteristic of human reality is its 'volatile' state in the world. Man is a self-surpassing being. He is stationed in the world, and yet the world cannot own him. Human consciousness is a ceaseless search for something beyond what is given as present, beyond the positive and worldly. We pass over every actualised possibility, every fulfilled state of our being. As a matter of fact, the entire history of mankind is basically an account of how human consciousness, in spite of its being anchored in the world, has moved toward a transcendental state. The world does not offer itself to us as a hard positivity. Underneath its apparent unmixed positivity, our world-experience hides an elusive hollowness against whose background what-is appears to endure as perishable and therefore contingent.

The originality of the philosophies of *śūnyavāda* and existentialism lies in their endeavour to comprehend the ultimate truth as something pre-reflective and inaccessible to intellectual formulation. To a disciplined inward-seeing act of consciousness, aimed at ascertaining from what transcendental basis our existential experience flows forth, and what generates the forms and contents of what we perceive, it is the ontological study of man that finally matters most in philosophy. Both Buddhism and existentialism are committed to such a study. By making the fragile life of man-in-the-world the starting-point of their thinking, the *śūnyavāda* Buddhists and the atheistic existentialists have sought to describe how man's estrangement from his ontological source has reduced him to a state of restlessness, affliction, despair, and anxiety. Man has lost his basis, which he is in search of. The ontology of Nothingness is an attempt to verbalise this basis.

Chapter 14

AESTHETIC EXPERIENCE AND BEYOND

by

S. VAHIDUDDIN

Man's experience of values has a diversity and variety which can never be fully exhausted. Friedrich Nietzsche is often given credit for his insistence on the plurality of values and value orientations and for his discovery of new dimensions of values. In contrast to the value of human proximity which is expressed in the love of one's neighbour he emphasised the value of the distant as expressed in the devotion to generations to come. Any attempt to consider one order of values as basic and all others as derivative leads to a position which is rightly considered the fanaticism of values and to an exclusiveness which might easily go beyond theoretical dogmatisms to practical and emotional attitudes which are indifferent and hostile to cultures other than their own. The German poet Schiller distinguished between barbarians and savages. The barbarians fight for one principle whilst savages know no principle. From a different angle of thought Hegel considered it the function of the philosopher to fight against abstraction, and by abstraction he meant indifference to wholeness both as conceptual exclusiveness and practical fragmentariness. 'To think abstract is to see in the murderer nothing but the abstract fact that he is a murderer only and to eliminate all human quality from him on the basis of this abstraction.' Hegel called celibacy an abstract human condition, but abstraction might easily go beyond intellectual confines, and a thinker who sees only in thought the reconciliation of the heterogeneous moments of spiritual life, as Hegel did, is no less abstract than the artist or the religious man for whom thought is suspect and who considers a philosophic evaluation of religious or aesthetic experience an unwarranted intrusion or even a sacrilege.

Among modern philosophers Immanuel Kant is rightly considered a thinker for whom each aspect or phase of culture is autonomous, and his three *Critiques* are sustained attempts to emphasise the autonomous regions of theoretic knowledge, moral commitment and aesthetic appreciation. It is also true that even Kant failed to assign to religious life any significance independent of moral consciousness and religion had to subsist only in the shadow of hope. Kant's philosophy is always sustained by a spirit of tension, in the theoretical realm by a conflict of knowledge and faith, in the practical sphere by a conflict of duty and inclination, and even in the third *Critique* Kant is faced with antinomies no less rigorous than in the first two *Critiques*.

It is to be noted that the attempt to analyse the irrational sphere of human experience cannot be carried into these domains without introducing an element of artificiality. Further these experiences show a diversity which is truly baffling for intellectual scrutiny. Our experiences of the graceful, the tragic, the comic and the sublime, though including the pervasive moment of beauty, have a distinction of their own and with the experience of the sublime we may even doubt whether it is the experience of the beautiful as such. When William James in his famous Gifford lectures insisted on the varieties of religious experience he leaned heavily on psychology to make intelligible the diversity of mystic and religious life. Religious life accordingly changes its character with the variations of personality, and the main patterns of religiosity find their explanation in the typical differentiations of man's psychic life. That psychic life is understood in an individual context or in a collective framework makes no difference to the understanding of man's experience of values through psychological categories. It is a further step to show that man's experiences are conditioned and that they change not only with persons and types but also with the diversity of history and culture. Recent philosophies have often vacillated between psychologism and historicism. Edmund Husserl's was a classical attempt to combat psychologism which he understood as the reduction of logic to psychology. But every attempt to understand art and religion has the same tendency, and subjectivistic analysis has vitiated modern philosophies of art and religion. Hence it is not the object but the mental act which is held to be decisive and even in the moral sphere where acts are really decisive, there is much more at stake than a pure psychological explanation can hope to deal with.

It would be highly presumptuous to pretend to exhaust the variety of aesthetic experience. What we can at the most attempt to do is to call attention to certain factors which are often neglected in the analysis of aesthetic experience. An effort will be made to see religious experience in relation to the traditional aesthetic categories, the tragic, the comic and the sublime, and second to examine their fusion with experiences which are supposed to be extra-aesthetic. The interpenetration might go so deep that we are not sure whether we stand in the realm of the holy or that of the beautiful. This is especially true in our experience of the tragic and the sublime. Our experience of the tragic is primarily aesthetic, but with a slight shift of accent the tragic might easily assume the form of the sublime where the religious moment becomes dominant. Kant was aware of the category of the sublime as a category in its own right, but allowed it to get totally absorbed in moral experience. Strangely enough the example that he gives clearly shows that it is really the religious moment that is decisive. He wrote: 'No more sublime can be the words than those written on the temple of Isis: I am all that is, all that was and no man has ever lifted up my veil.' Rudolf Otto[1] has therefore rightly considered the sublime as the most effective means by which the irrational moment of religion is expressed in art. Through the representation of darkness and silence the

[1] R. Otto: *The Idea of the Holy*, Oxford University Press, 1958, pp. 70 and 71.

numinous or the irrational and mysterious moment of religion assumes the form of the sublime. Thus he observes:

'The darkness must be such as is enhanced and made all the more perceptible by contrast with some lost vestige of brightness, which it is, as it were, on the point of extinguishing; hence the mystic effect begins with semi-darkness. Its impression is rendered complete if the factor of the sublime comes to unite with and supplement it. The semi-darkness that glimmers in vaulted halls, or beneath the branches of a lofty forest glade, strangely quickened and stirred by the mysterious play of half lights, has always spoken eloquently to the soul, and builders of temples, mosques and churches have made full use of it.'

The same impression is created through the representation of emptiness and empty distances. Thus Otto continues 'Chinese architecture, which is essentially an art in the laying and grouping of the buildings makes a wise and very striking use of this fact. It does not achieve the impression of solemnity by lofty vaulted halls or imposing altitudes but nothing could be more solemn that the silent amplitude of the enclosed spaces, courtyards and vestibules which it employs'.[1] And again: 'Still more interesting is the part played by the factor of void or emptiness. In Chinese painting, there it has almost become a special art to paint empty space, to make palpable and to develop variations upon this single theme. . . . For void is like darkness and silence, a negation, but a negation that does away with every "this" and "here", in order that the "wholly other" may become actual.' This reminds one of the famous exclamation of Pascal: 'The eternal silence of these infinite spaces frightens me.' This means that here silence, emptiness and also vastness contribute to create the impression of the sublime.

Now we are led to consider another type of mixed experience which may also take the form of the tragic or sublime and this is our experience of history. That knowledge of history and

[1] R. Otto: *The Idea of the Holy*, Oxford University Press, 1958, pp. 70 and 71.

our response to historical process requires appreciation in terms of art is responsible for the neglect of history as an area of philosophical understanding *per se*. What matters most in history is the individuality both of events and persons and not the uniform recurrence characteristic of nature. History requires that time should be taken seriously. But that just mere concern for duration does not suffice in understanding history is eloquently shown in the philosophy of Bergson whose insistence on duration as what is really real in life did not enable him to understand the historical process as over and above the organic process. The limitation of the psychological understanding becomes most striking in the face of historic personalities. Our historic understanding requires above all the categories of aesthetic relevance such as sympathetic imagination, empathy or intuition. This is because historic personalities are not just the duplication of their factual reality but historical constructions which differ from one historian to another. It is, therefore, erroneous to think that history is a simple reconstruction by memory. If it is preservation of the past in memory which makes history it is not the individual memory that preserves the past through the supposed psychological traces left in the organism but an impersonal memory enshrined in language, tradition and artistic moments, in a word the persistence of spiritual life in objective structures.

The experience of history takes us to another experience which is not typical but which is aesthetic none the less. It is our experience of ruins. It is not always clear what it is that constitutes the aesthetic moment, what makes the delight that we take in such a spectacle. Is it its tragic character or is it our association with the past which seems to live in the present in all its fullness? It is, perhaps, the presence of the past which makes us reflective without making us melancholy. Ruins are found and cannot be made. There is a spontaneity which they share with all life. Here nature has triumphed over man's work though in the victory of nature over man there seems an inner justification. Simmel subjected our appreciation of ruins to a penetrating analysis. 'The peculiar equilibrium between mechanical pressure of the passively resisting matter and the formative swing of the spirit breaks down the moment the edifice collapses. This means that the forces of nature have begun to master the achievement of man; the equilibrium which architecture represented is disturbed, in favour of nature.'[1] It is the vengeance of nature. It looks as if the stones had only unwillingly submitted to the violence of the spirit and have at last recovered their freedom. This cannot be brought about voluntarily. What has nature done but to convert a piece of art into material for its further formation as earlier art had taken hold of nature as a stuff for its creative expression. That the overpowering of human achievements by nature should work aesthetically has one condition: one must feel a sense of inner justification as is the case with ruins where nature seems to assert its claim on the stuff which is really hers. This is the reason why ruins invoke the tragic but not the sad. On the other hand, according to Simmel, if a man is considered a 'ruin' he cannot have any aesthetic appeal. The fact that the instinctive and natural forces have at last over-powered the rational or the spiritual forces in man seems to be lacking in justification. Here the spectacle is sad but not tragic. As regards ruins they appear as structures which were once the abode of life and are now bereft of life. What was once throbbing with life is brought back to view in indica-tions, traces, memory and imagination. This is equally true of antiquities. With the piece that we hold in our hand we really capture a wide span of the past and all its vicissitudes. Now the difference between thought and perception, past and present seems artificial; all is fused in the unity of aesthetic enjoyment which really beckons to a unity deeper than aesthetic unity.

But Simmel's foregoing analysis leaves unconsidered one important factor. The aesthetic delight is not born of the victory of nature as such but issues from the persistence of the work of man in spite of nature. Nature's vengeance is not complete and absolute and man's defeat is not total and final.

In our appreciation of relics there is not only a communica-

[1] G. Simmel, Ruine, *Philosophische Kultur*, Dritte Auflage, 1923, p. 135.

tion with the past but a *participation mystique*, a mystic communion with the divine. It seems somehow that the non-sensuous has assumed a sensuous form, and has literally enshrined itself in the material object and persists in spite of the ravages of time. Here again it is not just our surrender to beauty but our encounter with something beyond the senses. The feeling that the intangible is made tangible through the senses gives a new dimension to our consciousness. The aesthetic experience then imperceptibly merges in the religious experience.

Thus we are brought back to aesthetic experience both in their typical and atypical, pure and mixed manifestations. What really can hinder and disturb the possibility of these experiences is the conceptualistic and voluntaristic attitudes. They can neither be brought into a conceptual scheme nor produced deliberately by a fiat of the will. Their affective saturation is not of their essence, although it is a necessary moment. Much confusion in aesthetic theories is caused by a wrong approach to the affective bedrock of aesthetic experience.

Feeling is used, on the one hand, to indicate a confused or obscure cognitive state, on the other it may even be contrasted with intellect and may lay claim to be a higher source of knowledge. It was against the enthusiasm of some of his contemporaries for 'feeling' (Gefühl) as the higher source of knowledge that Hegel reacted so sharply. But in the context of aesthetic considerations we may safely restrict feeling to its affective dimension. Here again even in its affective restriction it may be easily confused with emotions especially when it is used in the plural form. What is called feeling in its primitive reference cannot be equated with emotions. In its relation to emotions it only serves as the core element of a complex in which affective, cognitive and conative elements blend together. The dichotomy of pleasure and pain does not at all exhaust the subtle feeling component of aesthetic enjoyment. Sweetest songs are carried by saddest thoughts and what has the character of pleasure and pain are only the affective elements most accessible to intellectual analysis. Since William

Wundt a dissatisfaction with the dichotomy of pleasure and pain as exhaustive of the rich complexity of man's feeling has been felt, and an attempt has been since made to see the essence of feeling in the total quality which overshadows all our personal experience. The aesthetic response is then marked by affective saturation though the product of aesthetic experience itself stands unconcerned with its affective accent.

The affective moment of aesthetic experience has only an empirical necessity. The values which are responded to in aesthetic experience are indifferent to any affective involvement. That they are experienced affectively is only a factual characterisation of the human response. Aesthetic experience is primarily a 'vision', an awareness or apprehension of a novel quality on its appreciative and creative side. So far as it is appreciation it may be called contemplation in the sense of persistent awareness which may have been provoked by a concrete object or an imaginary construct. In painting or sculpture the aesthetic quality of a concrete object is intuited and contemplated, while in fiction and poetic creation or music, the aesthetic quality apprehended is the product of creative imagination which constructs its objects. The perception of real objects and the perception of the same as aesthetic objects is distinguished by a qualitative difference. Even when nature is perceived aesthetically it is not perceived as 'real', as a configuration of quantitative relationships but as something other than the physical complex. In such cases our aesthetic experience has a twofold layer, one belonging to the real world as the possible object of productive or active imagination as contemplative vision. This does not mean that we first perceive the object as real and then a new 'perception' is imposed on the normal perception. The awareness and contemplation of an aesthetic quality has an immediacy which is characteristic of sense perception but a *novum* which is not produced by the senses. Though in all aesthetic experiences the senses are involved directly or indirectly through memory, the aesthetic quality as such is not produced by the senses but apprehended and contemplated through imagination. Aesthetic apprehension cannot be equated with contemplation. Unless the aesthetic quality is first apprehended it cannot be contemplated. Logically apprehension is prior to contemplation though in actual aesthetic experience both may coincide. Unlike the aesthetic contemplation of nature the aesthetic apprehension of objects of art may be delayed. It may take considerable time to appreciate the aesthetic quality or the significance of a poem or a dramatic piece or a painting. No doubt understanding is considerably involved in the appreciation of works of art but even understanding as an intellectual function is not enough. The words of a poem are heard and understood. But its aesthetic significance may still elude us. All of a sudden its beauty may capture us unawares and fill us with rapture. This means that not every aesthetic quality may be disclosed immediately, but once the disclosure is made it cannot elude us.

When I listen to a melody or see a painting or witness a drama, what is decisive is the apprehension of the aesthetic quality, the ability to participate in the vision of the artist by another vision in response. The artist is not conveying feelings but transmitting the vision which is embedded in feeling. I am not at all 'envisaging' his feelings, but partaking in his vision and only as a consequence responding to his feeling as a part of the total human involvement. But even in fiction, drama or poetry, where the portrayal of emotions is primarily intended, the emotions involved are not the empirically given matter of experience, but the imagined possibilities of emotional life in their hidden plenitude. My own response to the emotion portrayed may have a totally different emotional shift. If the situation is tragic I may not respond with simple sorrow but with sympathy. Hence my emotions may be more complex than the emotion which provoked it. The expression of a particular emotion need not evoke the same emotion in us. Unbridled and destructive anger may evoke repulsion or resentment, sorrow may evoke pity, and love sympathy or resentment varying with the circumstances and the moral or the psychological bias of the perceiver. Emotions are given expression in art not on their own account but as part of the total situation which involves any of them. The grief of Laocoon and the jealousy of Medea do not express emotions but the human situation to which man reacts through specific emotions. The poet is conveying not his emotions bu the vision of emotions while, at the same time, the empirical conditions do not allow the vision to be communicated in complete detachment but through the medium of his own factual affections.

The primitive experience of the beautiful is not that of nature but of art. Surprisingly enough we can respond to nature in its aesthetic worth only when we can appreciate the beauties created and revealed by art. It is, however, nothing short of human arrogance to consider not the sunset but only the poem or a painting about the sunset to be beautiful. It must be conceded that even in our appreciation of nature as beautiful there is an element of artistic evaluation. As Kant observed happily, we consider art beautiful when it appears as Nature, and Nature beautiful when it appears as art. The illusory character of aesthetic objects does not lead to the falsification of reality or to its duplication but to the disclosure of a new world with its own character and autonomy, with its own time and space. No wonder that man's proud claim to be a conqueror of nature on earth does not show so much in scientific discoveries as in artistic creation. In science man miserably lags behind nature. There he conquers nature by surrender and submission, whereas in art he creates nature, and his products can vie with nature in every way. The great characters portrayed in drama and fiction, in painting and sculpture, have a life and spirit all their own, a richness and complexity of character as great as in nature. Cleopatra of the poet's imagination may as much lay claim to life as the one who might have lived and died in the past; whilst the Cleopatra of history stands between the work of art and that of fact, between 'truth and poetry'. We may well be tempted to say that the feeling that the artistic creation evokes in us is only an apparent feeling lacking in reality and intensity. But to say that the feelings lack in intensity does not mean that they lack in depth or duration. The impact of imaginary existence on us may become part and parcel of our life, may even impart to our feelings a dimension hitherto unknown. To expect from art or aesthetic experience the revelation of a super-sensuous world is to belie the character of aesthetic experience. The aesthetic vision certainly breaks through the confines of discursive thought with as much vehemence as a religious experience, but its world cannot have more than a symbolic validity and cannot reveal any world of transcendental reality. The illusions created by art are not deceptions which mislead but possibilities indicated from our own experience of everyday reality, though it is given to art to create a new dimension or order of time and space where imagination can move with ever new freedom and spontaneity. Thus to speak of the objects of art as unreal or illusory is already to make use of a language borrowed from the extra-aesthetic sphere.

The association of the aesthetic moment with moral experience is not the same as the fusion of aesthetic elements in religious experience. Moral and aesthetic elements cannot always constitute a harmonious fusion. Conflict and tension may often mar their relationship. The obtrusive dominance of the ethical elements marks the end of art, though the absorption of an ethical element in art may contribute to its greatness. The difference cannot be overcome and this is well marked by Nicolai Hartmann who observes: 'The aesthetic value is not the act value, but the object value, whereas ethical value is essentially an act value. If in an aesthetic object certain acts also can function as the bearers of aesthetic value, as it is in the dramatic acts of all grades, the act is nevertheless the part of a whole and its ethical value or disvalue is not its aesthetic value or disvalue.'[1] Again Hartmann's observation is relevant. Aesthetic value can belong to anything, while ethical value can be associated only with persons. It is when we go beyond the confines of the beautiful to the area which is closely related to it and still different, the area of the sublime, that the moral and aesthetic elements seem to constitute a real unity. While every

[1] N. Hartmann, *Aesthetik*, Berlin, 1953, p. 344.

form of the beautiful, including that of the tragic, is characterised by freedom and spontaneity, the moral experience, in some of its characteristic phases at least, is the experience of an abiding tension and conflict. Kantian ethics with all its rigorism is an ethics of moral sublimity, and an outlook sustained be perpetual tension between duty and inclination, between ought and fact. Hence Schiller with his poetic perception rightly pointed out that Kant neglected the element of reconciliation in the moral character and ignored the 'beautiful soul' as the expression of a character in which conflict is overcome. The human character which is always split by conflict and tension and in which duty triumphs at the expense of nature, has something tragic about it. It can force our respect but cannot win our love. Moral experience touches only a cross-section of aesthetic experience. That we can judge characters created by art from moral standards and evaluate their action ethically shows strikingly that the so-called illusory form of aesthetic objects is nevertheless not quite alien to the moral situation. The feelings that they evoke are neither wholly apparent nor wholly real. They participate in the character of both. The place of ethical values in aesthetic situations can be best illustrated with reference to tragedies or comedies. Hegel saw the tragic in the ethical conflict of the family with the state, or as we would say, in the conflict of values. The conflict of the good with the good, of one value with another, is the highlight of tragedy. This means that we are, ultimately, bound to go even beyond the conflict of one ethical situation with another to a conflict of an ethical situation with aesthetic or other non-ethical requirements. But Hegel could not fully understand the nature of tragedy on account of his commitment to a metaphysic of reconciliation in which the element of negation has only a transitory character and conflicts are always resolved in a dialectical framework. But reality, as we know, is more ambiguous than Hegel's concept of the tragic conflict would make us believe. It has ample place for contradictions but their resolution is always suspect.

Moral experience is as much relevant and effective in comedies as in tragedies. Comedies cannot incorporate all that is comic but only that which can contribute to aesthetic enjoyment. The comic situation might easily conflict with moral requirements and often it is a more or less distinguished attempt to break through social and moral restraints without any apparent offence. But great comedies are often tinged with a deep ethical pathos. What marks the contrast to the tragic is not really the comic but the sublime. The great comic figures of artistic creation have a deep tragic strain. It is said of Gogol, the great Russian satirist, that tears are hidden in his laughter, and in Don Quixote we find the tragedy of idealism. The world is too small for the hero of Cervantes and what makes him really ludicrous is the seriousness with which he takes reality to be completely subservient to his ideas. This tragic dimension of laughter was noted by Nietzsche and expressed paradoxically when he said that the reason why man is the only animal who laughs is that he is the most miserable of all. Humour as an attitude to life is the capacity to laugh at oneself and to hold one's own against the heavy odds of life. The Socratic irony is not born of malice but produced by a deep metaphysical reaction against all pretensions. Great art always moves between the poles of a dual process, to catch the significance of the seemingly insignificant and, in the comic, to make the seemingly significant look insignificant. It is above all in the comic that the ability of a man to look at himself from a distance is brought out most clearly. He can stand apart from himself and can look at himself as an outsider. This is perhaps the quality which Plessner has called 'eccentricity' and which in another context is called by Heidegger 'man's quality of being ahead of himself'.

But it is indeed the religious consciousness which gives rise to a type of aesthetic experience where religious and aesthetic moments intermingle, shift and change. Often it may be difficult to say whether we are face to face with the religious or aesthetic moments of experience. A man without any concern for the ultimate may still hold aesthetic values as of ultimate concern to him. George Santayana with all his scepticism appreciated greatly the aesthetic value of religious rituals.

It is no secret that religions have historically used art and artistic expressions as the vehicle of their own aesthetic world, and the analogy between the prophetic and poetic inspiration is often drawn. Modern students of aesthetics have sadly neglected the religious moment in aesthetic experience. This is true as much of Kant as of Croce or Nicolai Hartmann. There is no denying that different phases of religious life might come very close to the aesthetic attitude and religion might assume a more contemplative or a more active manifestation. It may take the character of a vision which fights shy of action, or of action supremely unconcerned with aesthetic abandon. If the religious expression is more contemplative it comes close to the world of beauty; and if it is more active it comes close to the moral attitude. The diversity and conflict of these attitudes is well marked, in the historical religions, in the figures of Mary and Martha in Christian religiosity, in the difference of *Bhakti* and *Karma* in Indian religiosity, and in the conflicting attitude of sobriety and intoxication in Sufi religiosity. It is characteristic of the human situation that one type of experience can find such a successful expression in the language of another that it is identified with its expression exhaustively.

It is in the relation of the tragic and the sublime to the religious experience that the distinction, and yet similarity, of the two important areas of man's experience of values is brought out most clearly. The tragic can only figure as a moment of religious experience when it loses its finality, when it is subdued as a transitional phase and ultimately the possibility of its self-transcendence is indicated. One could only speak of divine comedy but not of a divine tragedy. As Karl Jaspers observes, the tragedy itself leads to transcendence and this means that the tragic cannot be absolute but only a moment in the foreground. It is not in the ground of being but only in the appearance of time. In all great tragedies there is not the sense of total loss, but the conviction of a gain in spite of apparent loss, a victory in spite of apparent defeat. The tragic, therefore, can only figure in the religious experience as an aesthetic moment which is not self-sufficient and which in isolation has even something anti-religious about it. Pan-tragism cannot fit in with the religious consciousness and in the artistic expression there cannot be any place for the tragic in its absolute finality. The tragic is often mellowed by the sublime. The sublime need not figure only in the tragic but can easily be found outside. All sublimity is august and serious but not tragic. The limitations of the given reality are somehow overcome and man's greatness triumphs in spite of the limitation of the human situation. Love defies death and death loses its sting. On its subjective side it is awe-inspiring, but a form of awe which is not simply over-powering but fascinating. The moment the tragic approaches the sublime it loses its gloom. The clouds dispel and, as in the end of Goethe's *Faust*, every phase of suffering seems to have been a step to salvation, a final reconciliation is reached, an inner telelogy is realised. And here it is that art and religion seem to part. This means that what divides religion and art is no less important that what binds them. The religious con-sciousness is committed to a deep sense of teleology, a freedom from empirical constraints and finally to a freedom from all possible empirical bonds. But the deliverance which religion aims at is totally different from the deliverance which art leads to. Art is the creation of another world, a world which is no less empirical, though imaginary. It is true that even our empirical world itself may be considered ultimately as an allegory, a *Gleichnis* as Goethe hinted in the concluding lines of *Faust*: 'Alles Vergängliches ist ein Gleichnis'.

But the teleology to which religious consciousness is committed is completely irrelevant to aesthetic appreciation and creation. It was Kant's enduring contribution to aesthetics that he dealt a death blow to the teleological conception of art and beauty with his concept of a purposiveness without a purpose. Unfortunately subjective bias vitiated much of the Kantian analysis, and added to this was his failure to overcome the rationalistic prejudice of the earlier generation completely. Hence it was freely assumed that the correspondence between the laws of understanding and imagination constituted aesthetic experience.

The objects of art, though originally the creation of aesthetic vision, take an independent character the moment they are expressed and objectified. They may reveal meaning and suggest feelings which have never been in the consciousness of the artist. The puzzling smile of a Mona Lisa may mean much more to the spectator than it ever did to the artist. Once they are produced, artistic creations have a life of their own which is quite independent of their creator.

This brings us to the crucial question of the relation that obtains between the personality of the artist and his work. The work of the artist can never be understood with reference to the personal life of the artist. His work of art is more than the artist. Among psychologists C. G. Jung has emphasised the super-personal character of works of art. The artist transcends himself in his own work. The personality of the artist as given through art is truly not that of his individual subjectivity but it is itself a piece of art. The person of Shakespeare that history or historical research might construct is irrelevant to the appreciation of his art, to his artistic creation. (He is as he is given in his work; his life as an artist is one with his art. We cannot go behind the mirror to see what it reflects.) The world of art is as different from the real world as the personality of the artist *qua* artist is different from the real person.

The temporal processes, the space, the feelings, the ups and downs of fortune have their own imaginary character. They are not borrowed from the real world but follow an order different from their real counterparts. The material is taken from the real world but formed into a world which is not real. The time process in the works of art is just a relationship between the present and past without any consequence for the future, or at the most it includes a reference to the future as expressed in the ending of the fairy tales, as 'ever after,' as something which is nothing but a postscript to the past. What matters in art is just present and past. No wonder that typical poetry leans so heavily on memories and reminiscences, and even in our day-to-day life, memory may impart an artistic touch to our commonplace encounters. They are seldom faithful records of events but an elaboration of imagination which is always saturated with feelings and emotions. The feelings which are imputed to fictional characters, though not real, have their own imaginary potency and can initiate movements and repercussions in the real world. Imagination might be so carried away by the characters of fiction, so overpowered by the moods of a poem, that real effects could be produced. No wonder Flaubert felt a bitter taste long after his heroine had poisoned herself. In other words the aesthetic experience, though belonging to an 'unreal' world, can still hit back and produce real consequences in the real world. Goethe once seems to have remarked that he did not write after experience but experienced after he wrote. The German romantic movement made much of the irresponsibility of the artist and in a way the artist is not responsible for the crimes committed by his creations. If they suffer he is not responsible for their suffering and if they die the loss is not his, and if they have children he is not responsible for their maintenance. But the unreality of aesthetic situations is not and cannot be indifferent to the demands of the real world. Indeed an artist is said to have exclaimed to his model; smile once and I will make you smile for ever. But this freedom from time is not absolute. It is, at least practically, subject to the laws which govern the real world and is limited by the conditions which prevail in the everyday world. Thus art has a dubious relationship to material conditions. The world in which we live is not just a stage for the performance of duties, as the ethical idealism of Fichte would make us believe. It is the locus of the realisation of art and appreciation of beauty. The artist's vision by itself can do nothing. It requires a foundation on which to stand. This is quite in keeping with the ontological analysis of recent times. Even the highest values require the lower for their foundation and even personal life with all its transcendental yearnings and aesthetic enthusiasm and ecstasy, has to flourish on the vital and physical plane.

Now we come back to our starting point. Aesthetic experiences do not show any uniform character. Each experience is the bearer of a unique vision which is informed with the all pervasive moment of an elusive significance which we call beauty. But no experience is sharply marked and there is a constant interpenetration. All that is sad is not tragic, and all that is comic cannot figure in a comedy without marring the aesthetic quality. Our experience of history is moulded by a curious interplay of factual reality and imaginative construction. We may even question the tragic character of the so-called historical tragedies and consider the tragic only as a concept which has relevance for aesthetic experience only. Thus we may conclude the the world of art has a structure which is neither of the real world nor of religious faith though touching both spheres. In art we encounter what Nicolai Hartmann called the immediacy of the mediate. If in the perceptions of everyday life we go beyond the given to what is not given this is especially true of the aesthetic situation. In a more pronounced and incomparable way our imagination carries us from one sensible world which is given to another world which is not given, but which is equally of the senses. The fact that art can easily take us from one order of the senses to another has been used by religion in making art the representation and the symbol of the transcendent. This is true of music above all. The spell of music lies in its highly evasive and other-worldly character which enables it to make us feel immune to 'the touch of the earthly years', and which instead of making us lose the world makes the world lose us. No wonder Schopenhauer saw in music the highest manifestation of art as it gives rise to a singular state of abandon where the will to live is silenced. Filled as we are with uncanny and elusive yearnings the normal agitations of the soul bound up with instinctive needs are neutralised and we seem to stand beyond all psychological dichotomies. The affective complex may now easily touch the mystic horizon and initiate mystic raptures. No wonder that some of the mystic orders made remarkable use of music in introducing ecstatic conditions. But aesthetic experience can only serve as the *vehicle* of religious or mystic experience without exhausting it. Hence Brémond's attempt to consider poetry as prayer is to be taken with reservation. He observes: 'If one has to believe Walter Pater all arts aspire to join in (or assimilate themselves) to music. No. They all aspire but each by the intermediary magic which is its own, the words, the notes, the colours, the lines, to join prayer.'[1]

Art as a vehicle of religious consciousness enables us to divine what cannot be immediately given, to experience the aesthetic appearance as a pointer to something which is not manifest. But the world of art may as well expose us to the temptation to lose ourselves in the world of aesthetic objects and abandon ourselves to the lure of beauty as a joy for ever. Paradoxically we may say that the greater the achievement of creative imagination is in art the closer it is to religion, whilst the deeper the religious experience is the more it sinks into silence and allows no access to art.

[1] H. Brémond: *La Poésie Pure*, p. 27.

Names Index

Abe, Masao 275n
Appar 103, 104
Appayya Dīkṣita 112
Aquinas 53
Aruni 76
Asaṅga 69
Aśvaghoṣa 275–7
Austin, J. L. 254–8, 263–4
Ayer, A. J. 167, 255, 257, 258,
  263–5, 269–70

Barnes, J. 97
Barrett, W. 121n
Belnap, N. D. 253
Berkeley, G. 277
Bergson, H. 281
Bharatitirtha-Vidyāraṇya 115
Bhatnagar, R. S. 36n
Bhattacharyya, Kalidas 35, 74, 75,
  118n
Bhattacharyya, K. C. 24, 74, 138–9
Boethius 53
Borst, C. V. 134n, 149n
Bradley, F. H. 37, 76, 116, 117,
  277
Brémond, H. 312
Brentano, F. 133–6, 152
Buddha 63–5
Butler, Bishop 177

Camus, A. 286, 287
Carlyle, T. 107
Carnap, R. 167
Cervantes 306
Chandrakirti 289–90
Chakravarti, A. 74
Chatterjee, Margaret 74
Chattopadhyaya, D. 74
Chennakesavan, S. 74, 75
Chesterton, G. K. 104
Chisholm, R. 133, 254–5, 258–9,
  265–6, 269–71

Dandekar, R. N. 75
Descartes 22, 79, 279
Devasenapathi, V. A. 75
Dharmendra Kumar 26n
Dīkṣita, Appayya 112
Dunn, J. M. 253

Eddington, A. 76
Einstein, A. 26
Eliot, T. S. 92

Feigl, H. 153
Fernando, Mervyn 75
Fichte 310
Fisk, M. 32
Flaubert 310
Føllesdal, D. 253
Frankena, W. K. 169n

Gaudapāda 109, 111
Geach, P. T. 253
Gettier, E. L. 259–63
Gilman, E. 173–6
Gogol 306
Goethe, J. W. von 308, 310
Goldsmith, O. 98n
Goodman, N. 23
Griffiths, A. Phillips 257n
Gupta, K. C. 75
Gurwitsch, A. 136n

Hare, R. M. 182, 189–90
Hartmann, N. 152, 189, 304–5,
  307, 311
Hegel 11, 116, 117, 118, 151, 294–
  5, 305
Heidegger, M. 119–21, 274, 277,
  284–5, 286, 287–90, 292, 306
Heisenberg, W. 26n
Hepworth, Barbara 198
Hick, John 102

Subject Index

This index includes the more important Sanskrit and foreign terms which occur in the text.